The Earthscan Action Handbook

For People and Planet

by Miles Litvinoff

Earthscan Publications   London

Dedicated to Cecilia, Angela and Daniel

Miles Litvinoff was born in London in 1950. He studied English at Liverpool University before going first into teaching and then into book publishing. He is now a freelance writer and editor and co-edited (with Czech Conroy) *The Greening of Aid* (Earthscan Publications, 1988). Married with two children, he lives in London and is an active member of the Green Party.

First published in 1990 by
Earthscan Publications Ltd
3 Endsleigh Street, London WC1H 0DD

British Library Cataloguing in Publication Data
Litvinoff, Miles
  The Earthscan action handbook : for people and planet.
  1. Environment. Conservation
  I. Title   II. World Wide Fund for Nature
  333.72

ISBN 1-85383-062-3

Production by David Williams Associates (081-521 4130)
Typeset by Bookman Ltd. Bristol
Printed and bound by Cox & Wyman Ltd, Reading

Earthscan Publications Ltd is a wholly owned and editorially independent subsidiary of the International Institute for Environment and Development (IIED).

Contents

Part One: Human Needs

The Problem:
Peoples of the past: in tune with nature; the first environmentalists; **Colonialism:** cash crops and commodities; **No food
for the landless; Farming for the rich:** International trade; Aid
and inefficiency; **Environmental destruction:** mechanized agriculture; wood for fuel; overfishing; escaping the consequences;
The "green revolution": miracle seeds?; new problems; pests and
pesticides; irrigation; who gained?; **Food aid:** "grain junkies";
political bias.

Action:
Hunger: children; women; land reform; soil restoration; rural
development; social change; the NGOs; self-reliance; Northern
production and consumption; fishing; food aid.

Getting Involved:
Consumer and lifestyle choices: buy direct; boycott products;
go vegetarian; buy organic; grow your own; your lifestyle;
Community and political action: videos; World Food Day;
Oxfam – Hungry for Change; tell them what you think; **Organi-
zations.**

Community and political action: tell them what you think; an end to secrecy; water contamination; waste dumping; nuclear power; **Organizations.**

4. Women – Present Burdens and Future Role   92

The Problem:
Discrimination under the law: the weight of tradition; work in the home; women's health; marriage and motherhood; domestic violence; divorce; **Women as farmers:** colonial disruption; ignoring women's role; **Women in the modern economy:** inequality in employment; obstacles for working mothers; new technology; unemployment and poverty; **Women in a man's world:** education; fertility; politics; rape.

Action:
Women's burdens and role: collective action; legal rights; culture; women and work; women and development; rural women.

Getting Involved:
Consumer and lifestyle choices: buy from women; changes at home; equal treatment for boys and girls; women's refuges; **Workplace, community and political action:** equal pay; co-ops; child care; self-development; **Organizations.**

5. Human and Civil Rights   118

The Problem:
Children and education: early drop-outs; child labour; street children; the adoption trade; victims of war; **Indigenous peoples:** European conquest; pushed into poverty; forest and mountain people; oppression worldwide; genocide; the cost; **The violent state:** political prisoners; Latin America; Asia; Middle East; Africa; South Africa; **Rights in the North:** poverty and injustice in the West; the high cost of Northern wealth; support for oppression; Eastern Europe; **The future**.

Action:
Human rights: making choices; rights of the child; community schooling; protection; indigenous peoples; a change in material values; political will; public opinion; strengthening the UN; better democracy.

the Warsaw Pact; nuclear test ban; dissolve the alliances; chemical weapons; disarmament and development; controlling sales; arms conversion; the peace movement.

Getting Involved:
Consumer and lifestyle choices: make do with less; avoid competition; oppose violence; **Workplace, community and political action:** international links; industrial conversion; lobby for peace; peace studies; **Organizations.**

About This Book

Everybody is "green" these days, but how much has really changed? True, there is an upsurge of interest in doing things to save the planet, and even our mainstream political parties and the multinational corporations say they want to help. Yet there has been a lot of talk and too little action. What we in the rich countries now think of as an environmental crisis is nothing new to the hundreds of millions of people in poor countries who have lived with hunger, poverty, the degradation of natural resources, physical violence, economic exploitation and political oppression for generations, *and whose suffering is in many ways increasing.*

Aims of the book

This book sets out to show the connections between the global crisis as we in the wealthy North see it and as those in the impoverished South experience it in the brutality of their everyday lives. A time of crisis is also one of opportunity, and this book tries to suggest remedial action for most of the major problems facing us, even if these are rarely simple, swift or conflict-free.

For the sake of clarity, the book is divided into two parts, although any separation of the planet's problems from those of the human race is artificial (neither can be eased without the other):

- Part One focuses on the denial of a decent life to millions of low-income people because of decisions made in boardrooms and parliaments around the world. It considers the upsurge of non-violent but determined effort needed to restore and uphold the rights of the world's oppressed majority.
- Part Two describes the well-documented problems of land, water and atmospheric degradation and pollution, as well

as species loss and the threat arising from the warrior mentality.

Action

Solutions

Solutions are suggested in every chapter. Most of them involve a change of priorities, and many demand apparent material sacrifices on the part of the industrialized countries, so much of whose wealth is wasted on misguided projects and short-sighted goals; many solutions also mean less material consumption by better-off people. Yet for every material loss, there will be more-than-compensatory gains of a different kind: healthwise, emotional, moral, spiritual and convivial.

Where possible, the book tries to link long-term solutions with action we can take as individuals, by adjusting our consumption and lifestyle and participating in campaigns and political life.

Letter-writing

There are suggestions in the "Getting Involved" sections at the end of each chapter for issues to raise in letters to local councillors, Members of Parliament and Members of the European Parliament, to UK government ministers, to the chairmen/-women of banks and multinational corporations, to newspapers and so on. Write to your MP at the House of Commons, London SW1A 0AA. You can obtain the name and address of your MEP from the European Parliament UK Office, 2 Queen Anne's Gate, London SW1H 9AA.

A few points about letter-writing:

• Be polite if you want your letter to have a constructive effect or to receive a reply.
• Make your points clearly and briefly.
• When you write to a person, rather than to the press, ask at least one specific question and ask for a reply.
• Keep a copy of every letter you send and file the replies.
• Be persistent; don't be put off if you're not satisfied with the first reply.

- Going to the "top" can be effective; if you want to write a critical letter to a multinational or any other organization, phone first to find out the name and job title of the company president, chairman/-woman or chief executive and write to them.

Campaigning

In the UK you can also arrange to meet your MP in the House of Commons lobby by writing first. Or you can visit the MP in his or her constituency "surgery". During elections, send a letter or questionnaire to each candidate, asking their views on the subject of your concern, or put questions to them at public meetings or when they canvass you. If you find yourself in broad agreement with a political party, become an active member and try to influence its policies.

Names and addresses of campaigning organizations and action groups are listed at the end of every chapter. When contacting them for advice, information or resources, bear in mind that many are run on tight budgets; if you want a reply, send at least a stamped self-addressed envelope or, better still, a donation. For more guidance about community action in the UK, see the books by John Button, Gavin Scott and Des Wilson listed in "Recommended Reading" (pages 324–9).

Definitions

The terms "North" and "South" became widely known through the Brandt Report (*North–South: A Programme for Survival*; London: Pan, 1980). I have used them in preference to "First World" and "Third World", although they mean more or less the same and, like all generalizations, are helpful only up to a point. "North" usually refers to the high-income industrialized countries (Western Europe, North America, Australasia and Japan), often in the context of the relationship dating back to the colonial era between European powers and colonies and extending to economic domination today. (Eastern Europe and the USSR account for only a tenth of world trade and have until recently traded chiefly between themselves.)

In chapters dealing with the relationship between the capitalist democracies and the (former) Communist bloc, I have used the

terms "East" and "West". "South" refers to the low-income countries of Africa, Asia, the Caribbean, Latin America and the Pacific,
and also usually to the high-income Middle Eastern oil states.

I have used "billion" and "trillion" in the North American
sense of 1,000 million and 1,000 billion respectively. All
monetary figures are given in dollars. Metric measures are used
throughout; a hectare is 10,000 square metres, roughly 2.5 acres.
For other definitions, see the "Glossary" (pages 299–305).

Acknowledgements

My thanks to Margaret Busby, Lavinia Greenlaw and their
colleagues at Earthscan Publications for their encouragement
and support for this book. Thanks also to Dave Bradney, Steve
Dawe, Penny Day, Felicity Edholm, Brian Horne (information
officer at the Centre for Alternative Technology, Machynlleth,
Wales), Bob Jones, Jane McIntosh, Aubrey Meyer and many of
the organizations listed in the book for their advice, help and
suggestions.

Grateful acknowledgements are made to *Housmans World
Peace Directory* for much of the data on organizations and
action groups listed at the end of each chapter. The full
Directory, listing some two thousand national and international
organizations, is revised and updated annually, appearing as
part of the Housmans Peace Diary. Contact: Housmans, 5
Caledonian Road, London N1 (071-837 4473).

Grateful thanks also to the *Spare Rib Diary* for data on
women's organizations listed at the end of Chapter 4.

Abbreviations

CFCs	Chlorofluorocarbons
CHP	Combined heat and power
CITES	Convention on International Trade in Endangered Species
EC	European Community
FAO	Food and Agriculture Organization of the United Nations
FOE	Friends of the Earth
GATT	General Agreement on Tariffs and Trade
GNP	Gross national product
HYV	High yield variety
IIED	International Institute for Environment and Development
IMF	International Monetary Fund
IMO	International Maritime Organization
IPM	Integrated pest management
IPCC	Intergovernmental Panel on Climate Change
ITDG	Intermediate Technology Development Group
ITTO	International Tropical Timber Organization
IUCN	International Union for the Conservation of Nature and Natural Resources
MEP	Member of the European Parliament
NATO	North Atlantic Treaty Organization
NGO	Non-governmental organization
NIC	Newly industrializing country
NIEO	New international economic order
ODA	Official development assistance
OPEC	Organization of Petroleum Exporting Countries
SDI	Strategic Defense Initiative (US)
TASM	Tactical air-to-surface missile
TFAP	Tropical Forestry Action Plan
UN	United Nations
UNESCO	United Nations Educational, Scientific and Cultural Organization
UNICEF	United Nations (International) Children's (Emergency) Fund
UV	Ultra-violet
WCS	World Conservation Strategy
WHO	World Health Organization
WWF	World Wide Fund for Nature

PART ONE

HUMAN NEEDS

1. Food – the Right to Eat

"Hunger…is almost always the result of people being too poor to buy food. In virtually every famine studied, food exports from the area have increased during the famine because local people could not buy the food being produced."

Lloyd Timberlake[1]

The Problem

In today's world of plenty, more people starve to death or die of hunger-related disease than ever before. Nine hundred and fifty million adults and children are undernourished, of whom 50,000 die each day; 20 children die because of hunger each minute. For most of these people, the lack of food is part of everyday life, not the result of famine. Millions of children grow up physically stunted and mentally retarded because they are underfed, and even unborn children suffer permanent damage if the mother is short of food. Yet most of this hunger and nearly all of these deaths are preventable. We have the means but do we also have the political will to act? Today hunger haunts the lives of the poor people of the South – the inhabitants of Africa, Asia, the Caribbean, Latin America and the Pacific. Have large numbers of people in these lands always been short of food; and if not, why are they hungry now?

Peoples of the past

History and mythology tell us that famines did occur in ancient times – for example, the Old Testament story of Joseph and the seven lean and seven fat years. Ecological catastrophe, crop failures and food shortages may have destroyed such civilizations as Minoan Crete and Mesopotamia. Smaller tribal groups may also have vanished as a result of drought and famine.

Untouched by the rise and fall of mighty civilizations, however, a great many local cultures of rainforest hunter-gatherers, island fisherfolk, farmers and nomads survived independently for thousands of years. These modest communities maintained their way of life uninterrupted (or resumed it as soon as any ruling civilization in the region had passed away) because they coexisted in harmony with their environment.

In tune with nature

Whether these communities inhabited moist forests or dry savanna, mountainous regions or fertile river valleys, they took no more from the land than they needed for survival and for occasional feasts and celebrations. Their way of life had evolved over countless generations and was rooted in an acceptance of the Earth's natural abundance, but they knew the importance of prudence. Where they did suffer harvest failure and food shortage, the Earth's natural resilience would usually recover quickly.

Land was owned collectively, if at all. In the rainforests there was no need for ownership, although within tribes different individuals or groups might by custom use the produce of particular trees. Elsewhere, as in Africa, a village might jointly own the land round about, the elders assigning temporary land-use rights to individuals according to need and capacity. Or the territory of a small nation might be symbolically owned by the king or queen but again assigned according to need.

As with the air, the waters and the animals, the idea that individuals could own the land would have seemed ridiculous to most traditional societies. Many never even considered the possibility until it was too late. In 1626 the Dutch bought the island of Manhattan from its Amerindian inhabitants for $24 worth of kettles, axes and cloth; a similar price was paid two centuries later by the British for Maori land in what would become New Zealand. In neither case did the sellers have any idea what was taking place. In the words of the Sioux chief Crazy Horse: "One does not sell the earth upon which the people walk."[2]

With their small populations, most pre-colonial peoples had enough land and water for all, provided it was used wisely. Food and other necessary items were obtained with the minimum disruption of nature. In most of Africa, the least populated continent, dry climates and fragile soils made it essential to use the land lightly. Farmers knew that after a few harvests a piece of terrain would be exhausted for some years, so they would shift to another place; grazers knew they had to keep their herds on the move to avoid stripping the vegetation bare.

The first environmentalists

All such subsistence cultures had a deep ecological knowledge and felt a closeness to and veneration for the Earth. This was practical common sense, not some mystical religion. They knew that only by preserving the systems of soil, water, plants and animals intact could human survival be safeguarded. The environment was to them the sum of all goodness, and their relationship with it was their morality. If people abused or degraded the world they lived in (although their capacity to do so was limited), their way of life would be endangered.

One important survival strategy was the deliberate cultivation of genetic diversity. Traditional Indian farmers, for example, could call on a "library" of perhaps 10,000 varieties of rice, many of which are now lost. Each household and community had its stock of different strains and would use a range of them each planting season; in dry years poor yields of some varieties would be compensated by the survival of hardier strains.

To this day many indigenous peoples maintain their traditional way of life. One such group, the Chagga of northern Tanzania, practise a sophisticated and complex form of "forest farming" on the slopes of Mount Kilimanjaro. Here they combine agroforestry (growing trees and crops together), polycropping (mixing together different varieties of plants) and organic composting. Complementary crops are grown at every height, from the forest floor to the tree canopy. Fifteen types of banana tree alone provide the Chagga with food, animal fodder and ingredients for beer, while stabilizing the soil and helping retain moisture. Other crops, such as coffee, are produced for sale to outsiders. Today the Chagga forest farms successfully support the highest population density in Tanzania.[3]

Colonialism

The regional civilizations and enduring local cultures of Africa, the Americas, Asia, the Caribbean and Oceania were disrupted for ever by a new force from the North. The coming of the Europeans would dislocate traditional ways of life in every continent and alter the world beyond recognition. European colonizers imposed new forms of landownership, agriculture and economic organization on their subjects. Some of the conquered peoples, such as the Caribs, were destroyed by genocide. Elsewhere, the Europeans enslaved or dispossessed the indigenous people, expropriating and enclosing the best land.

Poorer-quality or inaccessible land was sometimes left to the colonized populations as a source of the grains, vegetables, fruits, firewood, water, animal fodder and other goods they needed. Not surprisingly, however, the way of life these peoples had developed when land was more plentiful became less able to support many of them and began to damage the environment. Traditional communities increasingly knew hunger. As time went on, and more land was taken over by colonialist landowners and business interests, it began to appear to many of the subject peoples that there was no future for them on the land. But now there was an alternative – the towns that had sprung up as seats of government and as trade and industry centres throughout the South. Over the decades, millions of once self-supporting people left the countryside to become urban-dwellers, dependent on others for their food.

Cash crops and commodities

To the first European settlers and landowners, life was an adventure; but to succeed, the adventurer had to get rich. The fastest way to generate profit was to produce food crops and raw materials for sale in Europe and North America. This was the start of the international trade in "cash crops" and commodities – unprocessed food and agricultural products, timber, rubber and mineral ores – and it coincided with the beginning of the Industrial Revolution.

The rulers of the colonies geared themselves to supply what the newly industrializing powers wanted but could not produce sufficiently for themselves. The former croplands, woodlands and rangelands of pre-colonial peoples were thus adapted for the large-scale production of tea, coffee, tobacco, cotton, sugar, nuts, fruits, vegetables and, later, beef. Most of the wealth generated by primary production and export remained in the hands of the colonialist elites or was repatriated to Europe.

Once established, the cash crop/commodities sector took on

its own momentum. Myths of racial superiority were used to justify the theft of what had belonged to indigenous populations. If the Europeans were superior, then their profits and pleasure were more important than the survival of a few hundred, hundred thousand or million Africans, Amerindians, Asians or Australasians. Another myth, by-product of Europe's agricultural and industrial revolutions, was that indigenous people's farming methods were backward and that large-scale, modernized agriculture was more efficient. By taking over control of the world's land, the Europeans could therefore claim to be acting for the good of all.

As land use became further dominated by the rich and powerful, their ranks came to include favoured members of the indigenous populations and the mighty multinational corporations of the modern world. Europe was transformed, no longer having to support itself with food. Now that many of its primary supplies were produced in the hungry lands of the colonized peoples, it could use its own populations to produce industrial goods.

The pattern has continued to this day. In the 1960s, for example, Del Monte, the US fruit company, moved into pineapple production in Kenya by buying out the small local growers. This was "modernization". Now producing about 40,000 tonnes of canned fruit every year (more than the original growers did), Del Monte Kenya exports nearly all of it; so the land no longer supplies local needs. This might be acceptable if Kenyans earned a good income from the pineapples. However, using imported modern machinery and technology, Del Monte employs (at low Southern wages) only a fraction of the people who used to work the land as smallholders. Where are they now, and who is feeding them?[4]

No food for the landless

The international agricultural and trading system is usually justified on the grounds that it is "efficient" and the best way to feed all the world's people. The truth is that it fails to feed hundreds of millions in the South and several million elsewhere.

People go hungry when they lack both access to the means to grow food and the money to buy it with. Neither the land nor the money is evenly distributed. One hundred million hectares of Africa, Asia, the Caribbean and Latin America have been taken out of local production. The use of these "ghost acres", as they are sometimes called, is paid for by rich and densely populated countries such as Japan, the Netherlands and the UK to provide the food and other materials they want.

In some cases, such lands are taken out of productive use completely. Del Monte reportedly farmed only 4,000 of the 23,000 hectares of Guatemala it owned in the 1970s. Many large landowners and multinationals leave their land idle (but increasing in value) rather than allow it to be used by the hungry people whose parents or grandparents once farmed it.[5]

Farming for the rich

In all, three-quarters of the world's productive land is controlled by 2.5 per cent of all landowners. In Latin America 93 per cent of the farmland is owned by 7 per cent of the population. If present trends continue, there could be 220 million landless rural households – a billion people – by the end of the century.[6]

Much of the land left to peasant farmers and livestock herders is, or becomes, unproductive. To many of them, colonialism and land-theft are recent history. What will be taken from them next and when? Why work hard to manure the soil or plant trees if this will only make some future landowner rich? Insecurity of tenure leads in the long run to deforestation and soil erosion to the point where land has to be abandoned.

The one billion people of the North – in Europe, North America, Japan and Australasia – dominate the world's land use because food markets respond to cash, not to need. Take the consumption of cereals and meat, for example. In 1986 roughly 1.8 billion tonnes of cereals were grown worldwide. Between a third and a half of these grains were not eaten directly by people, although most were fit for human consumption, but were fed to animals on their way to the dinner tables of the rich. Brazil's plantation farmers grow enormous quantities of soya cattle-feed for North American and European livestock on land that could otherwise support thousands of peasants.

In Botswana, where large numbers of people are too poor to buy a decent diet, World Bank funding has helped set up a massive expansion of cattle ranching, mostly for export. Worldwide, as much land is now used for animal grazing as for food crops, and each kilo of animal protein is produced at a cost of five, ten or fifteen times its own weight in grain. Who said modern agriculture was efficient?

The same goes for fish. South American-based European and US companies export huge quantities of Pacific fishmeal to the developed countries for animal feed. Meanwhile in Chile and Peru, from whose waters the catch is taken, hundreds of thousands of people lack the daily protein they need.

International trade

The benefits of international trade are conventionally explained in terms of "comparative advantage". Africa, Asia, the Caribbean and Latin America, the theory runs, specialize in the production of agricultural products and other raw materials, while Europe and North America concentrate on manufactured goods. Each side sells its surplus to the other at a fair price, and both prosper. But as we have seen, the relationship has been one of dominance from the start. By the time slavery was abolished, the North had become so much wealthier than the South that its position was self-sustaining. Having cornered the market in manufactured goods, Northern industry kept prices cripplingly high. At the same time, it was relatively simple to play off one poor commodity supplier against another to keep prices of food and raw materials low.

On average less than a quarter of the value of Southern exports goes to the producer country; the rest is taken up by foreign shippers, processors and packagers. Also, food and commodity prices (with the exception of oil and precious metals) are unstable and have fallen almost from the first, reaching their lowest ever levels in the 1980s.

Huge food subsidies paid by the rich countries to their farmers ($26 billion in the USA and $21 billion in the European Community in 1986) help depress the prices of Southern produce by undercutting competition. At the same time, the overproduction of food in Western Europe and North America leads to the dumping of low-priced Northern produce on the poor countries, putting local small farmers out of business.

Despite major increases of world food output, the access of millions of poor people to land, food or cash has failed to improve. Even for those who survive as small farmers or obtain waged labour, the money they can earn usually buys a poorer diet than they previously achieved outside the cash economy.

After the postwar modernization of Indian agriculture, for example, India's grain stocks doubled, yet average food consumption among poor people fell. Many smallholders who had previously produced their own wholegrain rice now had to buy less nutritious, commercially milled grain from intermediaries.[7]

Whatever their cash income on paper, Southern households often reap little benefit. In general it is the men who control family cash crop sales or wage income, and it is widely recognized that men are as likely to spend the money on beer and prostitutes as on family nutrition. Even when rural women control cash income, those with little experience of handling money often misspend it, being easily tricked by merchants or misled by advertising. When a formerly self-reliant community is brought into the cash economy, the quality of the household diet invariably suffers.

Most low-income countries have long ceased to be self-sufficient societies where most people grow their own food. Instead, as in the North, a farming sector provides some of the country's food directly and, with an industrial and service sector, tries to earn enough foreign currency to buy from abroad whatever else is required. With local farmers forced out of business, and the export of commodities earning damagingly low prices, under the present system most developing countries cannot feed themselves properly.

The former colonies of Asia and Latin America generally have rural services such as roads, schools and health centres, although often of poor standard. Elsewhere, especially in Africa, they are non-existent. Lacking such necessary infrastructure, most of the South is just not equipped to participate as an equal partner in an international trading system built upon cut-throat competition.

Aid and inefficiency

With worsening balances of trade and payments, the countries of the South have looked vainly to the North for significant long-term assistance. Instead, the International Monetary Fund (IMF) offers short-term loans with nasty strings attached. In the early 1980s, for example, child malnutrition rose by 50 per cent in Botswana, Ghana and Peru after the IMF dictated cuts in food subsidies. When the Mexican government cut subsidies in 1986 there followed average price rises of 75 per cent for bread, beans, tortillas and rehydrated milk. The story has been repeated many times.[8]

Corruption, inefficiency and misguided priorities among Southern governments must take some share of responsibility for world hunger. These ruling elites are usually preoccupied with their power base in the urban areas and ignore the needs of people in the countryside. While the army and civil service are usually favoured, rural-dwellers are denied the basic amenities that would enable them to support themselves. In the meantime, poor countries build airports and hotels for the benefit of travelling salesmen peddling weaponry from the North.

Environmental destruction

Environmental pressures are reducing the planet's capacity to produce food. As trees have been felled and vegetation stripped, more and more soil has been eroded. Soil has also been degraded and lost through overgrazing by livestock and overcultivation by short-sighted landowners. On marginal lands, desperate small farmers, with little other choice, over-plough delicate soils or deny them the fallow periods they need to regenerate. As vegetation is removed, local climate becomes drier. Droughts increase, but so paradoxically do floods when it rains, because less water is absorbed by the ground. In Africa, the most damaged continent, food output per head of population has fallen since the 1960s, with drought the primary cause of the terrible famines of the 1970s and 1980s.

Mechanized agriculture

The impact of mechanized agriculture can be especially destructive. Unlike traditional farming communities, with their respect for the land, the first priority of commercial farming is to reduce cost and maximize output and profit. A classic example of this approach was the infamous groundnut scheme imposed on East and Central Africa by the British in the late 1940s. Valuable for their oils, groundnuts make hard demands on the soil, needing long fallow periods. Huge sums of money were spent on mechanically clearing more than a million hectares of Kenya, Tanganyika (Tanzania) and Rhodesia (Zimbabwe). Each groundnut farm in the region was to use as much machinery and chemical fertilizer and as little human labour as possible. Within ten years much of the ground had baked hard as rock, and the project had to be abandoned.[9]

Applied indiscriminately to fragile Southern environments, industrialized agriculture wreaks havoc, relying on chemical inputs and mechanical ploughing that poison the soil and turn it to dust. It rejects the mixture of livestock and arable farming to manure the ground; and it clears away the trees and hedges that shade the soil and keep it moist, provide natural fertilizer and harbour pest predators. Little wonder that modern intensive farming has produced a soil crisis; and as every traditional farmer knows, a soil crisis means a food crisis.

Wood for fuel

Matters are made worse by a severe shortage of firewood, on which a billion people depend for cooking and heating. As land is cleared of trees or privatized, the poor have to spend more and more time in search of wood to burn. When supplies of dead wood are exhausted, they are forced to cut live branches. When these cannot be found, they have to burn crop residues and animal manure, the natural organic matter the earth needs to maintain its fertility and structure.

The firewood shortage increases rural hunger in another way, too, as poor households are unable to cook often enough. Women, the food and fuel providers, are too busy searching for firewood to grow food or prepare it properly.

Overfishing

In the rivers and seas, sources of much of the world's protein, the pattern is similar. With the introduction of mechanized trawlers and factory ships by the industrialized countries in the 1960s and 1970s, the global commercial fish catch has increased dramatically to 80 million tonnes a year or more. The artisal or non-commercial catch by Southern people for their own needs is put at about 24 million tonnes a year. So overall we have probably exceeded the upper limit for sustainable fishing from the world's seas, estimated as a total annual catch of about 100 million tonnes.

Some fish populations are already well into a decline, as is the share of the total catch that Southern fisherfolk enjoy. The performance of Peru's anchovy fisheries, formerly a mainstay of the national economy, has steadily worsened; and offshore of West Africa only a third of the catch goes to local fisherfolk

– long-distance foreign fleets take the rest. Overall, a third of all the fish commercially caught is earmarked for animal feed and fertilizer, mainly in the North, rather than for direct human consumption. Besides overfishing, pollution and industrialization of river systems and coastal areas have done much to exhaust the productivity of the world's waters. Not surprisingly, from West Africa to South Asia (where ocean fishing supplies a high proportion of people's daily protein needs), traditional fishing communities are being forced into debt or out of business.

Escaping the consequences
The rich countries have so far escaped the consequences of the food crisis. Criticizing "ignorant" peasant farmers for cutting down too many trees, Northern consumers are themselves protected from feeling the pinch. When there are shortages, the available food goes to the highest bidder. If the lands become unproductive in one country or region, it is easy for the food multinationals to sell up and buy better land elsewhere. In the end, however, if enough of the world's fertile lands and waters are destroyed or endangered, these shortages will affect us all.

The "green revolution"

Before its official abolition in the nineteenth century, slave labour was the key to keeping costs low on the Northern-owned plantations and farming estates that covered the South. As time went on, however, it became harder to justify the enslavement of human labour. From the business point of view, in any case, human employees were increasingly expensive to pay and difficult to handle. But now there was an alternative – machinery and oil. In place of the human tasks such as ploughing, watering, weeding and spreading mulches by hand, oil-powered machinery, irrigation systems and chemical pesticides and fertilizers could be used. "Agribusiness" – industrialized agriculture – was born.

Miracle seeds?
To this capital-intensive method of farming was added one further component that launched what was to be called the "green revolution". The final element was specially developed genetic strains of wheat and rice that, given constant irrigation and enough chemical fertilizer, grew faster and produced larger

seed-heads than traditional strains. Some varieties could produce three crops in a year.

This was surely the "miracle" the world had been waiting for. It would both feed the hungry and make the agribusiness firms rich. No wonder the food scientists of the US government and the UN Food and Agriculture Organization (FAO) who developed the new strains in the 1940s called it a revolution.

The new "high yield varieties" (HYVs), as they were called, may have been useless in the rugged conditions in which most of the world's small farmers grew their cereals; but when the situation was right they seemed unbeatable. Introduced first in Mexico and the Philippines and then throughout Central America and South Asia, as well as in North Africa, HYVs caused an upsurge in the use of irrigation and agrochemicals. The world's area of irrigated land doubled in three decades, while chemical fertilizer and pesticide applications shot up by 900 per cent and 3,200 per cent respectively.[10]

New problems
True to predictions, yields have increased fast, but there have been many unforeseen problems. Because of their heavier seed-heads, HYVs would fall over were it not for the shorter stems bred into them. Shorter-stemmed strains, however, are easily crowded out by weeds, so extra doses of herbicide are needed. Again, water makes up a larger proportion of the magnificent size and weight of HYVs than of traditional strains (hence the need for constant irrigation); this means that their nutritional value is relatively lower, and they are more prone to destruction by moulds during storage. Another drawback for the world's undernourished people – although not for Northern agribusiness, which owns the seed patents – is that the characteristics of HYVs do not reproduce; instead of being able to rely on their own seeds, farmers have to buy new seeds each year from such global giants as Sandoz, Shell, Upjohn and Volvo.

There are further problems. Only two cereals have been developed in this way – wheat and rice – whereas most of the world's poor rely on other staples such as sorghum, cassava, millet and pulses; so millions of people cannot benefit from the "revolution" unless they change their eating habits. In any case, with its need for continuous irrigation and petrochemicals, HYV farming is out of reach of most small farmers. The "revolution's" founders argued in favour of "building on the best" – when the more prosperous farmers were successfully using the new techniques, other cultivators would follow. In the event, large landowners have benefited from increased yields and been able to expand their market share, forcing thousands of smaller farmers off the land.[11]

Blindly imposed on many developing countries, this uninvited revolution has rightly been called a "socioeconomic disaster".[12] The new techniques replaced the one resource there is plenty of everywhere – labour – with factors of production that are abundant only in wealthy countries: credit, technical know-how, machinery and petrochemicals. Nobody ensured that the increased food output was made available to the growing numbers of landless poor at fair prices. And as the price of oil and of Western manufactures climbed during the 1970s, poor countries that had enthusiastically converted to the "green revolution" found themselves hard pressed to pay.

Pests and pesticides
Worse still, the "miracle seeds" are unusually vulnerable to pests. Traditional cereal growing relies on planting several crops or varieties together or alternating them over time, with fallow periods, to prevent pest species finding a secure "niche" in which to multiply and cause serious damage. HYVs, by contrast, grown as uniform "monocrops" on vast, uninterrupted tracts of land with hardly a pause, provide ideal conditions for insect pests. (The application of herbicides can itself leave a residue on the ground that is a haven and breeding-ground for pests.)

Each application of pesticide destroys the weaker but not the stronger members of the target pest species. Free from competition, these stronger specimens enjoy a food bonanza and a population explosion. So a heavier pesticides dose is needed next time, and so the process goes on. By 1980 it was said that over 400 insect and mite species had developed pesticide resistance. Trapped on this pesticide treadmill, the insecticide expenditure of Philippines rice farmers shot up by 4,500 per cent during the 1960s and 1970s.[13]

Yet another problem arose in South-east Asia, where large areas of HYV rice paddy are stocked with edible fish. Masses of these fish have been poisoned with insecticide, causing losses of 600,000 tonnes of food a year in Indonesia alone.[14]

Dangerous as well as expensive, pesticides poison hundreds of thousands of people each year, in some cases fatally. Ironically, however, there is evidence that they are as good as useless. Worldwide crop losses to pests have remained at about 35 per cent since pesticides were first widely introduced in the 1950s, and only another 1 or 2 per cent of most crops would probably be lost if none were used at all.[15]

Irrigation

More harmful side-effects of the "green revolution" have been caused by large-scale irrigation. Many river ecosystems have been disrupted by the need for reservoirs. Areas flooded by the reservoirs include once-productive river valleys, sometimes destroying as much farmland as has been brought into use through irrigation. While new irrigation waters have allowed some farmers to increase their output, many small cultivators have been displaced by the reservoirs. The consequent clearing of new land on hillsides causes soil erosion that silts up the reservoirs, shortening their useful life.

Large reservoirs were to be a source of fish, but their yields are invariably lower than predicted, due to silting or to acidification caused by rotting vegetation in the water. As if this were not enough, life close to irrigation reservoirs and canals can be unpleasant and dangerous because these waters are breeding-grounds for malarial mosquitoes and disease-carrying snails. Finally, as with most components of the "green revolution", large-scale irrigation can rarely be sustainable in the long term; huge quantities of water are wasted through poor management and drainage, and this results in water shortages plus the salinization of soils, gradually rendering them sterile.

Who gained?

The "green revolution" has made some landowners and merchants wealthy. It has delivered vast profits to the multinational corporations that control agribusiness. Yet for hundreds of millions of the world's most needy people it has done nothing at all. As the writers Frances Moore Lappé and Joseph Collins point out, if the "revolution" could have worked, it would have by now.[16] Even the World Bank now admits that increasing food output alone cannot solve world hunger and that "redistributing purchasing power and resources toward those who are undernourished" is needed.[17] This idea is long overdue.

Food aid

Plenty of surplus food is produced – in the wrong places. Using hormone treatments, oil-guzzling machinery and agrochemicals as if there were no tomorrow, Western Europe and North America have given birth to monstrous beef, grain and dairy mountains. What could be wrong, an innocent might ask, with Northern growers giving this food surplus, currently worth about $2,600 million a year, as aid to the hungry of the South?

The main objection is that non-emergency food aid, like the dumping of low-priced food, is inflicted on poor countries at the whim of the rich and causes structural dependence. There is, in fact, little to choose between low-priced dumping and the supposedly humanitarian gift of non-emergency food aid. By undercutting local prices, both strategies put small farmers out of business.

The flood of cheap or free foreign food may dry up at any time if conditions, markets or foreign-policy objectives in the North change. But by then people in the recipient country or region may have got so used to Northern wheat that local producers cannot woo them back to traditional grains. Apart from during emergencies, a large temporary influx of food can reduce a country's potential to feed itself for years to come.

"Grain junkies"
The conscious promotion of food dependency is an unpleasant feature of US foreign policy. In the 1950s, worried by rising domestic wheat surpluses, the US government devised its Food for Peace Act. The Act aimed to prevent a crash in US prices by selling the wheat cheaply in Southern markets for local currencies. This would not affect US farmers' dollar incomes and would "make friends" abroad. The Americans knew exactly what they were doing; in the words of Senator Hubert Humphrey: "If you are looking for a way to get people to lean on you and be dependent on you...it seems to me that food aid would be terrific."[18] Whole regions became "grain junkies".[19]

Largely unchanged, this approach was adopted by the European Community (EC) for disposing of the food mountains and lakes arising from its common agricultural policy in the 1970s and 1980s. The reduction in storage costs for its meat, wheat, butter and milk was a major consideration in the EC's deciding in favour of mass non-emergency food aid.

With all their experience of giving food away, the North Americans and West Europeans might have been expected to snap smartly into action when a genuine emergency arose. Not so. In the terrible sub-Saharan famine of 1984–5, when up to 2 million people died, their indecision and inefficiency – as well as corruption and bungling among the beneficiary governments – made the disaster far worse than it might have been. Following warnings that a famine of extraordinary scale was at hand, it took two years before significant amounts of food aid arrived from the industrialized countries. Then it descended on Ethiopia and Sudan in an avalanche that overwhelmed storage and distribution facilities. (By 1989–90, however, lessons had been learned, and the EC and USA emergency response in Ethiopia was better organized.)

Wheat and rice have often been sent to the Sahel and West Africa, where the staple foods are millet, sorghum, cassava and pulses. In 1968 the Swiss government sent cheese to starving Biafra during the Nigerian civil war; like other West Africans, the Biafrans cannot digest dairy produce easily and become ill if they eat it. Some of the cheese was eaten by foreign aid workers, while the rest was burned.

Political bias
There is political bias, too. Egypt is a relatively affluent developing country. Because of its staunchly pro-Western government in a politically sensitive region, it receives a fifth of all World Bank cereal aid and in some years (including the catastrophic 1985) more US food aid than any other African country. Elsewhere, in 1986 the USA sent tractors and other farm machinery worth $2 million to impoverished Mozambique – on the condition that the aid was used in the private sector, which hardly exists there because rural communities pool their resources in the struggle to survive.[20]

Recipient governments themselves use food aid short-sightedly. With so many Southern cities sited close to frontiers or on the coast, it is easier to have the food consumed there rather than to pay for transportation into the countryside. Politically insecure governments also use cheap or free food to defuse urban discontent rather than to alleviate the misery of the rural areas. In early 1990 it was reported that Ethiopian government aircraft had knowingly bombed 50,000 tonnes of stored emergency grain in the Eritrean-held port of Masawa.[21]

Action

Hunger

Some people, who have full stomachs, say we should accept hunger as a fact of life, since we will never eliminate it. True, we cannot be sure we will ever abolish hunger completely, but it would be immoral not to try. Europe was once ravaged by hunger, as was China.

Children
The most vulnerable of the world's undernourished people are children. According to the UN children's fund UNICEF, the lives of most of the 15 million children who die of hunger annually could be saved at a cost of $5 each through simple rehydration therapy, breast-feeding, immunization and basic child care. With growth monitoring and supplementary feeding where needed, children's life expectancy would improve markedly. Women in developing countries would then choose to bear fewer children and be better able to feed their households.

Women
Women are the key to the welfare of poor households. If their control of cash, land or crops increases, levels of family nutrition improve. This means there must be more participation by women in all levels of decision-making, and a reversal of the decline in the status of girl children in much of the South.

Land reform
Most hunger is rural, and most rural households are small farmers, who can be helped to end their own hunger. First, land reform is essential so that rural people have enough land to sustain themselves (and perhaps grow a small surplus) with security of tenure. In China (as far as we can tell) a thorough redistribution of land helped release the country from chronic famines and give it low-level but adequate food security. With only 7 per cent of the world's arable land, China supports 22 per cent of the planet's population on domestic produce.

Wherever countries have successfully redistributed land, as in Cuba, Japan, South Korea and Zimbabwe, food self-reliance and rural well-being have been improved.

Counter to conventional myths, small farmers are probably more efficient than large ones. Small farms tend to be more labour-intensive, less dependent on chemicals and machinery and, crucial in the long run, kinder to the environment. The World Bank reports that small farms in Latin America produce on average fourteen times more per hectare than large ones. In Asia small farms are up to six times more efficient than large ones, despite, or because of, using much more labour. One study concluded that by distributing all the farmland among the peasant population Brazil's north-east region could achieve an increase in food output of 80 per cent.[22]

The reasons for the efficiency of small farmers are not hard to find. They make use of every spare patch of ground, while respecting the value of trees and hedges, for example, rather than clearing them. They usually have a detailed understanding of the needs and limitations of the soil; and as long as their land rights are secure, they are much better motivated than underpaid labourers working on large estates.

Land redistribution is a political problem. In many parts of the world, large landowners have proved unwilling to give up their power and wealth at any price. Nevertheless, the political pressures for reform must be sustained.

Soil restoration
In many places, the soil will have to be rehabilitated. Techniques to improve food output and restore soil productivity include:

- a return to traditional crop varieties and mixed cropping (to protect against drought, soil erosion, pests and other losses);
- agroforestry;
- the use of leguminous plants (such as lentils; legumes "fix" nitrogen in the soil and enhance fertility),
- organic mulches and animal manure (to reduce dependency on chemicals and restore soil structure);
- the planting of trees and hedgerows as windbreaks, to stabilize soils and retain moisture and for firewood, animal fodder, building materials and pest control.

All these are standard techniques drawn from the best traditional practice. This is not, however, to consign rural people to a life of drudgery. In many developing countries traditional practices are increasingly combined with small-scale modern techniques ranging from rock bund construction and contour terracing to windpumps, small tractors and micro-hydro dams for local irrigation. Simplicity and low cost are the key to what has become known as "appropriate development".

Rural development
Besides agriculture, complementary rural activities such as small industry, crafts, reforestation and fish farming can play an important part in the regeneration of the rural South. Other useful strategies (many of them common in Asia) are the use of all organic wastes (including human excrement) for fertilizer and methane generation, widespread small-scale irrigation and hydro-power, orchards, dairy farming and light industry.

Governments have a major role in guaranteeing fair prices for rural produce and providing funding for small-farmer credit and advice, as well as rural services such as roads, storage facilities, sanitation, schools and basic health care. Developing countries will have to change their investment priorities and put more money into the rural areas. (Currently no more than a fifth of their domestic spending goes to the countryside.)

Rural populations are being depleted and shanty towns are mushrooming as people migrate to urban areas in search of work. The cities cannot cope with the influx. Rural development must aim to slow and, in time, reverse this process. Nevertheless, in the towns and cities, too, a redistribution of income and wealth is essential if poor urban-dwellers are to live decently.

Social change
New forms of social organization have become necessary because of the fragmentation of traditional communities. Throughout the developing world more and more women's farming co-ops, tree-planting and livestock-lending associations, urban gardening groups, collective credit schemes and health clubs are starting up, often funded by non-governmental organizations (NGOs) such as Oxfam and World Neighbors. These groups

are rediscovering valuable principles of collective self-help and risk-avoidance.

The NGOs

NGOs are increasingly at the forefront of problem-solving in poor countries. Motivated by humanitarian ideals, they have an invaluable role as facilitators of grass-roots development. NGOs have shown themselves better able to understand and respond to needs at village and community level than national governments or institutions such as the World Bank. As an example of what can be done, a Colombian NGO has recently launched a low-cost rooftop food-growing scheme in the slums of Bogotá. Backed by the UN Development Programme, the project uses donated waste materials such as unwanted rice bran, wooden crates and recycled polythene to help poor urban dwellers grow fresh vegetables both to supplement their diet and to generate income. Trials have proved promising.[23]

Self-reliance

The international trade in cash crops (coffee, tea, sugar, cocoa and so on) will be a fact of life for decades but must not be allowed to expand further. Southern governments should be encouraged to resist any extension of their cash crop sector and instead work towards food self-sufficiency and regional co-operation in food provision with neighbouring countries. Self-reliance will depend on a move away from mechanization and agrochemicals back to low-input, labour-intensive agriculture.

The fear that developing countries will suffer by reducing their involvement in the international commodities trade is often unfounded. Throughout the US trade embargo, the well-being of Nicaragua's population compared favourably with that of the poor majority populations in El Salvador, Guatemala and Honduras, whose economies are closely tied to that of the USA. In Africa, rural nutrition in Tanzania improved when, unable to sell their cash crops because of depressed markets, peasants returned to growing food for home consumption. Niger survived the Sahelian famines of the 1980s better than some of its neighbours because of its earlier change of priorities from cash crops to food self-sufficiency.

Northern production and consumption

We cannot expect poor countries to go it alone. In the industrialized countries there must be an end to the overconsumption and overproduction that have caused untold harm. The subsidies that encourage Northern farmers to produce so much wheat, meat and dairy food must be phased out. Paying farmers to "set aside" land – now US and UK government policy – is the wrong approach, failing to discourage overproduction on the remaining land. Nor is "set aside" any help to Northern farmers who want to farm less intensively and use fewer chemicals. Northern governments must instead provide subsidies and grants to help farmers through the fallow periods needed for the change to organic methods – as is done in Denmark and Sweden. Such a reduction in output in the North will lead to more food being produced where it is needed.

Consumption patterns in the industrialized countries are changing but not fast enough. Northern consumers will have to cut down on the meat, dairy foods, foreign-grown fruits, exotic vegetables, convenience foods and other luxuries that they currently enjoy because of their monopoly of the world's wealth and land use. In the words of John Medcalf, a priest working in Central America: "Supermarkets stuffed with 35 different brands of chocolate bars and 22 assorted breakfast cereals are the *reason* why most people in most countries don't know what a chocolate bar is and don't eat breakfast at all."[24]

Instead, we will have to adapt to a simpler, plainer and healthier diet based more on local and seasonal produce. Total vegetarianism may not be needed, because a limited number of animals can be raised economically, manuring the soil and eating grass and foliage people cannot digest. But the world's livestock population is at present greater than the planet can sustain, and too many animals are raised wastefully. Pigs, for example, could be fattened on processed institutional waste foods, as they were in Europe during the Second World War, saving grain and cutting farmers' costs.

Because much more of the food produced in the developing countries will have to stay there to meet local needs, the North also needs to become more self-supporting. Land reform can help, enabling more people to produce the food needed; at present much of the land is wastefully farmed, left idle or preserved for the private pleasure of the rich.

Something could be learned from Sweden, where only working farmers are permitted to own farmland, and the government monitors and controls land sales and prices to protect small family farmers. A community land tax would dissuade large land-owners from keeping productive land unused (and unavailable to the public for recreation).

Fishing

As for fish, the shortage may be partly met by exploiting the Antarctic krill. Japan and the USSR already harvest large quantities; but research is needed into how much krill can be caught without adversely affecting the marine mammals, fish and seabirds that depend on it. More important, how-ever, would be a redistribution of the available fish away from the developed countries – especially a reduction in their use of it for animal feed and fertilizer – towards the peo-ple who need the protein most. The idea of 320-kilometre Exclusive Economic Zones, already internationally negotiated but not yet accepted as international law, offers a chance for Southern countries to control the fish caught in their waters; these zones could be used as the basis for an inter-national fishing policy aimed at keeping the world's annual catch below 100 million tonnes and ensuring its proper dis-tribution.

Food aid

The need to end all non-emergency food aid is a priority. According to the Ghanaian-born academic Edward Ayensu: "The greatest threat to Third World nations is the prolonged and unwarranted food aid from the rich nations of the North."[25]

Long-term reforestation and soil recovery programmes must remain an international priority in drought- and famine-hit regions. Where major crop failures do occur, early warning is essential to avoid a human disaster. Monitoring of grain and cattle prices in local markets has proved useful for predicting the approach of food shortages.

To reduce their reliance on foreign emergency aid, develop-ing countries can build up local and regional stocks of surplus produce in better years. Where emergency food aid is unavoid-able, it must be better managed than in the past. In cases of local food shortages, "triangular" emergency aid should be provided. This means buying the food from another developing country or, preferably, elsewhere within the famine-hit country to encourage local production and keep wealth in the region. Oxfam did this during the 1980s Ethiopian famine.

The changes needed seem immense. So too, however, is the power of public opinion expressed through political pressure, consumer action and the changing atmosphere of debate and concern. Every one of us can contribute to this force for change.

Getting Involved

Related subjects covered elsewhere in this book include: poverty, debt and development – Chapter 2; population, disease and pesticide poisoning – Chapter 3; rural women – Chapter 4; deforestation and soil erosion – Chapter 6; irrigation – Chapter 7. To find out more about hunger, world food production and food consumption, see "Recommended Reading" (pages 324–9).

Consumer and lifestyle choices

If we know where our food comes from and how it gets to us, we can put pressure on the food industry through our consumption decisions. There are consumer guides on the market giving useful information about the effects of different food products and companies on the welfare of poor people worldwide. In the UK try *The Green Consumer Guide* (London: Gollancz, 1988) and *The Green Consumer Supermarket Guide* (London: Gollancz, 1989) by John Elkington and Julia Hailes, and *How to Be Green* by John Button (London: Century Hutchinson, 1989).

Buy direct
A great deal of our food is unethically produced. For example, most of our coffee and tea comes from plantations in the South where people are paid near-starvation wages. But there are a growing number of non-profit fair-trading organizations selling food and other produce from low-income countries; you can be sure that purchases from them will help make the growers better off rather than enriching merchants and shippers. Most of these

suppliers have mail-order catalogues; some have shops. Many sell coffee, tea, grains, spices, dried fuits, nuts, honeys and so on. See the "Getting Involved" section in Chapter 2 for a full list of these organizations.

Boycott products

Where you learn that a particular food or drink is being produced in a low-income country at the expense of local people's food needs, boycott that product and explain your reasons to retailers, to other people you know and (in writing) to the wholesaler, supplier or manufacturer. In the UK, send a copy of your letter to the Food and Drink Federation, 6 Catherine Street, London WC2.

Go vegetarian

Reduce your consumption of meat; hungry people could grow food for themselves on the land now used for rearing animals and producing animal feedstuffs. There are plenty of good alternative sources of protein, such as milk, cheese, yoghurt, eggs, beans, peas, grains, soya, nuts and seeds. Ideally, cut down on all forms of animal produce; the UK could be self-sufficient in food if more land were used to produce vegetable rather than animal protein. Ask for vegetarian food in restaurants and suggest improvements if the choice is poor. More information on changing to a meatless diet is available in the UK from the Vegetarian Society, Parkdale, Dunham Road, Altrincham, Cheshire WA14 4QG (061-928 0793).

Buy organic

Buy organic rather than chemically-farmed food as often as possible and try to buy local produce rather than the mass products of the multinationals. Organic food is healthier and usually tastes better. For information about the availability of organic foods in the UK, see *Thorsons Organic Consumer Guide*, edited by David Mabey and Alan and Jackie Gear (Wellingborough: Thorsons, 1990).

Grow your own

You could also try to grow your own food organically. The day when governments recognize the importance of low-input farming and subsidize it properly cannot be far off. To learn about organic farming techniques and suitable varieties of fruits and vegetables in the UK, as well as to obtain supplies of seeds and tools, contact or visit:

- Henry Doubleday Research Association, National Centre for Organic Gardening, Ryton-on-Dunsmore, Coventry CV8 3LG (0203-303517).
- Centre for Alternative Technology, Machynlleth, Powys, Wales SY20 9AZ (0654-702400).
- Permaculture Association, 8 Hunters Moon, Dartington, Totnes, Devon TQ9 6JT (0803-867546).
- Soil Association, 86 Colston Street, Bristol BS1 5BB (0272-290661).
- Working Weekends on Organic Farms, 19 Bradford Road, Lewes, Sussex BN7 1RB.

Your lifestyle
Consider other ways you could increase your solidarity with the world's hungry people. Think about the consequences of your work or your lifestyle. What else could you do in either to contribute to the fight against hunger?

Community and political action

Videos
As a teacher or parent, encourage children to discuss, read or watch educational films and videos about hunger and produce their own drawings and writings on the subject. Here are some sources of videos for young people and adults:

- The Hunger Project (address below) will supply, for a small donation, a video and presenter's pack about world hunger and how people can overcome it. Use the video as a basis for viewings and discussion sessions in your school or college, in your family, among friends or in your community group.
- Another video available in the UK is *Everything Connects*, which links world hunger with unemployment, the environment crisis and the arms race. The video comes complete with study materials and is available from the General Synod Office of the Scottish Episcopal Church, 21 Grosvenor Crescent, Edinburgh EH12 5EE, Scotland.

Other videos on hunger, development and related issues are available in the UK from:

- Concord Videos, 201 Felixtowe Road, Ipswich, Suffolk IP3 9BJ (0473-715754).
- Oxfam Education Unit, Effra School, Barnwell Road, London SE2 (071-737 7967).

World Food Day

Every year 16 October is World Food Day, promoted by the UN Food and Agriculture Organization to increase public awareness of the world food problem and to bring people of all countries together in the fight against hunger. You can participate in World Food Day in a number of ways:

- Write to the press, pointing out how widespread hunger is and describing some of its causes and possible solutions.
- Write articles on hunger for community newsletters.
- Make contact with local or national organizations involved in the effort to eliminate hunger and join in their activities.
- Arrange meetings or workshops about hunger, perhaps with videos (see above).

Oxfam – Hungry for Change

Oxfam UK (address below) has run its Hungry for Change campaign since 1984, focusing on five causes of hunger in poor countries: debt, aid, trade, agricultural policies and arms. There are over two hundred Hungry for Change groups in the UK involved in mounting street stalls and public exhibitions, arranging vigils, street theatre, public meetings and home video shows, contacting MPs and MEPs, taking part in nationwide events, organizing media publicity and participating in the annual sponsored fast. There is a book to go with the campaign, *Cultivating Hunger*, available from Oxfam for £1.50, which focuses on the causes of hunger and poverty. People are welcome to participate in the campaign even if they have only a little time to spare; contact Hungry for Change through local area Oxfam offices, listed in the phone book.

Tell them what you think

Letter-writing to local councillors, MPs and MEPs, to the local and national press and to community newsletters, as well as calls to phone-in radio programmes, can help change public opinion. Or you can write directly to the Minister for Overseas Development (Foreign and Commonwealth Office, Downing Street, London SW1A 2AL). Subjects you could take up include:

- the connection between our overabundance of food in the North and starvation in the South;
- the need to end all non-emergency food aid to the South and to halt the dumping of cheap surplus food there;
- the importance of food labelling to show country of origin so that people know which country's produce they are buying;
- the need for guaranteed international prices for Southern foodstuffs;
- the importance of land reform in both South and North;
- the vast sums of money spent on weapons, of which only a fraction would help low-income countries eliminate hunger;
- the need for poor people in the South to be given a real chance to achieve food self-reliance.

Organizations

Organizations dedicated to the elimination of hunger throughout the world include:

UK and Irish Republic
Action from Ireland, PO Box 1522, Dublin 1, Irish Republic.
Catholic Fund for Overseas Development, 2 Romero Close, Stockwell Road, London SW9 9TY (071-733 7900).
Christian Aid, PO Box 100, London SE1 7RT (071-620 4444).
Hunger Project, 140 Cromwell Road, London SW7 4YZ (071-373 5066), and 7 Regents Terrace, Leeds LS7 4QL (0532-668448).
One World Centre, 4 Lower Crescent, Belfast BT7 1NR (0232-241879).
Oxfam, 274 Banbury Road, Oxford OX2 7DZ (0865-56777).
Quaker Peace and Service, Friends House, Euston Road, London NW1 2BJ (071-387 3601).
Save the Children Fund, 17 Grove Lane, London SE5 8RD (071-703 5400).
SOS Sahel, 1 Tolpuddle Street, London N1 0XT (071-837 9129).
United Nations Children's Fund (UNICEF) UK, 55 Lincoln's Inn Fields, London WC2A 3NB (071-405 5592).

USA and Canada

American Friends Service Committee, 1501 Cherry Street, Philadelphia, Pa 19102, USA.

Bread for the World, 802 Rhode Island Avenue NE, Washington, DC 20018, USA.

Canadian Friends Service Committee, 60 Lowther Avenue, Toronto, Ontario M5R 1C7, Canada.

Child Hope, 6th Floor, 331 East 38th Street, New York, NY 10016, USA.

Hunger Project, 144 Front Street West, Suite 520, Toronto, Ontario, Canada.

Hunger Project, 1 Madison Avenue, New York, NY 10010, USA.

Institute for Food and Development Policy/Food First, 145 Ninth Street, San Francisco, Calif. 94103, USA.

Oxfam America, 115 Broadway, Boston, Mass 02116, and Suite 8, 513 Valencia Street, San Francisco, Calif. 94110, USA.

Oxfam Canada, Room 301, 251 Laurier Avenue West, Ottawa, Ontario K1P 5J6, Canada.

Project Ploughshares, Conrad Grebel College, Waterloo, Ontario N2L 3G6, Canada.

Save the Children, Suite 6020, 3080 Yonge Street, Toronto, Ontario M5W 2B1, Canada.

World Neighbors, 5116 North Portland Avenue, Oklahoma City, Okla 73112, USA.

Australia and New Zealand

Action for World Development, PO Box 117, Fitzroy, Victoria 3065, Australia.

Australia Coalition for Overseas Aid, PO Box 1562, Canberra, ACT 2601, Australia.

Community Aid Abroad, 156 George Street, Fitzroy, Victoria 3065, Australia.

Council for the Organization of Relief Services Overseas, PO Box 9716, Courtney Place, Wellington, New Zealand.

Hunger Project, Suite 6, 3rd Floor, 154 Elizabeth Street, Sydney, NSW 2000, Australia.

Hunger Project, PO Box 2000, Auckland, New Zealand.

New Zealand Coalition for Trade and Development, PO Box 11345, Wellington, New Zealand.

United Nations Children's Fund (UNICEF) Australia, 14th

Floor, 80 Mount Street, North Sydney, New South Wales 2060, Australia.

United Nations Children's Fund (UNICEF) New Zealand, PO Box 347, 29 Brandon Street, Wellington, New Zealand.

Africa and Asia (Commonwealth)

Christian Service Committee, Box 551294, Limbe, Malawi.

Institute for Environment and Development Studies, Bangladesh, PO Box 4222, Ramna Dhaka 1000, Bangladesh.

International Council for Research in Agroforestry, PO Box 30677, Nairobi, Kenya.

Kagisong Centre, Mogoditashane, PO Box 20166, Gabarone, Botswana.

Lesotho Co-op Credit Union League, PO Box 439, Maseru 100, Lesotho.

Presidential Trust Fund for Self-Reliance, PO Box 70000, Dar-es-Salaam, Tanzania.

Research Foundation for Science, Technology and Natural Resources Policy, 105 Rajpur Road, Dehradun 248001, India.

Sarvodaya Shramadana, 98 Damask Mandira, Rawatawatte Road, Moratuwa, Sri Lanka.

Village Development Foundation, Box 113, Mungwi, Zambia.

2. Wealth – Greed versus Need

"If change is really to benefit the poor and powerless...real resources have to be massively diverted. That means that big industry, large-scale farming, expensive buildings, prestige medicine and academic education cannot expect to go on growing as before...Real powers have to be devolved to democratic organizations at the base."

Paul Harrison[1]

The Problem

Most people in the rich countries of the North enjoy the benefits of a world economy geared to their satisfaction, while millions in the South live like slaves. Western Europe, North America, Australasia and Japan, with about a sixth of the planet's population, account for 65 per cent of its cash income. Africa, Asia, the Caribbean, Latin America and the Pacific share just 25 per cent, half of which is OPEC oil money. The poorest seven-tenths of humanity survive on roughly an eighth of the world's wealth.[2]

The gap between rich and poor countries is widening. Economist Ted Trainer argues that early in the colonial era average incomes in Europe were perhaps less than twice those in Africa, Asia or Latin America. By 1960 gross national product (GNP) per person in the industrialized countries had climbed to twenty times that of low-income countries, and by 1980 it had shot up to forty-six times more. While average incomes of the rich have advanced annually by more than $270 since the 1960s, Southern incomes have crept up by only $7 a year. Incomes *fell* in at least forty countries during the 1980s, with the proportion of the world's population living in severe poverty increasing for the first time since 1945.[3]

World trade and modern economic development, in combination with rapid population growth, have "left hundreds of millions of people utterly destitute and raised an unprecedented spectre of perpetual famine, starvation and war".[4] How has this arisen, and what can be done about it?

Unequal partners

During the centuries of economic expansion and foreign conquest, Europeans' technical superiority (in navigation, ship-building, firearms and so on) over the peoples of other continents allowed them to build a system of trade and political domination that few could withstand. Apart from a few honourable exceptions, Europeans and (later) North Americans rarely concerned themselves with the needs of the lands and races they came to dominate. Whatever could be freely obtained or easily produced was to be taken.

"Western Europe and Africa had a relationship which ensured the transfer of wealth from Africa to Europe," the Guyanese historian Walter Rodney wrote. In Asia, European domination had less leeway but was still enough to enrich Britain enormously at India's expense. As for the Americas, "European society was thrown into a frenzy of greed and insatiable lust for riches ...Even more than Circe in the *Odyssey*, who turned men into beasts, the virgin Americas became a trough that turned Europeans of all nations into swine."[5]

Africa supplied ivory, gold, diamonds, cocoa, nut oils, timber and at least 10 million slaves. From Asia there came precious stones, spices, porcelain, silk, tea, coffee, cotton, timber and rubber. The Americas were a source of precious metals on a scale never dreamed of, as well as cotton, rubber, tobacco and sugar. As the Northern trading empires grew stronger, they crushed the traditional way of life of the South. This produced the international division of labour in which, to this day, "one participant of the team specializes in starvation while the other assumes the white man's burden of collecting the profits" (to quote economist Paul Baran).[6]

First Latin America and then Asia, the Caribbean and Africa came to achieve political independence, and slavery was outlawed. Western Europe and North America, however, continued to rely on the former colonies for cheap unskilled labour, agricultural produce, industrial raw materials and captive markets for their manufactured goods. The South was said to be "dependent", but it was the North that was hooked on the relationship.

Once converted to cash crops and commodities, the low-income countries were robbed of the right to determine their future. In Central America, Belize, El Salvador, Honduras and Panama were made to provide bananas, and all four still earn more than half their export income from that crop. Huge areas of Asia were planted with rubber, introduced from Brazil. In Africa 70 per cent of Gambia's agricultural land and 55 per cent of Senegal's were converted to groundnuts (peanuts). Ethiopia's export economy became 80 per cent dependent on coffee, Peru's 35 per cent on zinc, copper and lead, Chile's 40 per cent and Zambia's 85 per cent on copper.[7]

Multinationals

The multinational corporation developed as the most formidable agent of Northern economic power. The multinationals' forerunners were such early trading organizations as the British East India Company, which in 1815 ruled many millions of Indians and had its own army and navy. By 1936 US President Roosevelt was warning: "Concentration of economic power in all-embracing corporations...represents private enterprise becoming a kind of private government which is a power unto itself – a regimentation of other people's money and other people's lives."

Fifty of the world's one hundred largest economic units, including countries, are multinationals. Although supposedly competing with each other in a free market, the hallmark of these giants is domination and control. In many industries they regulate all stages of the supply and processing of raw materials and the marketing and distribution of manufactured products. They increase their power by buying out smaller competitors and diversifying across industries, sectors and locations.

Besides making motor vehicles, for example, Volkswagen has interests in tropical forestry. Coca Cola is involved in cattle ranching. British Petroleum manufactures fertilizers and holds the patents for high-yield cereal crops. Another multinational, the Anglo-Dutch Unilever Group, controls companies in more than fifty countries in every continent, with interests in foods and drinks, soaps and detergents, toothpaste and cosmetics, pesticides, plastics, paper and packaging.[8]

While multinationals make fat profits, the countries where they operate are mostly poor. Sources of their profitability include the power to bankrupt local firms; to impose low wages; to neglect employee health, safety and welfare; to take advantage of lax pollution controls; and to benefit from tax incentives granted by low-income countries desperate for investment. Among established multinational procedures are the repatriation of profits (ensuring that only the parent company in the North makes much money) and transfer pricing (fixing prices between subsidiary companies in two or more countries to maximize benefits from local tax arrangements).

Investment by these corporations can cost an arm and a leg. "To attract companies like yours," ran a Philippines government advertisement with unconscious irony, "we have felled mountains, razed jungles, filled swamps, moved rivers, relocated towns...all to make it easier for you to do business here." Or the price may include life itself. Union Carbide was making annual profits in the region of $86,000 *per employee* in 1984 when an explosion at its Bhopal pesticide plant poisoned and killed thousands of people.[9]

Under these conditions, inequalities of wealth within low-income countries are extreme. Northern exploitation is sustained with the help of collaborators such as Zaire's President Mobutu, described by George Bush as "a valued partner of every US President since Lyndon Johnson". With over $300 million of his country's export earnings unaccounted for, Mobutu is said to spend on himself and his presidency more than Zaire's entire social welfare budget. At the other end of the scale, Southern farmworkers earn on average only about 2 per cent of the retail value of what they produce; a Caribbean sugarcane cutter earns about $3 a day, a Philippines banana worker $1.50 and a Sri Lankan tea picker 72 cents.[10]

The World Bank

After the devastation of the Second World War, North America and Western Europe set about rebuilding world trade, supposedly for the benefit of all. Two major institutions were established: the International Bank for Reconstruction and Development (the World Bank) and the International Monetary Fund (IMF). The General Agreement on Tariffs and Trade (GATT) was also set up (in practice to safeguard the industrialized countries' monopoly of the trade in manufactured goods).

World Bank and IMF policies have set the development agenda for almost fifty years. Their lending and spending decisions are signals to the global financial community, opening the door to private investment by multinationals and commercial banks. Based in Washington, DC, headed by a US citizen and largely funded by the USA, the Bank makes long-term economic decisions affecting hundreds of millions of people. As for the IMF, just five of its 140 members (the USA, the UK, West Germany, France and Japan) dominate its decision-making on short-term loans. Bank and Fund activity has reflected Northern foreign-policy and business aims, not the needs of the world's poor.

The World Bank now invests well over $20 billion a year, mostly in low-income countries. What sort of "development" projects have won its approval? Massive and expensive hydroelectric and irrigation dams, mines, tropical forestry, cattle ranches, airports and international trade centres have been firm favourites.

Large-scale capital ventures usually take longer to complete, cost more and cause worse environmental disruption than budgeted for. The supposed benefits often do not materialize, but widespread human misery frequently does. Unforeseen costs – which the developing country, not the World Bank, has to cope with – may include: inflationary price increases for imported machinery; faulty planning, materials and construction; inadequate assessment of the environmental impact; the provision of alternative work and housing for people unemployed and uprooted as a result of capital-intensive projects; extra health and law-enforcement provision to cope with development-related problems.

Giant dams

Giant hydroelectric and irrigation dams were thought to represent the heights of economic progress during the 1960s and 1970s, and the World Bank has helped finance many of them. Egypt's Aswan Dam – which was built by the Soviet Union in perfect imitation of the World Bank approach – has become a symbol of what can go wrong.

When the Aswan Dam was opened in 1970 President Nasser declared it a source of everlasting prosperity for his country.

None of the projected benefits – flood control, easing of droughts, irrigation and hydroelectricity – has been achieved without a heavy price, however. Egypt still has droughts; more than a third of the irrigated farmland has been ruined by waterlogging; soil fertility downriver, which depended on the Nile's annual flooding, has declined; hydroelectricity capacity is decreasing fast because the reservoir has silted up; the rural poor cannot afford the electricity, but those living near the reservoir and irrigation canals have suffered an increase of water-borne disease (including malaria); Egypt's Mediterranean coast is being eroded because of the loss of river-borne sediment; the coastal sardine catch is, for related reasons, declining; and the country is more dependent on imported food than ever before.[11]

Or consider Ghana's Akosombo Dam on Lake Volta, which also reduced the flow of silt downriver, resulting in coastal erosion. Here the price was paid by the 10,000 people of Togo whose homes fell into the sea. Much of the electricity generated at Akosombo goes to Kaiser Aluminium, a foreign-owned multinational, at *one-twentieth* the average world price. Kaiser has taken most of its production out of the country, however, allegedly operating in Ghana just for the cheap electricity. The dam's high construction costs are thought to have contributed to the overthrow of President Nkrumah in 1966.[12]

The flooding of vast reservoirs for dams often results in the dislocation and resettlement of entire valley communities, without consultation or compensation, on poor-quality land. Tribal communities uprooted by Zambia's Kariba Dam development broke up amidst an outbreak of malnutrition, alcoholism, disease and allegations of witchcraft. The Aswan Dam is said to have displaced about 100,000 people, the Akosombo 75,000, and China's current Three Gorges project may dislocate as many as 2 million. Opponents of India's unfinished Narmada River development point out that as little as 1 per cent of the World Bank's funding has been earmarked for the rehabilitation of farming villages displaced by the reservoir. Major population upheavals are also forecast for proposed dams in Brazil, Nigeria, Panama, the Philippines and Sudan.[13]

Displacing people

The disastrous removal of large numbers of people is something that the World Bank must know a lot about. North-east

Brazil's Polonoreste highway was built with Bank funding to encourage the migration of half a million peasants. These people, who were landless because large fertile areas to the south were in the hands of the wealthy elite, cleared strips of Amazon forest alongside the road and settled there, as they were told to. It took only a couple of years to discover that, once cleared, Amazon soils are virtually useless.

Indonesia's World Bank-backed transmigration programme has been an even larger-scale calamity. Millions of landless people from Java and Bali have been uprooted from their rural shacks and sent to heavily forested areas of Sumatra, Sulawesi and other islands. Most find it impossible to secure a livelihood on the new land. The Indonesian government has provided few roads or health services. Armed clashes have taken place between the settlers and indigenous forest dwellers, who are also threatened by logging; and the Indonesian army sometimes intervenes with appalling brutality. The Bank gave its then biggest ever loan to the scheme ($160 million) in 1985, and more than 3 million Indonesians have been forced to migrate. The programme has reportedly had little useful impact on land pressure in Java, where 1 per cent of farmers own 35 per cent of the productive land.[14]

The World Bank used to deny that the social and environmental effects of development were its business. In the 1970s, however, Bank president Robert McNamara publicly admitted that economic growth alone could not benefit the poor countries. The redistribution of wealth, income and jobs was also necessary, he said. This revised approach has been acknowledged by World Bank staff many times since. Yet almost half of their lending is still for the "prestige" projects that do the most damage.

Southern debt

What is the reasoning behind World Bank policies? In the postwar world, establishment economists, politicians and bankers have mostly remained committed to the idea of export-led economic growth. World trade can and must expand indefinitely, according to this theory. We do not need to be unduly concerned if some countries are poor while others are rich, because every impoverished country can earn its way out of trouble. Wealth may be created at the "top" at first (among the business class, for example) but will gradually trickle down so that even the poorest people benefit.

The low-income countries of the South had a "natural" specialization in agricultural products and raw materials. They were encouraged to export more and more of these cash crops and commodities, to earn more foreign exchange and build up their technology and industries. If they worked hard enough, they were told, they would gain entry to polite society – the rich countries' club.

Has export-led growth enabled low-income countries to climb out of poverty? No chance. After nearly fifty years of trying, as the economist Susan George comments, "The 'foreign-exchange-for-your-essential-imports' gambit has proved a lie."[15] Why has it?

What went wrong?
To begin with, the theory was wrong. What we call economic growth cannot continue indefinitely and is already producing widespread human misery and environmental damage. The planet's less-than-infinite resources of fossil fuels, fertile soils, virgin lands, species-rich forests and oceans, purifying rainfall and rivers, and cooling atmosphere are being depleted and polluted too fast.

The average US citizen guzzles more than 7,000 kilos of oil-equivalent energy a year, for example. This is twice the rate for the average Briton and four hundred times more than someone in the world's poorest fifty countries. Each year in the rich North we consume fifty times the value of metals used by somebody in the South. Such rates of consumption could never extend to most of the human race and will never be repeated. It would, in any case, take most poor countries hundreds of years of rapid economic growth – if this were possible or desirable – to reach current material standards of living in the North.[16]

The South has indeed concentrated on producing agricultural output and raw materials for export. While some of its export prices held up during the 1950s and 1960s, but too many sellers of non-industrial produce were competing in a buyers' market, and the late 1970s and 1980s were disastrous for commodity exporters. Multinationals and middlemen had bought out Southern producers and could dictate prices; or they played off one competing supplier against another. World markets were swamped with cocoa, coffee, copper, cotton, fruits, groundnuts, iron ore, rubber, sugar, tea and tin. Prices fell as exporters competed to increase their market share; and according to the UN Food and Agriculture Organization, low-income countries' overall share of the volume of world trade in agricultural, fisheries and forestry products fell too.

The power of oil
A few commodities were different. Cheap oil was the indispensable raw material behind the postwar economic boom. It powered many of the factories of Europe, North America, Australasia and Japan, fuelled the world's ever-growing number of motor vehicles and was essential to the mechanization of agriculture (to run farm machinery and produce agrochemicals). Oil-derived plastics transformed thousands of industries and products.

Unlike other Southern exporters, the oil-producing countries had market leverage. In 1973 Middle Eastern-led exporters quadrupled their prices. This and the 1979 OPEC "oil shock" contributed to inflation, unemployment and recession in the industrialized countries. In reaction, Northern governments and multinationals squeezed the South harder, imposing import restrictions and other protectionist measures, buying fewer commodities and forcing down prices and Southern wages yet again. They also charged more for the manufactured goods and technical skills that the poor countries wanted.

Already depressed, commodity prices fell further. Average market values of metals and minerals fell by 55 per cent during the 1970s and 1980s. Prices for beverages (coffee, tea and so on) fell by 45 per cent. Fats and food-oils lost 72 per cent of their value, sugar 83 per cent and other foods more than 60 per cent. At the same time, of course, the South's imports from the North were costing more.[17] The real value of Southern wages tumbled. Latin America experienced annual inflation rates of thousands of per cent (as it still does). Unable to earn enough abroad to pay for their imports, low-income countries' trade balances plunged into the red.

Meanwhile World Bank investment and other forms of lending continued. Now there was a new source of cash: OPEC petrodollars – the profits from oil sales. Northern commerical banks were awash with them. International banking circles feared that recession would worsen unless this money was "recycled" to poor countries. This, people hoped, would keep world trade on the move. Few thought what might happen if the borrowers were unable to repay.

Money down the drain

Total borrowings by developing countries built up from about $76 billion in 1970 to more than $500 billion by the end of the decade. Since then the debt has advanced to $1.3 trillion (thousand billion). The loans were made at interest rates that in the early 1970s stood at around 6 per cent but within ten years had often risen to 15 per cent or more. It became impossible for most debtors to cope with repayments.

Where did the money go? Some of the loans were siphoned off into Swiss bank accounts or frittered away on luxurious living. In the Philippines the Marcos family is said to have privately accounted for $15 billion of the country's debt. Large weapons purchases were made, such as an estimated $10 billion worth by Argentina's military junta. Wasteful mega-projects ate up much of the rest – Brazil, the biggest Southern debtor, spending $40 billion on a nuclear power programme. "Such loans", the economist J. K. Galbraith has commented, "given by foolish banks to foolish governments for foolish purposes, generally are not – and perhaps should not be – repaid."[18]

Enter the IMF

As the poor countries struggled under the debt burden, the IMF stepped in. Under the Fund's usual procedure, wealthier members could borrow more, poorer ones less, to help meet short-term deficits until they could increase their export earnings and repay. Countries that wanted to borrow more than their entitlement were asked to make "structural adjustments" to their economies. That was the theory.

The conditions imposed for more IMF loans involve government spending cuts. However, the Fund does not normally ask borrowers to reduce expenditure on imported weapons, manufactured goods or consumer luxuries. It prefers instead to penalize "unproductive" economic sectors such as health, education, public-sector wages, food subsidies and rural development. Under IMF adjustment policies in the late 1970s and early 1980s, for example, UNICEF found that government health spending fell by 85 per cent in Ghana and 78 per cent in Bolivia.[19]

In country after country, as the debt burden built up, the

imposition of IMF austerity measures was followed by people protesting in the streets. The Moroccan government had already raised prices of staple foods by between 50 and 100 per cent when, in 1984, the Fund ordered further subsidy cuts; hundreds of people were killed in the disturbances that followed. Other "IMF riots" during the 1980s led to the military overthrow of the Sudanese government and to the death of 180 civilians in the Dominican Republic. Violent protests against loan conditions have also broken out in Brazil, Jamaica, Jordan, Nigeria, Venezuela and Zambia, in the latter case leaving thirty dead. An IMF economist who resigned in anger during this period, D. L. Budhoo, has compared the Fund's approach to a terrorist attack.[20]

(The IMF approach was mirrored during the 1970s and 1980s by the taxation and spending policies of conservative governments in the North, which have redistributed wealth upwards towards the rich. Public spending in the UK, the USA and elsewhere on education, housing, health, social welfare and public transport has failed to keep pace with rising need, sometimes declining in real terms.)[21]

The debt crisis
For almost a decade, the borrowing countries have been repaying more in interest and capital to the IMF and the banks than they receive in new loans. Latin America has had to use a third of its export earnings to keep its debts serviced, Africa a fifth. By 1987 the main debtor countries were: Brazil, owing $124 billion; Mexico, $108 billion; Argentina, $57 billion; Indonesia, $53 billion; India, $46 billion; Poland, $42 billion; Turkey, $41 billion; Egypt, $40 billion; South Korea, $40 billion; and Venezuela, $37 billion. Latin America owes $1,000 for every man, woman and child on the continent. None of these countries will ever be able to repay in full.[22]

Politicians and bankers in North America and Western Europe began speaking of a debt crisis in the early 1980s. If the South failed to keep up its repayments, what would happen to the banking system? This crisis, however, was not sudden; it was, as the UN Secretary-General has said, "the most visible part of a relentless process in which problems have accumulated, in many aspects foreseeably, for years".[23] The difference now was that for the first time the world economy was inconveniencing the banks a little.

Only a small percentage of commercial bank lending was to developing countries, and the banks were still making comfortable profits. Citicorp of the USA, for example, the world's largest commercial lender, declared profits of more than $1 billion in 1986. True, the banks were unsettled because they had not made proper provision for their bad debts. The real crisis, however, was and still is that of the world's poorest people. "A world war is being fought by 'the system that works' against the majority of humanity," writes the journalist John Pilger; "a war over foreign debt which has interest as its main weapon, a war whose victims are millions of malnourished and dying children."[24]

And the good news?

Can the global picture really be so bleak? Have not Brazil, Hong Kong, Mexico, South Korea, Singapore, Taiwan and other "newly industrializing countries" managed to modernize their economies and capture a share of the world market for manufactured goods? True, a few countries have achieved some export success, but mostly in poorly paid, labour-intensive industries (such as textiles) where their wage costs undercut those of their competitors.

Little prosperity has trickled down to ordinary people in these countries. South Korea has had the world's fastest-growing economy in recent years, but the price includes some of the longest industrial working hours and most dangerous factories in the world, as well as repeated outbreaks of violent protest and state repression. Besides, with world markets already overburdened with competition, there is little hope that the global "prosperity cake" can ever grow large enough to allow reasonable shares for all.[25]

What, then, about the economic aid given by rich countries to poor ones? Surely this must do some good? The value of North–South development aid has, in fact, stagnated or declined. In the 1970s the rich countries agreed a target of 0.7 per cent of their GNP to be given as official development assistance (ODA) each year. A number of donors – the Netherlands, the Scandinavians and Saudi Arabia – have been relatively generous, giving close to or over 1 per cent of GNP. Of the rest, only France has consistently met its agreed ODA target. The UK, the USA, Australia, Canada and

New Zealand have a much poorer record, several of them giving a smaller fraction of GNP now than they did in the 1960s.[26]

Also, government aid is often determined more by the donor's foreign policy than by the recipient's need. In 1986 Israel received a quarter of all official US aid, four times more than the total given to forty-five African countries. Two years later only 5 per cent of US aid went to the world's poorest ten countries, and nearly 40 per cent of that was used for military purposes. About 80 per cent of Canadian ODA is said to be tied to purchases of Canadian goods, and up to nine-tenths of UK government ODA has to be spent in the UK for similar reasons. Such aid is little more than an export subsidy.

A billion pounds' worth of official UK aid to India over ten years, much of it geared to selling UK products overseas, resulted in a whole catalogue of disasters, as an official report documents. These included violent clashes between local people and mine operators, non-compliance with reforestation and land reclamation conditions, severe air pollution, water contamination and the export of dangerous pesticides.[27]

Action

The wealth gap

The myth that wealth creation in the North and among Southern elites somehow trickles down to help poorer countries and needy people has proved false time and again. While a limited number of fortunes will always be made, growing numbers of the world's people are destitute. Where the worst-off people have benefited, however, this has been the result of a different process. Socially based reforms and programmes have been set in motion by international bodies, governments, non-governmental organizations (NGOs) and grass-roots community groups with the specific aim of improving human well-being not "from the top down" but "from the bottom up".

Human development

Writing during the 1970s of the need for a people-centred view of development, E. F. Schumacher argued that "Development does not start with goods; it starts with people and their education, organization and discipline...Development...can succeed only if it is carried forward as a broad, popular 'movement of reconstruction', with primary emphasis on the full utilization of the drive, enthusiasm, intelligence and labour power of everyone."[28]

Also during the 1970s, United Nations agencies adopted a declaration that put economic development in the wider framework of the "spiritual, moral and material advancement of the whole human being", with an emphasis on self-help, self-reliance and self-improvement. In recent years the importance of such approaches has gained wider recognition. "The failure of...growth oriented models...has led in the decade of the 1980s to the emergence of a concept of bottom-up participatory development in which the emphasis is on people," observes the Barbadian writer Pat Ellis.[29]

Grass roots

The readiness of the poor and powerless to organize themselves, given the chance, is the key factor. All around the world, groups of dispossessed people such as Kenya's Green Belt movement and India's Chipko have come together to improve their living standards, protect their environment and improve the social resources of their communities.[30]

The Green Belt movement focuses on the establishment of "green belts" of hundreds of trees in rural areas to provide low-income households with firewood and building materials and to halt soil erosion. Green Belt foresters teach mothers and their children, young adults, the elderly, the disabled and the very poor how to propagate native varieties and set up nurseries. Participants are paid according to how many of their seedlings survive and mature. Now funded by the United Nations, Green Belt has planted over 2 million new trees and in the process has strengthened Kenya's village communities.

The Chipko movement of the Himalayan foothills is another grass-roots success story. It began in the 1970s near the north Indian town of Gopeshwar. The state forestry department had licensed a non-local firm to fell trees in return for royalty payments; and the local women (joined by a few men), who attributed recent floods to deforestation, protested. "They will not fell a single tree without felling us first. When the men raise their axes we will embrace the trees to protect them," the women declared. After a series of confrontations with the loggers, Chipko ("to embrace") spread throughout the Himalayan region, and the state government suspended commercial forestry. Besides saving the remnants of original forest, Chipko has prevented the government from turning the hillsides into plantations of non-native eucalyptus; instead, the movement has planted indigenous species to provide shade, fodder, firewood, wild food and medicinal herbs. People have come from neighbouring Pakistan to learn from Chipko.

Latin America also has vigorous community movements, many of them in the cities. After Mexico City's 1985 earthquake, for example, speculating slum landlords wanted to evict their fixed-rent tenants from the ruins of their homes. The slum dwellers, led mainly by women, organized themselves, secured their tenancies with the city authorities and persuaded the government to finance a rebuilding programme under their supervision. Throughout Latin America, groups of homeless people have often staged mass occupations of unused urban land, as in Lima in 1971 and in Buenos Aires in 1981. Once established, many of these squatter colonies transform their living environments, planting trees, organizing rubbish clearance, setting up food co-operatives and distribution networks for milk for children and building their own schools, community centres and roads.

This grass-roots model of "bottom-up", socially based wealth-creation is now recognized as the best alternative to the bankrupt ideas that have dominated economic thinking for so long. Few projects set up by governments, aid agencies or the international community can work unless they are combined with popular participation. The message is getting through at the top, but there is a long way to go. "We must reshape... the customs and ingrained attitudes of hundreds of millions of individuals and of their leaders," says Barber Conable, the World Bank's current president.[31]

New priorities
Southern governments and their Northern advisers will have to abandon their faith in capital-intensive, high-technology investment. Instead, development choices must be made in terms of who will benefit directly from them. Whether designed and funded by the World Bank, foreign governments, NGOs, commercial banks or multinationals, projects must be assessed socially and environmentally as well as in narrow economic

terms if their impact on the poorest people is to be understood. Some recent development decisions have, at long last, been made that reflect these new priorities, among them the cancellation of such mega-developments as the Altamira Dam in the Amazon (Brazilian rainforest tribes threatened war if the project went ahead) and the Nam Choan Dam in Thailand.

Self-reliance
The South will never equal the present-day material prosperity of the high-income countries, but it is not necessary to achieve great wealth before all people can have a decent standard of living – as long as income-earning opportunities are fairly distributed. The often fruitless philosophy of export-led growth should be modified with an emphasis on import substitution, making do with what can be produced within poorer countries instead of trying to overspecialize. Using this approach, Brazil developed the production of vehicle fuel from sugarcane and reduced its dependency on imported oil. Several other developing countries have adopted import substitution with some success. Bangladesh and Nicaragua, for example, have relied on domestic production to overcome severe shortages of foreign pharmaceuticals, while China adopted the strategy to compensate for its lack of foreign currency.

The industrialized countries have generally opposed import substitution on the grounds that world trade must be increased to generate wealth, but the argument rings hollow. In fact, the policy of increasing self-reliance needs also to be applied to the North to help reduce the ravages of pollution and to revitalize declining regions and inner cities. Improvements in food and resource self-reliance, including the conservation and recycling of materials, will create jobs and new industries in the North, reducing both the waste of resources and the exploitation of the Southern population.

Regional co-operation
The governments of developing countries can help each other by working together in regional groupings to pool resources to improve their technology and industries. At present South–South trade is only a small fraction of world trade. More trade between poor countries, replacing North–South commerce, will help build self-reliance and reduce the exploiting power of the multinationals.

Controlling the corporations
Southern countries must reconsider their competition for multi-nationals' investment. Joint action by governments, trade unions and the public is needed to press for less multinational secrecy and more accountability, for better wages and conditions, compensation for job losses, environmental safeguards and tighter health and safety controls. Giant corporations will not give up their economic power without a struggle, but a redistribution of their wealth must be a long-term goal.

Internationally agreed codes of conduct for multinationals could be negotiated and enforced through the UN. The introduction of turnover taxes related to company size, an idea put forward by the UK Green Party, would ensure that the largest corporations – usually the worst abusers of the countries they operate in – made a fair contribution to the battle against poverty.

Appropriate development
The South has a shortage of capital but an abundance of labour. Nearly a billion more workers will join the labour force by the century's end. So development solutions – whoever pays for them – must be low-cost and labour intensive, focusing on small rather than large undertakings. This is the meaning of "appropriate development", and there is a growing body of practical experience in this area. As the economist George McRobie argues: "In practically every field of human activity...innovative, small-scale locally based technologies can create new opportunities for people to work themselves out of their poverty." The view is not new; Gandhi said: "Every machine that helps every individual has a place, but there should be no place for machines that concentrate power in a few hands and turn the masses into mere machine minders, if indeed they do not make them unemployed."[32]

Urban renewal / Rural investment
Besides the priorities for rural development considered in Chapter 1, the mounting problem of the South's overcrowded cities must be tackled. A reallocation of finance from the big-business sector to the needs of the urban poor is essential, and laws must change to recognize the rights of squatters to the land they live on. Governments and donor organizations

can provide advice, tools and materials to help shanty-town dwellers upgrade and improve their housing and local services. Meanwhile, by increasing investment in rural communities and in medium-size towns, Southern governments will slow the rate of migration to the major cities.

Exploited labour
More attention should be given to the underclass who work long hours for pitiful wages, often in appalling conditions, in both formal and informal employment. Aid workers and politicians are now considering ways to bring the informal economy into the mainstream without penalizing the people who work in it. The bargaining rights of the low-paid need strengthening, and stonger laws and law enforcement are required to ensure decent working conditions.

Rewriting debts
The continual rescheduling of debts to keep alive the fairy-tale that the South will one day repay all the money is senseless. Major initiatives by the rich countries are called for. As the development writer Lloyd Timberlake says: "Northern governments wanting to help Africa can always find scope for their 'big fixes' – the biggest fix of all would be a rewriting of Africa's debt so it bears some relationship to any possibility of repayment."[33]

Northern banks and governments can afford to write off many of the debts. Canada, France and West Germany have agreed to cancel some of the debts of the poorest countries; and further concessions, proposed by the UK, have been made to African countries (although these are tied to IMF conditions). By and large, however, Northern governments still insist that Southern debtors and commercial banks will have to sort out the problem between them. In what may herald a change of heart, in 1990 the managing director of the IMF gave his backing to debtor countries that refuse to comply with excessively high repayment demands.

Available solutions, requiring rather more imagination than politicians and bankers usually display, include debt/conservation and debt/development swaps. As an example of the first, in 1987 the US group Conservation International paid off a chunk of Bolivia's foreign debt at a reduced rate in return for the Bolivian government's protection of 1.6 million hectares of

rainforest. Similar deals have been struck by the World Wide
Fund for Nature in Costa Rica, Ecuador, Madagascar and
Zambia. The UK's Midland Bank set up a debt/development
swap by writing off an $800,000 loan to Sudan in return for
the Sudanese government's allocation of an equivalent sum to
a UNICEF project.[34]

In 1989 US Treasury Secretary Brady arranged for US
banks to make minor concessions on Latin America's debt
burden. Scornful of this piecemeal approach, the economist
Susan George suggests what she calls "creative reimburse-
ment". George's solution would be tried first in sub-Saharan
Africa, where the debt is relatively small, and then extended
elsewhere. Instead of having to repay their debts in hard-
currency pounds, deutschmarks or dollars, poor countries could
write off agreed amounts of their arrears by contributing sums
in their own currency to national or regional development
funds. Run by democratically elected non-government boards
representing all sections of the community and under United
Nations supervision, such funds would provide money, channelled through NGOs, to grass-roots community projects.[35]

Another debt solution George proposes is a variation on the
debt/conservation swap. Debtor and creditor countries would
negotiate and agree the monetary value of urgently needed
environmental projects, such as reforestation, low-cost house-
building or research into traditional medicine and nutrition.
With participants guaranteed a fair basic wage, the debtor
would undertake the project, while the creditor cancelled its
value of the debt.[36]

There must be an end to the structural adjustments that have
caused such misery when attached as lending conditions. Future
lending by the IMF should instead be based on assurances
that borrowing countries will devote the money to genuine
improvements in the living standards of the poorest people.

Reforming world trade
In the 1960s the "Group of 77" African, Asian, Caribbean
and Latin American countries came together to press for less
exploitative patterns of world trade. By the 1970s the changes
they demanded had become known as the "new international
economic order" (NIEO). Debate about the NIEO has per-
sisted but has borne little fruit, looking less realistic than
ever during the 1980s when the economics of self-interest

became dominant in the industrialized countries. However, the demands of the South for stable and guaranteed commodity prices, freer access to Northern markets, a larger share of the world's industry, the transfer of technology, reductions in the debt burden, increased economic self-determination and a greater say in international decision-making are as valid now as ever they were. Can it really benefit the North for its partners to remain impoverished and politically unstable?

What we owe the South
Public pressure in the rich countries can help bring about change. There needs to be more open discussion of the impact of government and commercial lending and multinational activity on the lives of poor people in the South. More discussion and understanding are also needed of how Southern poverty affects people in the North; for example, poverty causes deforestation, which is a problem for us all. Government agencies and big business must be persuaded to take greater responsibility for their activities.

It is time, too, for Northern governments to meet their commitment to give 0.7 per cent of GNP to help the South. More of this aid should be channelled through NGOs, which have the best record of assisting developing countries; no development aid should be tied to purchases from the donor country, and none should be spent on weapons. A worldwide programme to combat poverty, comparable to the postwar Marshall Plan, could be funded by just 10 per cent of the world's present arms budget.

Japan's growing role as a donor is only just coming into the picture. It now has the world's largest ODA budget; but the indications are that Japanese aid has often done more harm than good. Now that there is greater awareness of the damage caused by inappropriate development policies, the international community must persuade the Japanese to change their approach.

More aid money should become available if better East–West relations are allowed to produce reductions in military spending during the 1990s. US and Japanese help for the reforming countries of Eastern Europe has so far been given at the expense of the people of the South. The USA is said to have cut development assistance, but not military aid, to

Central America in order to help to Hungary and Poland.
This is robbing Peter to pay Paul. Once arms cuts are made
and the peace dividend comes on stream, there should be no
doubt about the people it needs to be spent on. The world's
poor have already been kept waiting far too long.

Getting Involved

Related subjects covered elsewhere in this book include: agribusiness and the causes of hunger – Chapter 1; poverty and
ill health – Chapter 3; the position of women – Chapter
4; social injustice – Chapter 5; land use, deforestation and
maldevelopment – Chapter 6; irrigation dams – Chapter 7;
energy conservation – Chapter 8; military spending and the
arms trade – Chapter 10. To find out more about the North–
South wealth gap and the development debate, see "Recommended Reading" (pages 324–9).

Consumer and lifestyle choices

Some people find economics dull, but it is a life-and-death matter for the world's poor and it affects us all in the long run. Think
about how your work or lifestyle may be part of the Northern
exploitation of the South. As a rule, the less goods and materials
you consume (within reason), the less you will be caught up in
the unjust global economic system and the more freedom you
will have to join with others in working for economic justice.

If you agree with those in the UK who believe that the
elimination of poverty involves people in the rich countries
adopting more modest standards of living, you might be inter-
ested in contacting the Lifestyle Movement, Manor Farm, Little
Gidding, Huntingdon PE17 5RJ.

Fair trading
Follow one of the green shopping guides mentioned in the
"Getting Involved" section in Chapter 1. Try to avoid buying
from multinationals; instead choose local produce or buy from
organizations, such as the following, that have established
fair-trading links with low-income countries. Some of these
organizations have shops and local agents; most run mail-order
catalogues:

UK
- Equal Exchange Trading, 29 Nicolson Square, Edinburgh EH8 9BX.
- One Village, Charlbury, Oxford OX7 3SQ.
- Oxfam Trading, Murdock Road, Bicester, Oxon OX6 7RF.
- Traidcraft, Kingsway, Gateshead, Tyne and Wear NE11 0NE.
- Twin Trading, 345 Goswell Road, London EC1V 7JT.

USA and Canada
- Bridgehead Trading, 424 Parkdale Avenue, Ottawa, Ontario K1Y 9Z9, Canada.
- Friends of the Third World, 611 West Wayne Street, Fort Wayne, Ind. 46802, USA.
- Pueblo to People, 1616 Montrose Street, Houston, Tex. 77006, USA.

Australia and New Zealand
- CAA Trading, PO Box 104, Enmore, NSW 2042, Australia.
- Trade Aid, PO Box 18620, Christchurch, New Zealand.
- Trading Partners, 101 Young Street, Annandale, NSW 2038, Australia.
- World Development Tea Co-operative, PO Box A559, Sydney South, NSW 2000; and PO Box 117, Fitzroy, Victoria 3056, Australia.

The choice of goods is wide. The Traidcraft catalogue, for example, includes soft furnishings and crafts, kitchen and diningware, children's toys, clothing, jewellery, gifts, food and drink, cards and stationery.

Traidcraft in the UK has launched a campaign to publicize and improve the exploitative working conditions in textiles and clothing manufacturing throughout the world by persuading clothing retailers to adopt the "Clean Clothes" code of practice. Traidcraft's campaign action pack describes the working conditions in textile and clothing factories in different countries, giving information on the profits, size and market share of the major UK clothing retailers, naming the countries the retailers obtain their clothing from and suggesting how people can get involved in the campaign – for example, writing to the managers of local clothes shops. For your campaign action pack, send Traidcraft (address above) 60p plus 35p p&p per order, marking your envelope "Textiles and Clothing Campaign"; posters and a video are also available.

Boycott the offenders
Be aware of the ethical conduct of multinational companies. Boycott the goods and services of those you know to be heavily involved in exploiting poor countries and explain your decisions to retailers, to other people you know and (in writing) to the companies themselves. Useful sources of information in the UK about the conduct of multinationals and current consumer boycotts are the magazines *Ethical Consumer*, *New Consumer* and *New Internationalist* (see "Recommended Reading").

Ethical investment
Put your savings in one of the growing number of ethical investment schemes. These unit trusts and pension funds undertake to research companies carefully before investing in them and will not invest in the tobacco or arms industries or in firms with poor human rights or environmental records. (Apparently not all ethical investment firms have equally stringent principles, however.) Among the UK's leading ethical investment, pension and unit trust funds are Friends Provident Stewardship Fund (the longest-established and largest ethical policy) and Merlin Ecology (said to be among the most principled). Details from the Ethical Investment Research and Information Service, 401 Bondway Business Centre, 71 Bondway, London SW8 1SQ (071-735 1351).

Community and political action

Intermediate Technology
At the forefront of the movement to make development serve the needs of the world's poorest people is the Intermediate Technology Development Group (address below). ITDG was set up in 1965 to put into practice the ideas of E. F. Schumacher, based on the philosophy "Find out what the people are doing and help them to do it better."[37] The Group researches, develops and helps poor countries install low-cost technologies for food production, water and sanitation, housing and small-scale industry. ITDG's education department in the UK produces

a range of materials for schoolteachers and adult discussion groups, including a set of colour slides and notes (price £12.50) on its work and on the wider issues of development and aid.

Young people in the UK can join the ITDG's youth branch, Youth TAG (Technology Action Group), which is run by a committee of 13-to-18-year-olds. Members receive a quarterly magazine and take part in sponsored cycle rides, canoeing, climbing, running and walks, raising money through their schools, colleges and youth clubs or with friends to help provide low-cost technology for poor countries. Details from ITDG.

Oxfam 2000
Oxfam UK (address below) has a campaigning network, Oxfam 2000, working to reform the aid-giving policies of the UK government and the World Bank and to end poverty and injustice. People who join the network take part in lobbies of Parliament and letter-writing to MPs, MEPs and embassies.

In Whose Interest?
In Whose Interest? is a petition campaign asking UK banks to reduce the debts owed by debtor countries by at least half and to write off the debts of the poorest countries entirely. Copies of the petition (which asks Barclays, Lloyds, Midland and NatWest branch managers to raise the issues with their head office) are available from Third World First or the World Development Movement (addresses below). A similar postcard-writing campaign to change the debt policies of UK banks is being run by Reforest the Earth (details in the "Getting Involved" section of Chapter 6). If you already know the points you would like to make to the banks, you could write politely to their chairmen at the following addresses:

Barclays Bank, 54 Lombard Street, London EC3P 3AH.
Lloyds Bank, 71 Lombard Street, London EC3P 3BS.
Midland Bank, Poultry, London EC2P 2BX.
National Westminster Bank, 41 Lothbury, London EC2P 7DR.

Tell them what you think
Help change the climate of opinion by calling attention to the North–South wealth gap in letters to local councillors, MPs, MEPs and the press, in community newsletters and in

contributions to radio phone-in programmes, or by writing to
the Minister for Overseas Development (Foreign and Commonwealth Office, Downing Street, London SW1A 2AL). Points
you could make include:

- the damage caused by multinationals in poor countries and
  the need for public pressure and international controls to
  improve their conduct;
- the destructive effect of World Bank and IMF aid and
  lending policies;
- the effectiveness of NGO projects and grass-roots, com-
  munity-based development;
- the UK government's moral obligation to meet its "0.7 per
  cent of GNP" official aid target instead of postponing its
  commitment;
- the need to free foreign aid from purchasing conditions;
  none should be spent on weapons;
- the need to allocate government-to-government aid according to recipient countries' commitment to economic justice,
  human rights and real democracy;
- the high profits made by commerical banks in the early days
  of lending to low-income countries, although poor people
  did not benefit from these loans;
- it would be fair and wise to write off past government
  and bank loans to the poorest countries to give them a
  breathing space;
- new aid should be provided by the European Community in
  the form of grants;
- preparations for the 1992 EC Single Market have ignored
  the interests of low-income countries; the EC should publish a report on the impact of the Single Market on
  low-income countries and prepare to compensate those
  whose interests are harmed.

Write to the World Bank, calling on it to stop funding socially
and environmentally destructive development projects and to
channel its money through NGOs to grass-roots development:
Barber Conable, President, World Bank, 1818 H Street NW,
Washington, DC 20433, USA.

Write to the Japanese Ambassador, too. The UK Japanese
Embassy is at 46 Grosvenor Street, London W1. Politely
point out:

- Japan now has enormous economic power in the world and must use this wisely and for the benefit of all.
- Reports indicate that most Japanese development aid goes to big-business high-tech projects that harm the environment and the welfare of poor people.
- Most people in low-income countries do not want large-scale industrialization financed by foreign aid, which does so much damage.
- The World Bank now agrees that development should be based on small-scale projects that have the support of local communities and should be accompanied by improvements in the education, health and welfare of the poorest people.

Organizations

Organizations working for reform of the international economy, an end to poverty and appropriate development include:

UK and Irish Republic
Action from Ireland, PO Box 1522, Dublin 1, Irish Republic.
Catholic Institute for International Relations, 22 Coleman Fields, London N1 (071-354 0083).
Christian Aid, 35 Lower Marsh Street, London SE1 7RL (071-620 4444).
Help the Aged, St James Walk, London EC1B 1BD (071-253 0253).
Intermediate Technology Development Group, Myson House, Railway Terrace, Rugby CV21 3BR (0788-60631).
New Economics Foundation (organizers of The Other Economic Summit, "TOES"), 27 Thames House, South Bank Business Centre, 140 Battersea Park Road, London SW11 4NB (071-377 5696).
Oxfam, 274 Banbury Road, Oxford OX2 7DZ (0865-56777).
Quaker Peace and Service, Friends House, Euston Road, London NW1 2BJ (071-387 3601).
Third World First, 232 Cowley Road, Oxford OX4 1UH (0865-245678).
Village Volunteers, 41 Miranda Road, London N19 3RA.
Voluntary Service Overseas, 9 Belgrave Square, London SW1X 8PW (071-235 5191).

Women's Environmental Network, 287 City Road, London EC1V 1LA (071-740 2511).

World Development Movement, Bedford Chambers, London WC2E 8HA (071-836 3672).

USA and Canada

American Friends Service Committee, 1501 Cherry Street, Philadelphia, Pa 19102, USA.

Canadian Friends Service Committee, 60 Lowther Avenue, Toronto, Ontario M5R 1C7, Canada.

GATT-Fly, 11 Madison Avenue, Toronto, Ontario M5R 7S2, Canada.

Institute for Food and Development Policy/Food First, 145 Ninth Street, San Francisco, Calif. 94103, USA.

Interfaith Center on Corporate Responsibility, Room 566, 475 Riverside Drive, New York, NY 10115, USA.

Intermediate Technology Development Group, 777 United Nations Plaza, New York, NY 10017, USA.

Taskforce on Corporate Responsibility, 129 St Claire Avenue West, Toronto, Ontario M5R 2S2, Canada.

Task Force on Latin America and the Caribbean, 515 Broadway, Santa Cruz, Calif. 95060, USA.

Ten Days for World Development, Room 315, 85 St Clair Avenue East, Toronto, Ontario M4T 1M8, Canada.

Transnational Network, Box 567, Rengeley, Maine 044970, USA.

World Neighbors, 5116 North Portland Avenue, Oklahoma City, Okla 73112, USA.

Australia and New Zealand

Action for World Develpoment, PO Box 117, Fitzroy, Victoria 3065, Australia.

Australia Coalition for Overseas Aid, PO Box 1562, Canberra, ACT 2601, Australia.

Community Aid Abroad, 156 George Street, Fitzroy, Victoria 3065, Australia.

Council for the Organization of Relief Services Overseas, PO Box 9716, Courtney Place, Wellington, New Zealand.

New Zealand Coalition for Trade and Development, PO Box 11345, Wellington, New Zealand.

Pacific Concerns Resource Centre, PO Box 9295, Newmarket, Auckland, New Zealand.

Transnational Corporate Research Project, University of Sydney, Sydney 20006, Australia.

Africa, Asia and the Caribbean (Commonwealth)
Afronomics Institute, Unilag Consult, 7th Floor, Senate Building, Lagos University, Akoka, Yaba, Nigeria.
Asia and Pacific Development Centre, PO Box 2444, Jalan Data, Kuala Lumpur, Malaysia.
Bombay Sarvodaya Friendship Centre, Shanti Kutir, Vasudeo Balvant Phadke Road, Muland-E, Bombay 400081, India.
Caribbean Women's Association (CARIWA), c/o The Social Centre, PO Box 16, 13 Turkey Lane, Ros'eau, Dominica.
Chipko Information Centre, PO Silyara, via Ghansali, Tehri-Garhwal, Uttar Pradesh 249155, India.
Christian Service Committee, Box 551294, Limbe, Malawi.
Green Belt Movement, c/o National Council of Women of Kenya, PO Box 67545, Moi Avenue, Nairobi, Kenya.
International Organization of Consumers' Unions, PO Box 1045, 10839 Penang, Malaysia.
Kagisong Centre, Mogoditashane, PO Box 20166, Gabarone, Botswana.
Planetary Citizens' Council for Peace, Development and the Environment, Robinson Road, PO Box 2753, Singapore 9047.
Sarvodaya Shramadana, 98 Damask Mandira, Rawatawatte Road, Moratuwa, Sri Lanka.
Self-Employed Women's Association, SEWA Reception Centre, opposite Victoria Garden, Ahmedabad 380001, India.

3. Population and Health

"Hygiene, not medicine, guarantees health – hygiene...in the original sense of all the rules and circumstances of life."

André Gorz[1]

The Problem

In 1987 the human population of our small planet reached 5 billion, and even the most cautious estimates indicate a doubling of this total by the mid-twenty-first century. How are we to cope with this growth in human numbers? How, when millions already die every year because of a lack of food, hygiene and basic health care, are we to help every person achieve the "physical, mental and social well-being" by which the World Health Organization (WHO) and the United Nations Children's Fund (UNICEF) have defined good health?

A major cause of the gradual acceleration of population growth over the decades has been the disruption of traditional lifestyles by "development", which has so often meant little except human greed and indifference. The same human failings have allowed identified risks to health and well-being to persist needlessly. Every child and every adult, however, could be guaranteed a fair chance of good health if the right social and economic choices were made.

Population – still soaring

Humanity reached its first billion in about 1800, its second in the 1930s, its third in about 1960 and its fourth in the late 1970s. Now carrying 5.3 billion people, the Earth will be home to a further 90 million-plus each year until the century's end. Depending largely on how effectively China, India and other populous countries reduce their birth rates, numbers are likely to reach between 10 billion and 14 billion before they stabilize, perhaps not before the twenty-second century.

How concerned should we be about population growth? Very concerned. The current rate of increase – three births a second, 250,000 a day, a million every four days – could lead to environmental and developmental catastrophe, especially through deforestation, says a recent United Nations Population Fund report. Within forty years there could be twice as many people on the planet as now, eating three times more food and using four times more energy. With the Earth's carrying capacity already overburdened, environment writers Paul and Anne Ehrlich believe that "If the human population cannot soon be curbed by humane means, Nature will do the job for us – and she is not noted for her kindness or compassion."[2]

It is a mistake to think that human numbers are a problem for the poor countries alone. Japan, the Netherlands and the UK are more densely populated even than China and India, while Africa and Latin America are the emptiest continents. Besides, during their lifetime children born in the North have a much greater impact on the world's resource base and environment than their counterparts in the South. The poor countries are short of food and other resources mainly because the rich take more than their share.

Population mathematics

Why have human numbers risen so fast? The reason is partly mathematical: exponential growth. Unchecked biological populations expand at a percentage rate. Each expansion creates a larger accumulated total on which the next is based; so numerically each increase is larger than the one before. The percentage increases have themselves been rising, too. World population grew by about 0.3 per cent a year in the seventeenth century, taking roughly 250 years to double; by the 1970s annual growth was 2.1 per cent, with a doubling time of just 33 years.[3]

Upsetting the balance

Why, then, has population growth been accelerating? Self-contained rural societies tend to have relatively stable populations; industrializing ones do not. During the Industrial Revolution human numbers in the British Isles almost doubled between 1760 and 1820. Village life was disrupted as rural people migrated to urban centres to become industrial workers;

earlier marriage, more illegitimate births and larger families became common, and the birth rate soared.

Similar forces have been at work in the South. Pre-colonial societies practised sexual abstinence, coitus interruptus, douches, late weaning and long breast-feeding, herbal contraception and abortion. Sexual activity during lactation and widowhood was taboo; late marriage was encouraged by the custom of bride prices. Colonialism and economic development overwhelmed these customs. Communities were broken up, their inhabitants forced into slavery or migrating to mines and plantations. Instead of clan or village mutual help, the guarantee of survival in old age was now to have grown-up children to look after you. Lack of access to "survival resources" (land, jobs, food, education and health care) became a prime reason why poor people had numerous children.[4]

Besides, poverty breeds ill health, and birth rates tend to be high where people fear that women or children may not survive. Catholic and Muslim countries, and regions where contraception is disapproved of and women are subservient to men, also tend to have high birth rates and produce large families.

Africa now has the world's fastest-ever rate of population growth. In places the disruption of family life has caused a labour shortage. With their men away as migrant labourers, African women farmers are often hard pressed to complete all their work, especially at harvest times. There is a temptation to have many children to provide extra hands.[5] Another factor in Africa, after decolonization, was that some politicians urged their people to have large families (understandably, after the slave trade had deprived the continent of millions of its inhabitants).

Much of Africa is inhospitable desert or dense forest. Habitable areas, mostly around the coasts, are already nearly half as heavily populated as Europe and will equal Europe's population density within about thirty years. The development writer Paul Harrison believes that Africa cannot support more than about a billion people, a total it will reach soon after the year 2000.[6]

High birth rates, as is well known, endanger family health. Large families mean relatively short periods between childbirth. Pregnancy, birthing and child rearing exhaust women and impair their capacity to care for their children. Child mortality rates for five-child families in Central America are double those for three-child families; and children born to teenage mothers are more likely to die in infancy than others are.

Disease in the South

Millions of people die annually from a shortage of food, clean water, medical care and shelter – in a word, from poverty. Inhabitants of the world's poorest continent, Africans, have an average life expectancy of 51 years, and for every 1,000 live births 101 infants die before the age of 5. In North America, the wealthiest continent, life expectancy is 75.5 years, infant mortality 9 deaths per 1,000 births.

"Wealth determines health, and the poorest of all...are the children," writes Lloyd Timberlake.[7] Simple childhood diseases become fatal because of poverty. Of the 15 million under-5s who die each year, one-third are killed by easily preventable diarrhoea caused by malnutrition and a lack of clean water, and UNICEF calculates that half a million of these infant deaths are the direct result of austerity measures forced on governments by the debt burden. Other major childhood killers are measles, respiratory infections, malaria, polio, tuberculosis, tetanus and diphtheria. Four-fifths of the world's children are not immunized.

Water and sanitation

Unclean water and inadequate sanitation are, together with malnutrition, the major cause of illness and premature death in the South, affecting well over half the population of Africa, Asia and Latin America. Millions of people are forced to use the same rivers, lakes and ponds for bathing, laundering, defecation and drawing supplies for drinking and cooking. Dirty water is a source of infection carried by parasitic insects, worms and snails, as well as in human waste, putting people at risk from malaria, cholera, hookworm, bilharzia, river blindness, dysentery, typhoid and hepatitis.[8]

Water-borne disease kills about 25 million people annually, of whom more than half are children. Malaria alone (advancing because of mosquitoes' genetic resistance to pesticides and because irrigation schemes provide the insects with new breeding grounds) causes a million deaths in the South each year and threatens 2 billion people.

In both town and country, rather than make ever-longer

journeys for clean water, people may knowingly use contaminated sources. The mushrooming growth of hundreds of Southern cities has completely outstripped urban public health facilities. Cairo's water and sanitation systems were planned for 2 million inhabitants and must now serve 11 million, for example; Mexico City, already unsuccessfully accommodating a population of 18 million, is forecast to reach 26 million inhabitants by the end of the century. Environmentally related illness may also result from a shortage of firewood or other fuel, because families then get fewer properly cooked meals.

Health care
What about health services? In 1986 Africa, Asia and Latin America spent four times more on their armed services than on health, with some African countries committing as little as $1 per person per year. A billion people, mainly in rural areas, have no access to health services. Health provision is usually city-focused, giving priority to high-tech hospitals and expensive treatments. Only 15 per cent of Ghana's health budget, for example, is spent in the rural areas, and rural East Africa has only one doctor per 60,000 people. Low-income countries' health care programmes are hampered by a shortage of essential medicines, while many of their expensively trained medical personnel join the brain drain from South to North.

South Africa is an example of Northern and Southern standards of health care coexisting in the same country. There are six nurses for every thousand whites but fewer than two for every thousand blacks in South Africa. Infant mortality for black South Africans is ten times worse than for whites, and blacks suffered the world's sharpest fall in life expectancy during the 1980s.[9]

The corporations
The activities of multinational corporations can badly damage people's health in poor countries. With Southern tobacco consumption rising anually by 2 per cent, a near-epidemic of lung cancer has been forecast as the cigarette giants launch a sales drive to compensate for lost markets in the North.[10] Little or no health labelling of cigarettes is enforced, and tobacco advertising has gone as far as the sponsorship of road signs in Ghana. Nor are food multinationals entirely

innocent. The aggressive marketing of low-nutrition foods has undermined respect for traditional healthy diets. "He'll go far. He'll eat white bread," is the slogan of one advertising campaign in Africa.

In the 1970s manufacturers of powdered baby milk, notably Nestlé and Wyeth, were found to be supplying their product free or at low prices to Southern hospitals. Mothers of new-borns who could have breast-fed were given bottled formula in hospital. Returning home, many would find that their breast milk had dried up, so they now depended on milk powder – although out of hospital they had to buy it. Nestlé and Wyeth had a captive market of hundreds of thousands of infants, many of whom are thought to have died as a result. Mothers would over-dilute the milk powder and starve their babies or inadvertently poison them with infected water.

When the baby-milk scandal first broke, a consumer boycott was launched, and Western countries banned the dumping of unsolicited baby foods. Even so, in the late 1980s Nestlé and other manufacturers were still sending free or cheap batches of milk powder to hospitals "if requested".[11]

Drugs multinationals have operated along similar lines. Modern pharmaceuticals are a by-product of the petrochemicals industry, and funding from the oil industry has helped focus Northern medical practice on drug treatments rather than on the less lucrative (but more effective) field of preventive and community medicine. Multinational drugs firms promote their products aggressively in Southern hospitals, exporting medicines that have been banned in the home country. Among these commercially promoted but irrelevant or even harmful treatments are expensive anti-diarrhoeal drugs of which the World Health Organization (WHO) said: "There is no evidence that they can shorten the course or decrease the severity of diarrhoeal attacks."[12]

Poisons on the land

Pesticides are used for killing insects, weeds, moulds, fungi and other unwanted organisms. Vast quantities are used in farming, to control disease-carrying mosquitoes and for such trivial purposes as clearing golf courses. Pesticides seep down into groundwater or are washed into rivers, entering the water-plant-fish-bird food chain and infiltrating the human body via drinking water. They may be blown on the wind, remain as residues on the land, persist on post-harvested food and enter the environment through industrial waste and accidents.

Although they target particular pest species, these chemicals threaten humans. Today's pesticides are mostly non-biodegradable (or slowly biodegrading) synthetic chemicals; once in the food chain, they become increasingly concentrated. Residues in grass may be absorbed by grazing cattle and concentrate in the cows' milk. When people drink the milk, the toxin further concentrates in their body fat and in mothers' breast milk.

With heavy pesticide use in cash crop regions of the South, high breast-milk traces are common. In India up to twenty times accepted safe levels of pesticide contamination have been found in breast milk, in Nicaragua forty-five times the safe level of DDT.[13] Even in the USA most women tested have shown breast-milk traces of the pesticides dieldrin, chlordane and heptachlor. The latter two were withdrawn in 1978 because of links with reproductive disorders, cancer and blood disease.

Many pesticides have been connected with cancer or shown to cause genetic mutations and birth defects. Other documented health risks include anorexia, diarrhoea, vomiting, cramps, seizures, hypertension, tremors, convulsions, sterility, blindness, coma, brain damage and death. Pesticide traces can be passed on to babies in the womb.

Hundreds of thousands of people die annually from pesticide poisoning, mostly in the South, and up to 2 million suffer acute symptoms. Yet most cases go unreported. Landowners may use threats of unemployment to prevent workers reporting poisonings, or persuade doctors to misrecord causes of illness or death. Government departments, anxious about food exports or tourism, hide the facts.

Legal standards
Many modern pesticides were developed as a by-product of chemical warfare research during the Second World War, and hundreds were licensed for use before testing became effective. Since then, many of the early prototypes – aldrin, dieldrin, malathion, parathion and others – have been banned in the North following discovery of their dangers. Such hazardous pesticides are still used in the South, however. Few low-income countries have the laws or resources to enforce controls, and

Northern manufacturers continue to export chemicals prohibited in their own countries. "The health of the Mexican
worker", it has been said, "has been subordinated to the health
of the tomato."[14] Ironically, banned-but-exported poisons can
sneak back in as residues on food imports; in 1988 beef bought
by the USA from Honduras had eight times US safety levels of
pesticide contamination.

Some countries try to save money by producing older-style,
more toxic pesticides of their own rather than importing more
expensive but safer ones. DDT and benzene hexachloride (both
outlawed in the North) are said to account for three-quarters of
pesticide use in India.[15] Lindane (banned in twenty countries)
is also widely used in the South, as is heptachlor (banned in
seventeen countries and linked to leukaemia).

Misuse and accidents
Poisoning often occurs when pesticides are applied without
proper precautions, or because of accidental spillage. Impoverished farmers have to use the cheapest, most toxic chemicals
and may skimp on protective clothing. Low-cost pesticides
are usually ineffective, so more dangerous quantities must be
applied. Illiterate farmworkers may not understand the risks,
and instructions and warning labels may be in the wrong
language. Pesticide poisoning was found to affect 80 per cent
of Filipino rice growers in the mid-1980s.[16]

The world's worst pesticide accident happened at Bhopal,
India, on the night of 2 December 1984. Forty tonnes of
explosive and highly toxic methyl isocyanide gas escaped from
a storage tank at Union Carbide's factory. Thousands of people,
mostly slum dwellers living near the factory, died immediately.
The authorities disposed of the bodies rapidly, concealing
the number of deaths. Those who survived suffered ulcers,
paralysis, eye disease, blindness and digestive, menstrual and
psychiatric disorders. Many Bhopal women have since had
spontaneous abortions, stillbirths or deformed babies. The
Union Carbide plant was operated with a disregard for safety
that would not be allowed in the West.

Different safety standards
Attitudes to safety vary in the North. The weedkiller 2,4-D
remains in use, despite links to cancer; combined with 2,4,5-T,
it was the basis for the lethal US defoliant Agent Orange used

in Vietnam. In 1989, after studying test results showing life-threatening tumours in mice, UK government advisers declared that the pesticide Alar (daminozide) posed no health risk. Identical evidence had led the US Environmental Protection Agency to the opposite conclusion. Alar was sprayed on to UK apple trees for several more months until voluntarily withdrawn by most growers.

US researchers have begun to investigate maneb and zineb, commonly used pre-harvest fungicides for cereals, fruit and vegetables, because of indications of a serious cancer risk to children. The US National Academy of Sciences says that 90 per cent of today's fungicides could be carcinogenic. Most food manufacturers and retailers – supported by the chemical industry – have opposed the public's right to know what chemicals are in its food.

Do pesticides work?

How necessary are pesticides? Would we face food shortages if we used less of them? According to international research, as little as *one-tenth* of all pesticides may reach their intended target. The rest drift across the land, especially when applied by aircraft, contaminating soil and water. In developing countries, the writer David Weir argues, only half the pesticides applied may be for essential food production.[17]

Nitrates

There is evidence that nitrate fertilizers also pose a health threat by seeping into underground water courses, rivers and reservoirs. Nitrate has been linked to the "blue baby" syndrome (blood-oxygen deficiency) and, by the WHO, to stomach cancer. There is uncertainty because of the time lags between the application of nitrate and its appearance in water and between the onset of cancer and its discovery. Levels of poisoning could rise because most farmers now use far more nitrate than they used to, and some research suggests that even low nitrate levels can impair children's development and reflexes.[18]

Chemical poisons in industry

A vast array of toxic substances have been developed and manufactured since the 1940s, their presence building up in our soil, water and air. Among the more dangerous industrial products are petrochemical derivatives, industrial solvents, heavy metals (such as mercury, cadmium and lead), asbestos, polychlorinated biphenyls (PCBs) and dioxins. Contamination enters the environment as liquid outflows from factories, as particle-laden atmospheric emissions, as impurities in other substances, from accidents and explosions and after land dumping.

Many of these chemicals are carcinogens, although the cancers they induce may not appear until long after exposure and may be unattributable. Cancer clusters have been found close to petrochemical plants, oil refineries, chemical factories and nuclear plants, as well as in the North's old heavy-industry regions.

Worldwide problem

Environmental contamination is a worldwide problem. In the mid-1980s, 7 per cent of the land in West Germany was found to be unfit for food production because of the presence of industrial heavy metals; the whole country could become unsuitable for farming.[19]

Eastern Europe has especially severe pollution because of its old-style heavy industry, its neglect of environmental controls and the widespread use of low-grade brown coal. In Poland, perhaps the world's most polluted country, only 1 per cent of the water is said to be fit to drink, and a quarter of the food production may be unsuitable for human consumption. The life expectancy of older Polish men has fallen, with Cracow and other cities now designated "catastrophe zones".[20] Children are threatened with pollution-induced leukaemia, asthma, bronchitis and mental handicap.

Matters are almost as bad in Czechoslovakia, East Germany, Hungary and the Soviet Union. Hundreds of children who attended kindergartens built on top of a disused military uranium dump in Narva, Estonia, for example, suffer from premature baldness. Millions of tonnes of oil shale are burned annually in the city's power stations, with the result, according to Estonia's Green Party, that "Ninety per cent of the children in this city are sick."[21] Narva has the USSR's highest rate of lung cancer.

Dioxins

Dioxins are a group of industrial chemicals that deserve special mention. Most of the bright white paper used in the North is bleached with chlorine gas, and this releases as a by-product the dioxin tetrachlorodibenzo-paradioxin (TCDD), allegedly the most dangerous chemical ever produced. Dioxins also result from the manufacture of some pesticides and are released when some plastics burn. The effects of dioxin poisoning, which can build up through the food chain, include cancers, birth and reproductive defects, skin disease and immune system disorders. Traces of these chemicals have been found in a wide range of paper products, including women's tampons and babies' disposable nappies.[22]

Landfill and contamination
The dumping of poisonous waste in landfill sites is a proven health hazard. In the 1970s people living over a disused waste dump at Love Canal, Niagara Falls, suffered a wave of illness ranging from blood disease and nervous-system disorders to miscarriages and deformed births. Residents took the US government and the chemical firm responsible to court until they got proper compensation. Another contamination scandal occurred in the early 1980s when residents of high-tech "Silicon Valley" outside San Francisco became aware of a rising incidence of miscarriages, stillbirths and genetic defects in the area. The cause was traced to industrial cleaners leaking from underground chemical storage tanks used by the valley's microchip factories, which had contaminated drinking water supplies.[23]

Accidents will happen
Industrial accidents often occur. During the 1950s seawater at Minamata, Japan, was contaminated with methyl mercury from a local factory. The poison was taken up by the fish that local people ate as their staple food. More than a thousand people died, and three times that number were blinded or brain-damaged. At Seveso in Italy a cloud of dioxins was released in a factory explosion in 1976. Hundreds of people were taken to hospital, and 1,800 hectares of land were contaminated. Defective births in the region subsequently increased by 40 per cent.

Weak laws
Laws governing the handling of toxic chemicals tend to be weak in Africa, Asia and Latin America, which is one inducement

for multinationals to cut costs by manufacturing abroad. The human consequences are often ignored. The Brazilian industrial town of Cubatão became known as the valley of death because of the respiratory diseases, cancers and birth defects that plagued its inhabitants as a result of industrial pollution.

The poison trade
Each year hundreds of thousands of tonnes of poisonous waste are shipped from North to South. Why? Landfill waste disposal is relatively expensive in most Western industrialized countries (costs of up to $300 a tonne) but cheaper elsewhere (as little as $20 a tonne). In 1987–8, 10,000 drums of highly inflammable and carcinogenic debris of Italian origin were illegally shipped to the small Nigerian port of Koko. Wrongly labelled and leaking, the containers were stacked close to a school playground. Local people emptied some of the drums to store drinking water. Amid outbreaks of premature births and cholera in Koko, the Italian government reluctantly removed the waste.[24] In another incident, hazardous incinerator ash from Philadelphia was peddled on the ship *Khian Sea* to the ports of fifteen countries in five continents.

Some higher-income countries are less choosy than others. East Germany for years absorbed much of West Germany's contaminated waste, and the UK (which also accepts nuclear waste) imports hazardous debris from a number of countries. During the 1980s the volume of the UK's trade in toxics reportedly increased at least sixfold. Until 1989 dangerous consignments were shipped in (or sometimes flown on passenger aircraft) from Canada.

Among these imports were PCBs, lethal chemicals used in electrical work that are indestructible except by high-temperature incineration. Now banned in many countries except for use in sealed equipment, PCBs have been blamed for children's loss of learning and athletic ability in Canada, and traces have been found in the body fat of the Arctic Inuit people.

Other disease-causing substances exported to the South include asbestos, whose hazards are now well recognized. Over a thousand people die each year in the UK and eight times that number in the USA from asbestosis, which attacks the lungs; a cancer link is also suspected. Yet rich countries sell asbestos to poor ones as a cheap building material. Customers of the world's leading exporter, Canada, include Chile, Malaysia and Thailand.[25]

Contaminated air

Atmospheric poisoning is a major burden on human health. According to the UN Environment Programme, the health of 600 million people in urban areas is imperilled by high levels of atmospheric carbon monoxide (a lethal poison) and sulphur dioxide, and a billion people breathe air dangerously over-loaded with smoke, soot and dust. The US-based Worldwatch Institute puts the number of people at risk at one billion. Urban smog is worst in Eastern Europe and the South. The inhabitants of Mexico City breathe possibly the world's most contaminated air and, because of their petrol's high lead content, have the highest blood-lead count. During 1988 the city exceeded WHO atmospheric safety levels on 312 days. Illness resulting from lead poisoning includes kidney and nervous diseases, epilepsy and brain damage, with children especially at risk.

Radiation

The Earth's natural background radiation comes from space, the soil, rocks and buildings. Uranium mining and processing, X-rays, nuclear weapons tests and explosions and nuclear power generation and waste disposal have added to radiation levels. In the 1960s Rachel Carson's book *Silent Spring* publicized the connection between radiation, cancer and genetic deformities.[26] The risk increases as radiation levels rise, although even low exposure can stimulate cancerous cell growth. Other consequences include hair loss, vomiting, bleeding, heart disease, diabetes, arthritis, asthma, allergies, stillbirths, infant deaths and mental and physical retardation.[27]

Much of the radiation produced during a nuclear reaction can penetrate lead or concrete, and some of the isotopes used remain radioactive for immense periods of time. Uranium 233 and plutonium 239 have "half-lives" (during which radioactivity declines by half) of 162,000 and 24,000 years respectively.

The quantity of nuclear waste and the problem of disposal are growing. The worldwide volume of high-level debris is likely to reach about 15,000 cubic metres by the end of the century. In the words of a former science adviser to ex-US President Nixon: "One has a queasy feeling about something that has to stay underground and be pretty well sealed off for 25,000 years before it is harmless."[28]

Higher-than-average radiation doses are received by nuclear industry workers and, probably, by people living close to nuclear installations. According to its critics, the civilian and military nuclear industry has suppressed widespread evidence of illness and premature death caused by radiation exposure.[29] In reply, the pro-nuclear lobby has usually argued that properly managed nuclear activities are safe.

The anti-nuclear case

Who is closer to the truth? Consider some of the evidence. The Irish Sea, into which the UK's Sellafield reprocessing plant in Cumbria discharges its liquid waste, is the most radioactively contaminated anywhere. Along Ireland's east coast there has been a wave of Down's syndrome children and cancer deaths. Six Irish women who have all had Down's syndrome babies (usual incidence: one birth in 600) were at the same girls' boarding school on the coast, directly opposite Sellafield (then called Windscale), on the October 1957 night when an accident there released a cloud of radioactive fallout.[30]

Leukaemia, a cancer of the blood, occurs in heavy "clusters" in the proximity of nuclear plants. The adult male leukaemia rate near one US plant is more than 700 times the national average. In 1987 a UK government report confirmed that children born near Sellafield had ten times the average risk of contracting leukaemia, in many cases fatally. The nuclear industry protested its innocence, but new research in 1990 showed that children whose father had worked at Sellafield before their conception were two and a half times more at risk of contracting leukaemia than other children. If their father had received a large radiation dose they were up to eight times more at risk.

Nuclear tests

There have been hundreds of nuclear tests since the 1940s. Until 1963 testing was often done above ground, filling the stratosphere with radioactive dust. The research scientist Dr Rosalie Bertell estimates that there have so far been about 13 million serious casualties of nuclear weapons. These range from the hundreds of thousands of people killed or sick as a result of the US bomb drops on Hiroshima and Nagasaki (many have

passed genetic deformities to their children) to current cancer
victims and the genetically damaged children likely to be born
until the year 2000 even if all nuclear activity were stopped.[31]

Among the worst-hit victims are the Marshall Islanders of the
South Pacific, where the USA tested weapons in the 1950s. Miscarriages, stillbirths, deformities, thyroid disease, tumours and
other ailments are commonly reported, and the islanders' urine
contains abnormal levels of plutonium. One island, Rongelap,
has been evacuated twice – the second time, in 1985, after
its inhabitants had been assured it was safe. When the US
government refused to help, the Greenpeace *Rainbow Warrior*
took the people to the relative safety of another island.[32]

France has suppressed all attempts to discover the health
status of the Polynesian islanders living close to where it tests
nuclear weapons.

Nuclear accidents
Like every industry, nuclear power generation has had its
accidents. Near-disasters at Browns Ferry in 1975 and Three
Mile Island in 1979 led to the US nuclear programme slowing
to a standstill. Details of an explosion at the Urals city of
Chelyabinsk in the USSR in 1957, when 17,000 people had to
be resettled away from the area, were hushed up for years.

The reactor explosion at Chernobyl in the Soviet Union
in April 1984 was worse still. Cesium 137 (radioactive half-
life: thirty years) and iodine 131 (an eight-day half-life) were
released into the air over ten days, producing long-term radioactive fallout now estimated as fifty times greater than that
of the Hiroshima bomb. Thirty-one workers and emergency
personnel were killed and 200 hospitalized during the first
weeks; at least 250 people present at the site have since
died. The health of between 2 and 3 million Ukrainian and
Byelorussian children and adults is now said to have been
seriously damaged by radiation contamination, partly through
the consumption of contaminated food and drink; symptoms
include failing eyesight, swollen thyroid glands, anaemia and
psychological disorders. Soviet scientists have predicted 49,000
extra cancer deaths over the next few decades as a result of the
accident.

After the explosion, wind-swept radioactive rain descended
on Europe. Laplanders and their reindeer received massive
radiation doses. Within weeks, airborne radiation had spread

to the USA. In the UK radioactive contaminated lamb was sold and eaten for a month after Chernobyl before the government imposed restrictions. This followed the pattern set after the 1957 Windscale (Sellafield) fire, when milk with three times official radioactive safety levels was kept on sale – to avoid "alarming the public". West Germany sold radiation-contaminated powdered milk to Egypt as cattle fodder, and Poland appears to have sold the same to Nepal.[33]

In France, which has gone further down the nuclear-energy road than any other country, a semi-secret government report leaked in 1990 warned of the risk of a serious reactor accident unless work was done immediately to improve safety throughout the nuclear industry.[34]

Action

Population and health

Will world population stabilize in time to avert catastrophe? We cannot be sure, but every voluntary reduction in birth rates worldwide will help. To be morally acceptable and have a chance of success, efforts to slow population growth must be accompanied by improvements in health and women's status and by reductions in social and economic inequalities. Motivation is the key: people must *want* to have fewer children.

Appropriate family planning

Access to birth control is every woman's right. About half the world's women of child-bearing age are said to want to limit their number of children, but Northern-style contraception is often unavailable to, or disliked by, women in the South. Some women try modern contraception but abandon it because of the side-effects. Oxfam found that Kenyan women abandoned family planning because of a lack of sympathetic and well-informed staff and clinics within reach of their homes. Better advice and aftercare, more education about side-effects and access to choice of methods all encourage contraceptive use. Greater efforts should be made to develop male contraception.

Despite its problems, birth control is said to be less dangerous than childbirth in poor countries. Contraceptive use also tends to make each child wanted, expected and provided for. With fewer children and longer intervals between births, mothers and children are healthier, rates of child mortality lower and pressure for numerous offspring less. Indian children born after a two- or three-year interval following their mother's previous delivery have twice the chance of surviving infancy as those born after less than a year.

Every country that has achieved a significant reduction in its birth rate has reduced infant mortality first. Successes during the 1960s and 1970s included Burma, China, Colombia, Cuba, Kerala state in India, North and South Korea, Singapore, Sri Lanka, Thailand and Tunisia, although in some of these countries the trend has partly reversed. Funding and advice should be directed to support women's self-help efforts in promoting nutrition, preventive health care and family planning.

Better opportunities for women

Women need access to alternatives to child bearing. Better education, especially literacy, and improved employment opportunities undermine fatalism about "biological destiny", enhance women's decision-making capacity and increase their status and independence. Educated women in the South are usually more able to persuade their husbands to use contraception or to agree to their using it. Studies show that educated women also have healthier children. Also, when the income and security of poor people improve, they usually want fewer children.

Worldwide, a responsible approach to sex and health education would make all young people aware of the limited capacity of the planet to provide for ever-growing human numbers. With abortion terminating roughly 50 million pregnancies each year, half of them illegally, its worldwide legalization (with suitable provisos) could make a contribution to women's fertility rights and to maternal health. Legalization in the USA in 1973 is said to have cut the number of abortion-induced deaths by about 90 per cent.

In 1987 the WHO, UNICEF, the World Bank and the International Planned Parenthood Federation agreed steps along many of the above lines for population control. In addition, financial incentives could be worked out to encourage smaller families, such as larger pensions for people with fewer children, or government allowances for women of child-bearing age who avoid pregnancy.

Birth control programmes have sometimes been implemented

by coercion or by taking advantage of people's vulnerability, neither of which is justifiable. Non-voluntary sterilization programmes have been run in Bangladesh, El Salvador, Mexico, Puerto Rico and, using the high-risk Depo-Provera drug banned in the West, Thailand. In India famine relief and the promise of jobs were used as incentives. In South Africa a government programme to curb black birth rates also involved using Depo-Provera.

Preventive health care

The world's annual health budget is only a fifth of its arms spending. Along with a major reallocation of resources (which the North should lead), Southern health spending needs to be redirected from cure to prevention, with more emphasis on combating the social and economic causes of illness. Costly health care for the wealthy should not be provided at the expense of low-cost services for the majority. Hospital services need to be decentralized, based on regional networks of smaller health centres.

Water and sanitation

Social and economic improvements, especially in sanitation and housing, are often the best weapon against infectious diseases. In 1981 the United Nations launched its World Drinking Water Supply and Sanitation Decade. The Decade's aims – clean water and adequate sanitation for all by the year 1990 – have not been fully met, although some success was achieved. Reasons for the partial failure are thought to include underfunding, the North's tying of aid to rigid purchasing conditions, Southern politicians' lack of interest in sanitation and a failure to connect one development problem with another.[35]

Many countries made progress nevertheless. Virtually every Thai village now has clean drinking water for each person and one latrine per household; Malawi is close to providing clean water for all; and India provided efficient handpumps for an estimated two-thirds of its villages during the 1980s. In the years before the Decade, a UNICEF-backed programme of well construction provided 75 per cent of Bangladesh's households with safe water. The Decade's aims are thought to be achievable worldwide if one month's global weapons spending were used for the purpose.[36]

Local solutions
Much has been learned about water and sanitation provision
in poor countries, for example about the need to involve
rural communities in decisions about the citing of wells and
in the construction work. Paid, trained and equipped with
basic tools, "barefoot mechanics" can be given responsibility for well and pump maintenance. Low-cost water-supply
technologies include hand- and wind-pumps, bamboo pipes and
simple filters using sand, coconut fibre or rice husks. There
are valuable traditional practices, too, such as Indian women's
use of natural coagulants to clarify muddy water, seeds to
inhibit bacteria growth, burnt coconut shells to clear wells
and water containers made from copper and brass (metals
with antiseptic properties, unlike plastic). As for sanitation,
inexpensive alternatives to piped sewage systems include the
Vietnamese composting latrine.[37]

Primary health care
In 1978 the World Health Organization launched a campaign to
bring primary health care to all by the end of the century, and
a number of Southern countries have committed themselves to
this approach. Emphasis on primary health care in China, Cuba,
Nicaragua, Thailand and elsewhere has produced benefits.
Cuba has health standards superior to any comparable poor
country. Several countries have set up nationwide networks of
primary health care workers or "barefoot doctors" to take basic
medical treatment and advice into the countryside.[38] According
to the WHO, a trained village health worker with only twenty
drugs can treat most common illnesses. Such health workers can
be trained for a fraction of the cost of a Northern-style doctor,
but the benefits are frequently greater; many doctors take up
lucrative private practices and are indifferent to primary care.

Primary care means healthier women and children. Many
countries now recognize the key role of midwives and traditional birth attendants, and millions of infant deaths are
preventable through the elimination of malnutrition, the early
treatment of diarrhoea and dehydration and the availability of
vaccination and immunization. Infant malnutrition can be prevented by the promotion of breast feeding, care in pregnancy,
home hygiene, growth and weight monitoring and special supplementary feeding.

Oral rehydration therapy, using a sugar/salt solution, is very cheap. According to the WHO: "For $50 million, or the cost of a modest commercial building in New York City, we could cut deaths from diarrhoeal diseases by 2 million children per year."[39] UNICEF has estimated that the treatment would prevent up to 20 million further *births* by the end of the century.

The multinationals
The threat to health in the South from multinationals is unacceptable. Ways to reduce the power of these commercial giants were suggested in previous chapters. Consumer boycotts can be effective when governments fail to act. Yet countries should do more for themselves, such as Nigeria, which has banned tobacco advertising.

The WHO's Essential Drugs Programme recommends that doctors have a short list of essential medicines to help eliminate the problem of over- and mis-prescription. Since Bangladesh introduced a basic list of 250 drugs for hospitals and clinics in 1982, domestic medicine production has strengthened, prices have fallen, and quality has improved. About forty countries now have a similar policy.

Traditional medicines
The South can also learn from its own medical traditions. There is renewed respect worldwide for homoeopathy, yoga, herbal medicine and other complementary treatments. Government-sponsored research into traditional medicines is under way in Ghana (where herbal cures are used for malaria and asthma) and Nicaragua.

Fewer poisons
"It would be unrealistic to suppose that all chemical carcinogens can or will be eliminated from the modern world," wrote Rachel Carson nearly thirty years ago. "But a very large proportion are by no means necessities of life...The most determined effort should be made to eliminate those carcinogens that now contaminate our food, our water supplies, and our atmosphere."[40] (Lifestyle factors also play a part in people's vulnerability to cancer-causing substances.)

Dangerous pesticides – with their widespread use for non-essential purposes, the small proportion that reach their target and the speed with which pests sometimes develop immunity – are largely unnecessary. It has been calculated that pests reduced crop yields by about 30 per cent before chemical pesticides were developed, which is the same loss rate as now occurs *with* them.[41]

Integrated pest management

Despite what the agribusiness lobby says, there are workable alternatives to killer chemicals. Integrated pest management (IPM) is a far safer approach that combines biological pest controls with the minimum use of chemicals. IPM schemes have been launched with United Nations backing in sixty countries and probably save money in the long run.[42]

How do they work? IPM uses natural pest–predator relationships to control pest populations. In Gujurat in India, for example, mosquito-eating fish are introduced by farmers into ponds where the insects breed. In China yellow citrus ants have been introduced to protect mandarin crops from caterpillars, and ducklings are herded into rice fields to destroy grasshoppers. Sometimes IPM simply means careful farming. The planting and harvesting of crops can be timed to avoid periods when pests breed. Crop rotation, fallow periods, intercropping and a reintroduction of traditional crop varieties all help reduce pest damage. Trees and bushes in and around fields provide habitats for birds and other pest predators.

Tighter controls

Research into the dangers of agrochemicals has been a low priority, partly because of the political clout of the agribusiness lobby. In the UK such work has been underfunded and understaffed; there is a backlog of half-untested chemicals in use; research is based on animal experiments and so not entirely valid for humans; and test findings, as well as the relationship between government officials and agribusiness, are shrouded in secrecy under the Official Secrets Act.[43] (In 1990 the UK government announced some improvements in its pesticide-testing procedure, including higher staffing levels.)

European Community regulations may soon oblige food packagers to list any post-harvest pesticides used. Other useful recommendations were made by the Brundtland Commission: no sales of new pesticides without satisfactory health testing; restricted use of existing chemicals prior to full testing; no exports of pesticides banned in the producer country; regional advice centres to advise governments on health hazards; international standards for pesticide packaging and labelling; and international compensation for injury or accidents.[44]

In the meantime, legal, political and consumer action may be needed. Banana workers in Costa Rica went to court against the use of one dangerous pesticide, and in California a trade union campaign and consumer boycott were organized in the 1970s until the state tightened up its pesticide controls.

In 1989 the international chemical industry accepted a partial limitation on its powers to sell the most dangerous pesticides to unwary importing countries. Under the UN Food and Agriculture Organization's new "prior informed consent" arrangements, manufacturers must notify customers about health hazards and withhold sale until the importing country replies that it still wants the pesticides. It is thought that some manufacturers will just ignore the rule, however.

Farmworkers compelled to use pesticides need training, protective clothing and regular health checks. China, Indonesia, Kenya and Nigeria have reduced the frequency of poisoning through such measures. Safety does not come cheap, and an enlarged WHO or FAO budget or a pesticide sales levy could provide the funding.

With nitrate fertilizers posing possible health risks, we should be wary of them. "Water protection zones" near sources of underground drinking water, where nitrate use is restricted, are one solution (the UK has established some zones). In the long term, a steady reduction in nitrate use is preferable, achievable through a tax on chemical fertilizer sales to help subsidize farmers converting to organic methods. This is especially appropriate in North America and Western Europe, where nitrate use to boost yields has led to overproduction.

As with pesticides, so with industrial chemicals, tighter controls on manufacture and sale have been recommended by the Brundtland Commission.[45] Industries should have to prove the safety of new techniques or materials before obtaining an operating licence, and be legally accountable for waste disposal and for health and safety monitoring of sites.[46] If recent government proposals come into effect, UK factory and waste site managements will have to record pollution information on local open-access registers. Similar measures are thought likely to come into force throughout the European Community.

Alternative processes

There are nearly always alternatives to the most toxic chemicals. When the health risks caused by dioxins were discovered in Sweden, for example, a switch was made from bleached to unbleached paper products; now hardly any chlorine-bleached paper is used in Sweden. Printing and writing paper can be safely whitened with hydrogen peroxide instead of chlorine-bleached.

After years of dumping toxic waste into holes in the ground, the industrialized countries are seeing the need for safer disposal (particularly as they are running short of suitable landfill sites; it is predicted that Japan will have run out of sites in two years' time). Future waste-handling should include: separation of biodegradable and non-biodegradable materials; recovery and recycling of metals, oils and plastics; high-temperature incineration; re-use of treated waste water for irrigation; re-use of organic waste for animal feed, fertilizer and packing material; and safe landfill in sealed and monitored sites. A great deal of money will be needed to detoxify disposal sites. Such action could be partly self-financing, however; jobs will be created, materials and energy saved through recycling, health protected and environmental damage reduced. (See Chapter 7.)

Some reductions in pollution can come relatively cheaply, and resources can be conserved by using more labour and less capital equipment, a switch that can generate profits for low-income countries. In Shanghai, for example, a government-run network recycling and reselling metals, rubber, plastics, paper, rags, cotton, glass and waste oil has generated thousands of jobs.[47]

Polluter pays

Despite future technical improvements, few industrial or waste-handling processes can be guaranteed perfectly safe. Incineration of PCBs, for example, leaves a highly toxic ash residue. We must make and use fewer harmful chemicals in the first place. Governments can help by introducing taxes and charges on the consumption of materials, energy and water and the generation of waste. This is the "polluter pays" principle, championed for years by environmentalists and at last gaining ground. The money will help pay to clean up present damage and be an incentive for industry to reduce its consumption and pollution.

It can be done: Japan's rate of raw materials consumption fell by 40 per cent in a recent ten-year period.[48]

The international trade in toxic wastes must be halted. When countries have to dispose of their own waste on their own soil, they will work harder to conserve and recycle materials and manage waste safely. Local authorities and communities should be involved in waste-dump siting decisions and in accident contingency planning. Thirty-nine developing countries have banned toxic waste imports. An international treaty launched in 1988–9 and signed by a hundred countries restricts shipments, requiring advance notification and consent and environmentally sound disposal. Several Northern exporters of waste refused to sign.

Air pollution can be reduced with tighter industrial emission controls, increased fuel efficiency, clean-burning technology, the fitting of catalytic converters on motor vehicles and a switch from private vehicles to public transport. (See Chapter 8.)

Nuclear waste
Radioactive waste should not be allowed to cross frontiers. On-site disposal and monitoring will oblige countries and industries to take full responsibility for their waste. Workers in the nuclear industry must be given better protection against routine exposure to radioactivity. As the health dangers become increasingly clear, opposition to all forms of nuclear activity is likely to increase. With some countries heavily committed to nuclear power, however, and the world's abundance of nuclear weaponry, a complete winding down of the nuclear industry will not come easily; but it should remain the long-term goal.

Getting Involved

Related subjects covered elsewhere in this book include: malnutrition and agrochemicals – Chapter 1; poverty in the South – Chapter 2; women's burdens – Chapter 4; indigenous peoples – Chapter 5; water pollution and supply, waste conservation and recycling – Chapter 7; air pollution and low energy paths – Chapter 8; the social costs of military spending – Chapter 10. To find out more about population and health questions, see "Recommended Reading" (pages 324–9).

Consumer and lifestyle choices

Small families
A contribution every adult can make to avoiding a catastrophi-
cally overpopulated world is to have no more than two children.
If you want more than this, why not foster or adopt one or more
of the great many children in need of a loving home? Discuss
population questions with your children as they grow older.

Wealth and income redistribution
Ideas for consumer and lifestyle decisions that can help bring
about a fairer distribution of the world's wealth and income, and
therefore reduce the pressure on people in low-income countries
to produce large families, are given in the "Getting Involved"
sections in Chapters 1 and 2.

Consumer boycotts
Resist the power of those multinationals that you know are
involved in the unscrupulous marketing of health-endangering
foods, medicines or other products in the South. Boycott their
products and explain to retailers, to other people you know and
(in writing) to the companies concerned what you are doing
and why. More information about consumer boycotts is given
in Chapter 2.

Don't buy brand-name medicines when generic drugs (usually cheaper) are available. Oxfam UK (address below) is
campaigning to get the European Community to prohibit the
export to low-income countries of drugs that are banned in
EC countries. Letters to your MP and MEP in support of this
campaign (more details from Oxfam) would be helpful.

Avoid buying or using chemical pesticides, including fly- and
other household insect-sprays, and chemical fertilizers, even
for flower gardening. Natural substitutes include soft soap for
pesticide (washing-up liquid is often effective) and such natural
fertilizers as animal manure, plant and vegetable compost and
wood ash. Organizations in the UK giving advice on chemical-
free gardening are listed in Chapter 1.

Buying safely
Buy fresh, organic and local rather than pre-packed and
imported foods. Chemicals are often used to improve the
look of and to preserve pre-packed and imported foods during

storage and transportation. Organic food is far healthier both for growers and for eaters. For more about buying organic food, see Chapter 1.

As for industrial poisons, use emulsion paint, which is lead-free, rather than gloss. Keep your use of dangerous household chemicals to a minimum and reycle as much of your domestic rubbish as you can (see Chapter 7). The more recycling there is, the easier it will be for the remaining small quantity of refuse to be safely dealt with.

Buy non-chlorine-bleached paper products. In the UK the Women's Environmental Network (address below) has been campaigning to end the chlorine-bleaching of sanitary towels, nappies and so on; alternative products marked "unbleached" or "chlorine free" are now on the market.

Converting / giving up your car
If you have not already done so, convert your vehicle to unleaded fuel and fit a catalytic converter. Better still, walk, cycle or use public transport rather than driving. Support campaigns for better public transport and cleaner air (see Chapter 8).

Water quality
Domestic water in the UK is sometimes contaminated with agrochemicals and industrial toxins. Over a million people in the UK are said to drink water contaminated with nitrates above European Community safety levels (the EC is currently prosecuting the UK government). If you are concerned about your domestic water quality, write to your regional water company or the local environmental health department and ask them to carry out a test and show you the results. If you are still dissatisfied or left in the dark, try contacting the regional office of the National Rivers Authority (the standard-setting body) or Friends of the Earth (address below).

Advice on bottled water and domestic water filters is available in the UK to members of the Consumers Association (2 Marylebone Road, London NW1) and is usefully summarized by Frances and Phil Craig in their book *Britain's Poisoned Water* (London: Penguin, 1989), pp. 115–17. The Craigs rightly point out, however, that healthy water should be everybody's right for no extra cost; and to achieve this, campaigning is needed (see below).

Better personal health
Personal health is, of course, affected by lifestyle factors such as diet and exercise. These are beyond the scope of this book, but a useful guide is *Holistic Living: A Guide to Self-Care* by Dr Patrick Pietroni (London: Dent, 1986); there is also a section on personal health in *How to Be Green* by John Button (London: Century Hutchinson, 1989).

Community and political action

Every contribution that we make to the alleviation of hunger and poverty in low-income countries helps reduce birth rates and enables people to achieve better health (see Chapters 1 and 2). Ways to improve nutrition, health care, sanitation, water supply and housing are being carefully studied and worked on, in consultation with local people, by such UK organizations as the Intermediate Technology Development Group, Oxfam, the Panos Institute (which publishes the health-oriented bi-monthly development journal *Panoscope*), Population Concern, Save the Children and Water Aid (addresses below). Write to any of these organizations, offering to become a financial supporter and asking what else you can do to help people in the South achieve better health.

Tell them what you think
Raise the issue of health in poor countries by writing to your MP, MEP and the press or joining in radio phone-in programmes. Points you could mention include:

- Poverty is the worst enemy of health in poor countries. By keeping them poor, we in the rich countries are consigning millions of people to disease and premature death.
- Most illness among the Southern poor results from hunger and lack of clean water.
- Millions of the world's rural and urban poor lack 5 litres of clean water a day, while we in the industrialized countries use an average of 200 hundred litres each.
- Half a day's world weapons spending would pay for malaria to be eradicated worldwide; the cost of one jet fighter (about $25 million) would fund 40,000 village pharmacies.[49]
- Large development projects in poor countries contribute to

ill health: irrigation reservoirs and canals encourage malarial mosquitoes and other parasitic creatures to breed; export farming results in widespread pesticide poisoning; rural unemployment leads to urban overcrowding in disease-ridden housing.

- Few countries in the South have the resources to provide basic sanitation and health services for all.
- The governments of high-income countries should give world health a far higher priority; they could offer increased finance for the World Health Organization and provide more funds for public health programmes in poor countries.

An end to secrecy

Join the campaign to end agribusiness and industrial secrecy in the industrialized countries. In the UK one organization working for better information about the chemicals in our food is Parents for Safe Food (address below). Many people believe that the UK needs a Freedom of Information Act so that companies are obliged to disclose such information; Charter 88 (see Chapter 5) is campaigning for such an end to official secrecy.

In 1989 Greenpeace activists visited Czechoslovakia and worked with local environmentalists to distribute information (previously kept secret by the Czech government) about the dangers from a uranium ore processing plant, as well as presenting the new government with a dossier of information about past accidents at the plant.[50]

Water contamination

In the UK, if you know the water in your area is badly contaminated with nitrate, ask your local councillors, MP and MEP what they are doing to put this right. Send copies of your letters to the regional water company and to the National Rivers Authority's regional office. Friends of the Earth (address below) can give advice on your campaign. Efforts along these lines by a tenants' federation in the London borough of Tower Hamlets helped bring about a lowering of nitrate levels.[51]

Waste dumping

Are there landfill waste dumps in your area? If so, try to discover who operates the dump, what wastes are accepted (household or industrial or both) and what safety standards are in force. Ask your community organization, local councillors or MP to investigate the site unless you are sure that public health is properly protected. In the UK Friends of the Earth and the *Observer* newspaper have launched an investigative campaign aimed at cleaning up the UK's toxic waste sites; for details, write to FOE, marking your envelope "Toxic Tips Campaign".

Do any industrial firms in your area produce or use hazardous materials? If you know of any, write to the firm and politely express your concern as a local resident, asking how they dispose of such materials and what their attitude to safety is. Keep copies of any correspondence. If you are not satisfied with replies, get your community association, local councillors, the local press or your MP to take the matter up. Try Friends of the Earth if you need advice. Campaign in your own workplace to improve your company's handling of toxic substances.

Greenpeace UK (address below) is running a Waste Trade Campaign and would like to be informed of any schemes to import toxic or other waste into the country.

Nuclear power
Add your voice to those calling for a phase-out of nuclear power and an expansion of energy conservation and renewable energy (see Chapter 8). Campaign, too, for a halt to the transportation of nuclear and other hazardous waste within or between countries. Write to your MP, MEP and the press, and contribute to radio phone-ins, calling for the banning of shipments of nuclear waste between countries, an end to the UK's importing of radioactive waste for reprocessing at Sellafield and the banning of the world trade in non-nuclear toxic waste. Points you could raise include:

• Any movement of nuclear or toxic waste increases the likelihood of dangerous accidents.
• Nuclear reprocessing actually increases the overall quantity of dangerous waste.
• It is now about ten times more expensive to reprocess nuclear waste than to dry-store it.[52]
• It is wrong for the health of people in one country to be put at risk by any kind of waste produced for the benefit of another country.

Organizations

Organizations campaigning for fertility rights and better health worldwide include:

UK and Irish Republic
Cumbrians Opposed to a Radioactive Environment, 98 Church Street, Barrow-in-Furness, Cumbria.
Earthwatch, Harbour View, County Cork, Irish Republic.
Friends of the Earth, 26–28 Underwood Street, London N1 7JQ (071-490 1555); and Bonnington Mill, 70–72 Newhaven Road, Edinburgh EH6 5QG (031-554 9977).
Greenpeace, 30–31 Islington Green, London N1 8XE (071-354 5100).
International Planned Parenthood Federation, 18–20 Lower Regent Street, London SW1 (071-486 0741).
Intermediate Technology Development Group, Myson House, Railway Terrace, Rugby CV21 3BR (0788-60631).
London Food Commission, 88 Old Street, London EC1V 9AR (071-253 9513).
Oxfam, 274 Banbury Road, Oxford OX2 7DZ (0865-56777).
Panos Institute, 9 White Lion Street, London N1 9PD (071-278 1111).
Parents for Safe Food, Britannia House, 1–11 Glenthorne Road, London W6 0LT (081-748 9898).
Pesticides Trust, 258 Pentonville Road, London N1 9JY (071-354 3860).
Population Concern, 231 Tottenham Court Road, London W1 (071-637 9582).
Save the Children Fund, 17 Grove Lane, London SE5 8RD (071-703 5400).
Water Aid, 1 Queen Anne's Gate, London SW1H 9BT (071-222 8111).
Women's Environmental Network, 287 City Road, London EC1V 1LA (071-490 2511).

USA and Canada
Canadian Coalition for Nuclear Responsibility, PO Box 236, Snowden, Montreal, Quebec H3X 3T4, Canada.
Coordinating Committee on Pesticides, #505, 942 Market, San Francisco, Calif. 94102, USA.
Greenpeace, 1436 U Street NW, Washington, DC 20009, USA.

Greenpeace, 578 Bloor Street W, Toronto, Ontario M6G 1K1, Canada.

Health Action International Canada, 6th Floor, United Church House, 85 St Clair Avenue East, Toronto, Ontaria M4T 1M8, Canada.

Intermediate Technology Development Group, 777 United Nations Plaza, New York, NY 10017, USA.

National Women's Health Network, 45 Sutton Place South, New York, NY 10022, USA.

New York Public Interest Research Group, 9 Murray Street, New York, NY 10007, USA.

Nuclear Information and Resource Service, Suite 601, 1424 16th Street NW, Washington, DC 20036, USA.

Panos Institute, 1409 King Street, Alexandria, Va 22314, USA.

Pollution Probe, 12 Madison Avenue, Toronto, Ontario M5R 2S1, Canada.

Rachel Carson Trust, 8940 Jones Mill Road, Chevy Chase, Mass 20815, USA.

Save the Children, Suite 6020, 3080 Yonge Street, Toronto, Ontario M5W 2B1, Canada.

Australia and New Zealand

Australian Conservation Foundation, 672B Glenferrie Road, Hawthorne, Melbourne, Victoria 3122, Australia.

Australian Consumers' Association, 57 Carrington Road, Marrickville, New South Wales 2204, Australia.

Campaign against Nuclear Power, PO Box 238, North Quay, Brisbane, Queensland 4000, Australia.

Friends of the Earth, PO Box 530E, Melbourne, Victoria 3001, and GPO Box 1875, Canberra, New South Wales, Australia.

Friends of the Earth, PO Box 39-065, Auckland West, New Zealand.

Greenpeace, Private Bag No. 6, 134 Broadway, Sydney, New South Wales 2007, Australia.

Greenpeace, Private Bag, Wellesley Street PO, Auckland 1, New Zealand.

New Zealand Coalition for Trade and Development, PO Box 11345, Wellington, New Zealand.

Pacific Concerns Resource Centre, PO Box 9295, Newmarket, Auckland, New Zealand.

Africa and Asia (Commonwealth)

Asian and Pacific Centre for Women and Development, c/o Asia and Pacific Development Centre, PO Box 2444, Jalan Data, Kuala Lumpur, Malaysia.

Centre for Science and Environment, 807 Vishal Bhavan, 95 Nehru Place, New Delhi 110019, India.

Friends of the Earth Bangladesh, PO Box 4222, Ramna Dhaka 1000, Bangladesh.

Friends of the Earth/Sahabat Alam Malaysia, 43 Salween Road, 10050 Penang, Malaysia.

Friends of the Earth, PO Box 3794, Ghana.

Friends of the Earth, PM Bag 950, 33 Robert Town, Freetown, Sierra Leone.

Health Action International, PO Box 1045, 10830 Penang, Malaysia.

Kenya Water for Health Organization, PO Box 61470, Nairobi, Kenya.

Pesticide Action Network, PO Box 1045, 10830, Penang, Malaysia.

Tanzania Environmental Society, PO Box 1309, Dar es Salaam, Tanzania.

4. Women – Present Burdens and Future Role

"It seems almost certain that sooner or later [women] will arrive at complete economic and social equality...When we abolish the slavery of half of humanity, together with the whole system of hypocrisy that it implies, then...the human couple will find its true form."

Simone de Beauvoir[1]

The Problem

The first human societies are thought to have valued women highly. Women were the biological life-givers and, some say, the earliest farmers. A major change seems to have begun in about 3000 BC. The first urban civilizations arose, based on more sophisticated farming techniques, metalworking, warfare, slavery, religion and law, controlled largely by men. "The mother fell to the rank of nurse and servant, while authority and rights belonged to the father," writes Simone de Beauvoir of this transformation, and the status of women's occupations has remained low. "There are villages in which men fish and women weave," the anthropologist Margaret Mead remarks, "and those in which women fish and men weave; but in either type of village, the work done by men is valued higher than the work done by women."[2]

What if equality existed between women and men? Girls and boys would be brought up identically. Adults of either sex would work in the same occupations for equal pay. Both would have the right and duty to earn their own living. No woman would be forced into marriage, and maternity would be voluntary.[3] Such a future may sound remote, but increasing numbers of people are working for it.

Discrimination under the law

In many societies women are legally, culturally and economically subordinate to men, and this lower status begins in the
family. Millions of rural women in Africa, Asia and Latin
America have little or no legal entitlement to own land or other
forms of wealth or to control its use. Colonial and post-colonial
laws have everywhere been biased in favour of men. In some
African countries, for example, according to laws drafted both
before and since independence, women are legal minors, unable
to enter contracts or raise loans. Other basic rights denied by
backward legal codes to women in different parts of the world
include choice of where to live and the right to work outside
the home.[4]

The weight of tradition
Tradition and custom may be equally oppressive. Few Indian
women choose their own husband; most marriages are arranged
or forced. An Indian bride is the property of her husband, and
most newly weds live with the husband's mother. Mothers- and
sisters-in-law commonly victimize their weaker female relatives
"in retaliation for their own lifelong subjugation by the male
members of the family". Despite the legal prohibition of
dowries, Indian wives have been beaten, tortured, harassed into
suicide or murdered because their dowry was considered too
small by the new family. The practice of *sati* (widow burning)
also continues, although laws have been passed against it.
Fatalism sustains these customs: "Women themselves help per-
petuate the myth that their sufferings are divinely ordained."[5]

The life of millions of Arab Muslim women is one of "renun-
ciation, of captivity", during which the woman must "atone for
her sin of having been born a woman in a hyper-male society".
Women endure "a kind of life sentence in jail – behind a dark
veil, behind the thick walls of the family house where the men
act as jailors". Most Arab Muslim girls are married before or
soon after reaching puberty. Until old age, few Muslim women
can take part in activity outside the home. Among the freedoms
Muslim men are said to permit themselves, on the other hand,
are concubines and up to four wives.[6]

Work in the home
Who does the housework? In the oldest indigenous cultures,
life's necessities seem to be provided equally by women and

men. Child care is still a man's task among tribal peoples in Indonesia and Zaire. As more complex societies have evolved, however, the routine drudgery on which family welfare depends has fallen increasingly to women. In Southern rural societies today, women are almost universally responsible for collecting firewood, although in many cases only men have the right to plant or own trees.[7]

Over the centuries, colonization, economic development and population growth have made increasing demands on rural women's sources of wood, water, wild food and other necessities. Collecting fuel and water can consume up to a third of a meagre daily diet of 1,500 calories. Some Indian women walk 10 kilometres a day for firewood, returning with 35- or even 50-kilo bundles, and women in Africa may live 15 kilometres from the nearest well. The development writer Paul Harrison considers that the domestic burdens of African women are "enough to break a camel's back".[8]

In the North the idea that women naturally belong in the home is partly a myth. Until the early years of the Industrial Revolution, men, women and children were often employed together as farm labourers and in mines and factories. With advances in machine technology, industrialists needed fewer workers and laid off the women and children. Between 1737 and 1911 the number of married Englishwomen working outside the home is said to have fallen by almost 90 per cent.[9]

Women's housework would make up an estimated third of the value of industrialized countries' GNPs if it were paid for. Northern women who do not work outside the home have been found to do up to 99 hours of domestic work each week, while employed women average between 30 and 50 hours. The average man's weekly contribution is 11 hours.[10]

Paid employment and control of household finances are widely regarded as male domains. This housework/paid-work division of labour and economic power is said to benefit both parties, but the results can be one-sided. Southern men's wages are often spent on beer and prostitutes; their Northern counterparts may prefer pubs and smart cars; both plead work commitments to avoid domestic duties. Child-care responsibilities alone can make it impossible for mothers to gain economic independence.

Women's health

Women's health suffers, too. Despite their greater natural longevity, women's life expectancy in low-income countries can be as short as, or shorter than, that of men. They are often the last of the family to eat. In Asia two-thirds, in Africa one-half and in Latin America one-sixth of all women are reportedly anaemic from poor diet, overwork and the strain of pregnancy and childbirth. In the industrialized countries women are twice as likely as men to be diagnosed as mentally ill.[11]

Marriage and motherhood

Single and childless women are despised in many societies. Not surprisingly, most women accept marriage as the only realistic course. Sex becomes destiny – hence the importance of pre-marital female virginity. Among religious fundamentalists, parents may inflict brutal punishments on, or even kill, a daughter who has lost her virginity before marriage.

High birth rates occur wherever women lack independence and respect. "The low status of women has made childbearing the only rite of passage for girls" in many developing countries, says the Worldwatch Institute.[12] Boy children are more highly valued than girls. They have better earning potential and in most societies pass on the household property (as well as the family name). It is said to be a sign of a man's masculinity to father a son.

Preferential treatment of boys over girls starts early. When food is short, boys are generally fed first. Undernourishment is more severe in girls than in boys in Bangladesh, Botswana, northern India, Nepal and Turkey. As for housework, girls in Zaire do 55 per cent of their mother's chores, boys 15 per cent. Caribbean girls are brought up to cook, clean and wash (time-consuming tasks), boys just to sweep the yard and take out the garbage. Many girls but few boys miss school on account of household duties.[13]

Domestic violence

Domestic violence against women is widespread. In Peru 70 per cent of reported crimes are said to involve women attacked at home by their husband or partner; in São Paulo, Brazil, more than 700 wife-killings occurred in a single year. Wife-beating is a frequent reason for divorce in Japan, while in the UK about one wife in ten is raped by her husband. Worldwide there is still too little legal protection for women against male domestic violence.[14]

Divorce
Marriage break-up and divorce affect about one married woman in seven in the South and as many as one in two in the North. In Africa marriages are disrupted by male migrating work patterns. (Women of Lesotho whose husbands go to work in South Africa's gold mines are known as widows of gold.) Latin American female-headed households tend to be city-based rather than rural, with women leaving the countryside to work as domestic servants. In Muslim countries men divorce their wives simply by announcing the intention to do so; Muslim women cannot initiate a divorce.

Divorce leaves women and children worse off than men. In the USA women's average incomes have been found to fall by 42 per cent after divorce, while those of men rise by up to 73 per cent. Many legal codes give divorced men the greater share of jointly owned property, although most oblige men to support their ex-wives – a duty commonly ignored. By custom, African men often keep possession of children after divorce. Neither divorced women nor widows can remarry in some societies.[15]

Women as farmers

Women grow about half the world's food. They do three-quarters of the farmwork in Africa, half in Asia and three-quarters of the work on family smallholdings in Latin America. In parts of Africa four times as many women as men work the land.[16]

Women's agricultural work is generally unpaid and overlooked, yet women were probably the first farmers and, in terms of conservation of resources, are still probably the best. The psychologist and philosopher Erich Fromm writes: "Following the older division of labour, where men hunted and women gathered roots and fruits, agriculture was most likely the discovery of women." How important was this discovery? "Considering the fundamental role of agriculture in the development of civilization, it is perhaps no exaggeration to state that modern civilization was founded by women," Fromm believes.[17]

Women's farming is said to have a history of more than forty centuries in Asia, during which their knowledge of seeds, crops and soils has protected the environment. The physicist and environmentalist Vandana Shiva claims that the world's eight most important cereals (wheat, rice, maize, barley, oats, sorghum, millet and rye) were domesticated by women, and that women invented the hoe, spade, shovel, plough, fallowing, crop rotation, terracing, contour planting and irrigation.[18]

Where traditional agriculture persists in the South, tree felling, ploughing and looking after draught animals are men's tasks. Women are usually responsible for the more time-consuming work of clearing, planting, sowing, manuring, weeding, thinning, transplanting and threshing. Women hill farmers in northern India reportedly do around 3,500 hours' farmwork a year, their menfolk just over 1,200 hours. Javanese women work an average of eleven hours a day on the land, men less than nine.[19]

In Africa the division of labour is especially one-sided. "When one speaks today of 'the African farmer', one is talking about a woman," says the IIED's Brian Walker. Traditional African agriculture was based on shifting cultivation and little use of draught animals. African men tended to be hunters rather than farmers. In many areas, while men fell trees, women are left to clear the ground, sow, weed, harvest, carry and store the crops. "African women...work longer days than most slaves," the writer Susan George comments.[20]

Colonial disruption

Pre-colonial Southern agriculture was generally subsistence farming, serving local needs. Not much was grown for trade outside the immediate area, and little money changed hands. Collective or extended-family land rights in Africa and the Americas guaranteed women access to the land. With the impact of colonialism and economic development, this changed; subsistence farming, in which women played a leading role, was relegated to second place by cash crops and the modern market economy.

Why did this happen? Colonialist administrators and post-colonial modernizers saw men, not women, as the productive labour force to be exploited. Much of the best land was taken over by white settlers for their estates; poorer soils were allocated to local men to farm for cash. Most of the workers on the new export plantations were men, drawn away from family landholdings to work for wages. Even where women were recruited, as in Asia, they were paid less than men for similar work. (Women sugar workers still earn no more than two-thirds of men's wages in the Philippines, for example.)

Men who had been given land by the new administrators to farm for themselves often enlisted their wives to help, especially in Africa. So the women, now with less male assistance than ever, had little time to grow food for home consumption. African women sometimes resisted turning family land over to men for cash cropping, staging protests in Cameroon, Nigeria and Zambia.

The use of new agricultural technology benefited men more than women. When tractors and mechanized ploughs were introduced in West Africa, men's tasks became easier, so fields were enlarged. Women's drudgery increased, however, because no technology was introduced to help them weed and maintain these greater areas. In general, settlers and agricultural advisers from the North taught new techniques and skills to rural men but not to women. The belief that men made better farmers (women came to be seen as backward and not worth teaching) was a self-fulfilling prophecy.[21]

Ignoring women's role
After the colonies achieved political independence, development policies continued to allocate land, technical support and loans to men in preference to women. Women farmers were almost completely overlooked by rural training and extension schemes. Less than a tenth of all trained agricultural advisers in the South were women in the mid-1980s, with the smallest proportion in Africa. Even land reform, while apparently of benefit to all the rural poor, was frequently discriminatory. Latin American plantation land, for example, has been redistributed on the basis of continuous employment; so women, whose employment is interrupted by childbirth, fail to qualify.

Lack of legal title to the land, difficulty in getting loans and a shortage of technical support have made smallholder farming difficult for Southern women. Most are unable to invest the extra time, cash or labour in the drainage, tree planting, soil terracing, tools and small machinery they need to ease the back-breaking nature of the work and improve crop yields. And with access to firewood diminishing, many rural women burn animal dung or crop residues as fuel, leaving nothing organic to put back into the soil.

Women farmers have been among the chief victims of the "green revolution", which has lowered the value of their traditional skills. In India the "revolution" resulted in a 100 per cent rise in paid farmwork for women between 1961 and 1981 (naturally at lower wages than men earned); but the number of self-employed farming women has decreased by more than a third, and landlessness among rural women has increased substantially. Rising prices and competition from neighbouring high-input farms have pushed many women farmers into poverty.[22]

Overall, the development process has been "gender-blind" in ignoring women's place in and contribution to rural life. A recent seminar report comments: "Men are usually the prime benficiaries of deforestation and cash-cropping projects, while the complex ecosystems cultivated by generations of women are wiped out to make way for them. Women's agricultural knowledge is devalued as 'traditional', 'backward' or 'unscientific' because although their techniques produce food, sustain the soil and preserve the ecosystems they have no commercial value."[23] The result has been a disaster for the quality of the world's vegetation, soil and water.

Women in the modern economy

According to official statistics, women make up about a third of the global labour force. In the Soviet Union roughly half of all paid workers are women; in Western Europe, North America, Australasia, Africa and Asia a third; and in Latin America a quarter. These figures underestimate the extent to which women are involved in the informal economy and fail to reflect their unpaid contribution. There is no reason to doubt the accuracy of the UN Development Fund for Women's statement that women do two-thirds of the world's work, earn a tenth of its income and own a hundredth of its property.[24]

Inequality in employment
A narrower occupational range is open to women than to men. The majority of women in paid employment do work similar to housework – as cleaners, waitresses, domestic servants, launderers, nurses, food and textile workers, child minders, primary teachers, social workers and secretaries. Much of this is menial, repetitive, service-oriented, low-skilled work and considered by

men to be beneath their dignity. Paid domestic work alone is said to occupy about three-quarters of employed women in Latin America and the Caribbean. Women form the majority of part-time workers, too. Ninety-four per cent of part-timers in the UK are said to be women, 79 per cent in Australia and 70 per cent in the USA.[25]

Despite sex equality laws in many countries, few women enjoy equal employment status or prospects. Women are often willing to settle for poorer pay rates than men. Wage legislation in the developed countries, much of it dating from the 1970s, has not yet brought women's earnings into line with men's for the same work. In 1981, for example, while women made up more than 78 per cent of clerical workers in the USA, their average earnings in this job sector were 67 per cent of men's. The pay gap may be slowly narrowing; in the UK in 1986 average earnings of full-time women workers were 74 per cent of those of men. Even so, in some parts of the North, such as southern Italy and the west of Ireland, women still lag way behind men in terms of pay and work opportunities.[26]

Managerial occupations are dominated by men, and in only a few countries are more than a quarter of managers women. In the industrialized countries there are also few women in the most senior positions in manufacturing, mining, transport, science, medicine, law, architecture, finance, property dealing, public administration, the mass media and most other high-status occupations.

During the twentieth century women have gone out to work in increasing numbers, and more than half the female adult population of most higher-income countries now earns money outside the home. Yet the myth of the bread-winning male and the home-bound female persists. "Most social structures and government policies are constructed as though the stay-at-home wife was the norm," conclude researchers Joni Seager and Ann Olson. The purely domestic female role "is sharply at odds with the reality that many women *have* to seek employment in order to feed their children and themselves", agree development writers Gita Sen and Caren Grown.[27]

Obstacles for working mothers

With child care the most time-consuming family task, a lack of adequate nursery facilities nearly everywhere hampers working mothers. Where extended family networks remain, aunts, sisters and grandmothers usually provide back-up. Nevertheless, with the dominance of the nuclear family in many societies, a rising divorce rate and increasing numbers of female-headed households, a great many mothers are unable to work as they need or wish to.

Working mothers have handicapped job prospects because they are unable to travel, work overtime, go on training courses or do whatever else it takes to secure promotion. As part-time workers they automatically tend to receive little training and encouragement, few benefits, inadequate pensions, weak union protection and poor job security. This creates a vicious circle. Women's low occupational success restricts their opportunities for advancement because employers and managers believe that they make poor workers.

New technology
New technology has done little to help women at work. Unskilled women workers have often lost their jobs because of the technological advances that supposedly improve human welfare. The introduction of rice-hulling machinery in Indonesia, for example, is said to have reduced by two-thirds the amount of paid work available to a million women, cutting their incomes – and increasing men's – by an estimated $55 million. Much the same is reported from Latin America: "The idea that increased industrialization results in greater participation in the economically active population by women is...erroneous."[28]

Where industrialization does create jobs for women, these tend to be as cheap, exploited labour, while the controllers of the new technology are usually men. Multinational corporations operating in poor countries often prefer a young female workforce (except at managerial levels): "nimble-fingered", docile, non-unionized and easily disposed of. Unskilled work in the electronics industry is one such female job ghetto in Brazil, South Korea and other newly industrializing countries.

Unemployment and poverty
Widely thought of as a problem for men, unemployment is increasingly one for women, too. The rising tide of joblessness in the industrialized countries during the 1970s and early 1980s was borne as heavily by women as by men, more so in Belgium, Italy and the UK.[29] Although women's paid work is seen as supplementing that of their menfolk, millions of them are today

the sole supporter of their family. Many fail in the struggle to balance the conflicting demands of home and workplace, losing their jobs as the result of pregnancy and maternity. In the USA there is still no automatic right to maternity leave.

Poverty affects women far more than men, because of men's greater access to waged work and higher wages. As the market economy expands in the South, cheap and locally produced everyday goods are replaced with more expensive, mass-produced items obtainable only in the towns and often beyond women's means to buy. Women's greater responsibility for supporting children is another factor; a third of all households are headed by single mothers, and female-headed households are the leading poverty group worldwide. The elderly make up another large poverty group, so women's longer natural lifespan also tends to place them among the poor. In the USA 78 per cent of people living below the official poverty line are women and children.[30]

The proportion of the world's poor comprised by women is said to be growing, partly because Southern and low-income Northern women are pushed into poverty every time governments respond to economic crisis by cutting food, housing, health and other subsidies. Most women who become prostitutes do so through poverty. Poor parents in Latin America, South-east Asia and elsewhere may deliberately sell their daughters into prostitution. Or the girls are sold to domestic employers or marriage bureaux with the same result.

Women in a man's world

Education
All over the world, women's subordination is maintained through a wide variety of cultural and social channels. One such is the education system. Despite advances in recent decades, two-thirds of women in the South remain illiterate, and two-thirds of the world's illiterate people are women. Twice as many European women as men can neither read nor write, in the South one and a half times as many.[31]

In the mid-1980s there were seven girls for every eight boys in primary education and five girls for every six boys in secondary schools worldwide. Ratios in the poorest countries were the worst; five times as many boys as girls were at school in the Yemen. In more than seventy developing countries, less than 50 per cent of girls are enrolled in secondary school.[32]

Parents in the South often do not want their adolescent daughters to mix with boys of the same age, and they usually favour the education of boys over that of girls as an investment. The money needed to pay for uniforms and materials is thought to be wasted on girls, who will later have only a slim chance of finding employment. Besides, in many cultures girls' economic contribution to the household ends when they marry into their husband's family.

Wherever they go to school, the nature of girls' education is more limited than that of boys and directed towards domestic roles. In the early 1980s in Norway, for example, girls comprised 98 per cent of high-school domestic science students but only 10 and 15 per cent respectively of those studying fishery and industrial technology.[33] Girls are often categorized as educational under-achievers and receive less teacher attention in mixed-sex schools.

As for adult educational opportunities, women's housebound role can prevent them from becoming literate through non-school channels. Young men from poor families sometimes gain an education through the army or the churches, institutions that provide fewer opportunities for young women; others may learn to read and write at work. University education in the West was almost exclusively for men until the end of the nineteenth century. Women nowadays make up between 40 per cent and 50 per cent of Western students in higher education but only 33 per cent of students in Asia and the USSR and just 29 per cent in Africa.[34]

Women's lack of access to education reinforces their dependency. Millions lack the skills and qualifications to find decent employment, are ignorant of their legal rights and cannot get the support they need to resist ill treatment.

Fertility

Men have considerable power over women's fertility. Among the most influential opponents of voluntary birth control are the Catholic Church, Islam and some sections of the medical profession, all male-dominated institutions. Within the family, men may insist on having more children as "proof of virility", because they have not yet fathered a son or in the belief that a wife who uses contraceptives will be unfaithful. Female circumcision is widespread in Africa and the Middle East, fairly common in South-east Asia and not unknown in Latin America. This painful and health-endangering practice reduces women's sexual desire and thus serves as an extra instrument for the preservation of female virginity or fidelity.

Politics

Women's political emancipation is not yet complete. Kuwait will not allow them the vote. In Hong Kong property restrictions mean that fewer women than men can vote. Bhutan allows just one vote per family, usually exercised by the male of the household. In Jordan and Liechtenstein women gained the vote only during the 1980s. (There are, of course, other countries, such as Iran and Saudi Arabia, where nobody can vote.)[35]

Despite their enfranchisement in most societies, however, women participate in the political process less than men do, standing for office and voting more rarely. Their political priorities are said to be often different; policies found to attract women voters more than men include stronger environmental controls, improved child health care and protection, better nursery and education provision, progress in human rights, abolition of the death penalty and arms control. Women comprise only a small minority of the world's political decision-makers; only Scandinavia has a good record on the proportion of parliamentary seats and cabinet posts they hold. (There are signs of change; many of North-west Europe's environment ministers are women.)

The oppression of women can be politically both a tool and an end in itself. In Chile after the 1973 coup, for example, a propaganda offensive was launched to return women to the narrow domestic role from which the elected Allende government had done so much to free them. Leading figures of the regime (including the wife of the dictator) spoke about women's "purity" and "delicacy". In the words of one apologist for the military junta: "Unlike some women in other countries, [Chilean women] do not seek an illusory emancipation based on demands for rights which can only divert them from their essential femininity." Meanwhile many of the social reforms of the previous government – including equal pay legislation, free health care, increases in family allowances and nursery provision – were reversed.[36]

We may find such political manipulation offensive. Yet the

portrayal of women in the mass media of the industrialized democracies, especially through advertising and pornography, is not so different. Although there has been some change, women are still more often than not depicted as domestic and passive, men as work-oriented and assertive.

Rape
More than 90 per cent of the world's violent crimes are committed by men. Still not recognized as a serious problem in many countries, rape is said to be the world's most under-reported crime. Many women are said to hesitate to report rape because of feelings of shame or fear that their account will be disbelieved, because they fear reprisals on the part of the rapist or because of a lack of faith in the legal system.

According to UK research in the mid-1980s, one in six women has been raped, but less than 10 per cent of rapes are reported to the police. US studies indicate that one in four women is a rape victim, but only 21 per cent of rapists are convicted of the crime. An estimated 100 million young girls are raped at least once by adult men - usually their fathers or stepfathers. Most rapes are premeditated, most rapists known to their victims.[37]

Action

Women's burdens and role

If the human race is to progress, as much value must be placed on women's contributions inside and outside the family as on men's. Greater respect for domestic responsibilities is one side of the coin, as the Nigerian novelist Buchi Emecheta suggests: "Giving birth and nurturing the young should not be looked down upon. It is not a degrading job...We think it is low because society says so. But it's about time we said: '...We will train *all* people, men and women, in housework.' "[38]

False praise for female domesticity should not be allowed to obstruct women's progress in other fields, however: "As long as greater importance is placed on women's reproductive role than on their economic and civic roles, women will continue to be excluded from greater involvement at the level of policy- and decision-making."[39]

Collective action

To achieve this non-violent revolution, many women believe that joint action is essential: "One woman on her own cannot defend herself; a group of...women, on the other hand, can quell a brutal husband or work together to earn the money which can free them from a fatal dependence on the earning power and uncertain generosity of their men...[Women's needs are best met] within the framework of collective action for social change."[40]

Women are increasingly working together to achieve improvements in family, social and political life. Worldwide there are now thousands of support groups for battered women and rape victims. Communally run all-women refuges give safety from male violence while residents reorient their lives. These organizations offer physical and emotional support, legal advice and practical help for those in need of divorce, paid work, medical treatment or a new home.

The number of women's co-operatives and other grass-roots organizations is increasing. Throughout the South groups of women are establishing themselves in poultry raising, vegetable growing, dairy farming, tailoring, handicrafts production and marketing; in the North there are successful women's publishing, transport, retail and building co-operatives. Southern women have set up savings clubs (to pay for cattle, farm implements or school fees), health clubs (to promote nutritional education, family planning and preventive health care), rural associations (to fight for land rights), political committees (to protect detainees and demand information on the "disappeared" and the prosecution of human rights offenders), information and educational networks and resource centres, environmental groups and peace committees. There have, of course, been both successes and failures, but the successes are impressive; perhaps the best known, Chipko and the Green Belt movement, were described in Chapter 2; here are three more examples:

In India, Gujurati women formed the Self-Employed Women's Association in 1972 in response to their low working status. Membership has grown to 40,000, and the association has set up a co-operative bank, provides business start-up loans and welfare benefits and negotiates minimum earnings with employers. Association members work in handblock printing, weaving, milk and vegetable production and marketing.[41]

Japan's Seikatsu Club Consumers' Co-operative was founded by a Tokyo housewife and is organized largely by women. In the 1970s, concerned about pollution and health, the club began to market biodegradable detergents, to invest in organic farming (raising money through subscriptions and interest-bearing bonds) and set up a dairy plant to produce additive-free milk. Seikatsu now has an annual turnover of $250 million, serves 150,000 member households (half a million people) and has a nationwide network of community, business, health and cultural centres, wholefood restaurants and nursery schools. Members have been elected to local councils (their slogan: "Political reform from the kitchen") on a platform of women's rights, employee health and safety, environmental protection, peace, social welfare and citizen participation in civic life.[42]

Despite their poverty, the women who run the "popular dining rooms" of Latin America's shanty towns have achieved comparable success. Buying cheap fresh food in bulk from local markets, these women's groups – of which there are said to be almost a thousand in Lima alone – provide low-cost wholesome meals for their families and communities. Some receive food aid from NGOs and distribute powdered milk to slum children. Larger collectives have their own premises, often self-built, and provide, besides the food itself, a focus for community action in some of the world's worst urban environments. They support the families of people who are sick or out of work; provide nutritional advice and health education; set up literacy schemes; campaign for improvements in housing and legal status; counsel battered wives; organize waste disposal, build roads and plant trees.[43]

Legal rights

What are we aiming for? First, women's legal rights must be secured. Long-established repressive laws and customs in the Middle East and parts of Asia will take generations to remedy, yet in most countries there have been advances. Work by women's organizations in India, for example, is beginning to give hope to women oppressed within the family. The international picture has improved since the United Nations adopted the Convention on the Elimination of Discrimination against Women in 1981, defining discrimination in such areas as traditional family law, education, health care, employment and social life. By 1988 the Convention had been ratified by ninety-one countries.

Rape is taken increasingly seriously in the North, and wife-rape is being made a criminal offence in more countries. The justice system needs to be able to deal with crimes of violence against women speedily and effectively (the introduction of family courts will help). All women, particularly the Southern poor, need free legal support.

Culture
Cultural patterns must change, too. The more that women have a say in all fields of human activity, the less men will be able to get away with physical or institutional violence against them. Family and educational stereotypes are more likely to be broken first in the higher-income countries, where there is generally greater freedom of personal choice. Girls must be given a chance to grow up into the woman they want to be (with appropriate guidance). In place of the exaggerated concern with gender differences that still often dominates girls' upbringing and education, children of both sexes should be treated similarly, within reason.

Girls should be taught that large families are usually a liability and that there are other worthwhile goals to strive for besides wifehood and motherhood. In the South literacy programmes need to be specifically designed for and targeted at women; higher rates of female literacy will increase women's control over their fertility and other apects of their lives. In the North women need more awareness of their value as women, of their legal rights and of how to achieve independence.

Teachers and creators of educational materials are increasingly conscious of the mistake of gender stereotyping and now provide a more open curriculum, but the process has not gone far enough. In the developed countries the study of history, for example, still tends to emphasize "men's history" of royal lines and battles rather than women's contribution in such fields as agriculture, health and social and political reform.

Women and work
The status of housework has to be raised if women's opportunities are to extend beyond the home. Men must do much more of it.

Far more state-subsidized and workplace child care is wanted.

Governments and employers are beginning to recognize the need, although until recently few countries made this a priority. Subsidized workplace and state nurseries are preferable to tax exemptions on private child care because, as evidence from North America has shown, the latter tend to benefit well-paid middle-class women disproportionately. While still providing less state-funded child care than its EC partners, in 1990 the UK government took a step in the right direction by removing the tax on employers' subsidies for workplace nurseries; this may encourage more organizations to provide them, although only a minority of parents will probably benefit.

A minimum wage, increasingly discussed in progressive political circles, would help eliminate the poverty trap in which so many low-income women find themselves. It would reduce both their dependence on men's wages and their vulnerability to extremely low pay in the informal economy.

Not only do women need to go out to work; the rest of us need them to do so. Male domination of economics, journalism, administration, finance, medicine, banking, art, environmentalism, crafts, education, farming, policy-making, trade unionism, science, law and other occupations and activities has failed to benefit not just women but the greater part of the human race, as well as the planet itself. Studies have shown that the fields of science, technology, health and medicine, for example, would be very different today had women influenced them as much as men have.[44]

Male-dominated trade unions have often failed to protect women at work; but in the right political climate, women can change all that. In Nicaragua during the 1980s, pressure from women members led to the rural workers' association setting up communal washing, cooking, cafeteria and child-care facilities on co-operative and state-owned farms, giving women more time to participate in community affairs. By 1986 it was reported that more than half the union's leaders were women.[45]

Women and development
The need for more women to be involved in development in the South comes alongside the realization that "top-down", growth-oriented economic strategies have failed (see Chapter 2). Self-reliance – the area in which women usually outperform men – is the key to future well-being. Rural women's ability

to provide food, health and communal welfare with the barest of resources has so far been under-used. But the world is beginning to discover women's potential; as the World Health Organization has put it: "Women are the vast untapped resource for development."

Southern women's development priorities tend to differ from those of men, placing emphasis on basic needs, a more equal distribution of resources and wealth, improvements in quality of life for the poorest and environmental protection. "Women are bringing the concern with living and survival back to centre-stage in human history," comments Vandana Shiva.[46]

The 1989 UK seminar on Women, Environment and Development proposed a new definition of development to help undo past damage. Development, the seminar agreed, should be defined as a process of change that "safeguards the natural environment, enables women's self-empowerment, and balances social and economic needs".[47] The change is taking place. Governments and NGOs now recognize the importance of gender factors in development and try to involve women at every stage. Even the conservative World Bank has stipulated that teams of forestry-outreach workers must include at least one woman. When every development project is planned, implemented and evaluated by local women as well as by outside male specialists, we will know that gender-blind policies are a thing of the past.

Rural women

Formerly self-sufficient Southern women farmers need help to overcome the problems caused by men's past mistakes. The UN Food and Agriculture Organization agrees that the key to rural development is for women to be guaranteed access to land, loans, training and other resources independently of men. Women's income-generating schemes must involve better access to technology and markets, fair prices, encouragement for traditional skills, advice in the setting up of co-operatives, protected firewood and water sources, literacy and awareness-building programmes and family planning support.

Lateral thinking is sometimes required. Where in Africa a taboo remains against women planting trees, large shrubs can be planted and harvested instead. Land redistribution does not have to be discriminatory. Nicaraguan women are entitled to their own land in their own right, whether or not there is a man in the family. The redistribution of land to women farmers in Zimbabwe since independence, with government provision of seeds and fertilizer, has helped the country regain self-sufficiency in grain.

The burden of the "double day" of rural women, who work in the household and also in the fields, will be reduced when men accept a fairer share of domestic responsibility. Meanwhile, low-cost appropriate technology helps ease the drudgery. Water filters, maize shellers, iron handmills for flourmaking, raised washstands to keep utensils out of the dirt, pest-proof food safes, solar water heaters and cookers, fuel-efficient stoves and two-wheeled carts – all these cheap technologies have been designed and built.[48] It is high time they were brought more widely into use.

Getting Involved

Related subjects covered elsewhere in this book include: hunger – Chapter 1; poverty and development – Chapter 2; population, fertility and health – Chapter 3; human rights – Chapter 5; deforestation and soil erosion – Chapter 6; water pollution – Chapter 7; the social costs of military spending – Chapter 10. To find out more about the position of women worldwide, see "Recommended Reading" (pages 324–9).

Consumer and lifestyle choices

Buy from women
Buy food, drink and other goods from fair-trading organizations such as those listed in the "Getting Involved" section in Chapter 2. Some of these organizations make a point of buying produce from women's co-operatives in low-income countries; you can be sure, anyway, that none of their goods are produced by exploited female labour.

When you next need an electrician, a computer engineer, financial advice, a printer or any other product or service, try a woman-run business or women's co-operative. In the UK there is a directory of classified information on hundreds of women-run businesses, with addresses and full details of services offered: *Women Mean Business 1990: The Everywoman Directory of Women's Co-operatives and Other Enterprises*, published by Everywoman and available in bookshops or from 34 Islington Green, London N1 8DU.

Another UK organization that can put you in touch with a tradeswoman, as well as giving advice on training, is Women and Manual Trades, 52–54 Featherstone Street, London EC1Y 8RT (071-251 9192).

Changes at home

In the household, women and men can make a personal commitment to sex equality by sharing or rotating domestic tasks and responsibilities. Women can encourage men to bath and feed children, clean the home, shop for food and prepare meals; in return men can encourage women to change a bicycle tyre, use an electric drill, check the bank statement, fill in the income tax forms, and so on. This will give women a fairer chance of success in paid work outside the home and make both partners balanced human beings.

Equal treatment for boys and girls

If you are involved with children as a parent, guardian, teacher or child worker, try to treat girls and boys fairly and without gender stereotyping. Encourage (within reason) toys, books, activities and games that can be enjoyed equally by either sex (but do still respect individual preferences). Avoid stereotyped messages of the "boys don't cry"/"girls don't get dirty" variety. Teach boys to respect and not despise girls. In the UK a good source of anti-sexist children's books is Letterbox Library, 8 Bradbury Street, London N16 8JN (071-254 1640).

Women's refuges

There are a growing number of support groups for women who are oppressed by male behaviour within the family and elsewhere, including refuges for women who have suffered physical violence, sexual harassment or rape. In the UK many of these groups and refuges, including those run by ethnic-minority groups, are listed in the annual *Spare Rib Diary*, available from bookshops or from 27 Clerkenwell Close, London EC1R 0AT. You can make contact with a network of local women's refuges via the Women's Aid Federation (address below).

Workplace, community and political action

Try to get your workplace, your trade union or any community group or voluntary organization you are involved with to adopt equal opportunities policies. A first step could be finding like-minded people to help you set up an informal equal opportunities working group. Literature on equal opportunities at the workplace in the UK is available from the Equal Opportunities Commission (address below). If your organization already has such policies, how well does it act on them? Raise the question with colleagues and discuss how improvements could be made.

Equal pay
Under the UK's equal pay legislation, women who do the same or broadly similar work as men and work for the same employer are entitled to the same rate of pay and terms of employment. If you think you are not receiving equal pay and terms of employment to men for similar work because you are a woman, contact the Equal Opportunities Commission and ask for their "Equal pay for women: what you should know about it" leaflet, which explains the legislation and what action you can take if you think you are being discriminated against.

Weekend training programmes for legal practitioners and advice workers on the subject of employment sex discrimination and equal pay under UK legislation are run by the Women's Legal Defence Fund, 29 Great James Street, London WC1.

Co-ops
If you are a woman worker, consider setting up a women's co-operative. Advice about establishing women's co-operatives is available in the UK from the Industrial Common Ownership Movement, Vassalli House, 20 Central Road, Leeds LS1 6DE (0532-461737), which has a "women's link-up" section.

Child care
Investigate whether you could make arrangements for workplace child care at your organization or see if you can set up a local self-help child-care network. Possible approaches include nurseries run jointly by employers and local authorities. A pilot scheme has been set up by the Sainsbury food chain and West Lambeth Health Authority in London, at which nursery fees are subsidized according to employee pay levels. For more details, contact the

National Childcare Campaign at the London Women's Centre or, for advice on self-help, the Working Mothers' Association (addresses below).

The tax on employer subsidies for workplace child care has recently been removed in the UK. Join the campaign for tax relief for child care for working parents (not just for mothers) as a legitimate expense, for a nationwide employer levy to fund nurseries, for government subsidies for local authority nurseries and for substantial increases in child benefit. Write to your local councillors and MP and the press, raise the issue in community newsletters or on radio phone-in programmes, or write direct to the Secretary of State for Education and Science (Department of Education and Science, Elizabeth House, York Road, London SE1). Points you could raise include:

- The removal of the tax on employer subsidies for workplace child care will only benefit mothers of the few children under 5 who are in subsidized workplace nurseries (about 3,000 out of a national total of 5.5 million).
- Increases in child benefit will ensure that one of the leading poverty groups, women and children, are better off; this is good "targeting".
- Employer levies to fund nurseries already operate in France, where 95 per cent of 3- to 5-year-olds are in full-time state day care, and most other EC countries.
- Studies show that, besides freeing mothers to work, children under 5 who attend nurseries tend to become more confident and faster learners than those who do not.
- In the UK only 44 per cent of this age group attend nurseries, many of them only part-time.

For more information, contact the National Childcare Campaign at the London Women's Centre (address below).

Self-development
Women's centres in many countries offer women-run self-development courses in many subjects and a focal point for meeting others. In the UK, the London Women's Centre runs courses, workshops and other events in computers, performing arts, race issues, assertiveness, self-defence, health, child care, housing, literacy and numeracy, careers, money management and disability issues.

Spare Rib Diary, published annually in the UK, has a classified directory section that gives names, addresses and telephone numbers of scores of women's groups and organizations throughout the UK and abroad (some of which are listed below). Categories included in the diary include: abortion help/advice, black and Asian women, bookshops, child care, contraception, education, law, health, housing, international groups, parents, rape crisis centres and violence against women.

Every year, 8 March is International Women's Day in honour of a group of women workers who organized a strike against poor working conditions on that day in 1907. Find out what events are taking place in your area or get together with a group of like-minded people and organize something.

Organizations

Organizations working for a better deal for women include:

UK and Irish Republic
Campaign against Pornography, 9 Poland Street, London W1.
Cork Federation of Women's Organizations, Winnipeg, Ballea Road, Carrigaline, Cork, Irish Republic.
Equal Opportunities Commission, Overseas House, Quay Street, Manchester M3 3HN (061-833 9244).
Feminist Library (resource centre; open Tues. 10 am–8 pm, Sat. and Sun. 2–5 pm), 5 Westminster Bridge Road, London SE1 (071-928 7789).
International Planned Parenthood Federation, 18–20 Lower Regent Street, London SW1 (071-486 0741).
Legal Action for Women, 71 Tonbridge Street, London WC1H 9DZ (071-837 7509).
London Women's Centre and National Childcare Campaign, Wesley House, 4 Wild Court, London WC2B 5AU (071-831 6946).
Northern Ireland Women's Rights Movement, 18 Donegall Street, Belfast (0232-243363).
Population Concern, 231 Tottenham Court Road, London W1P 0HX (071-637 9582).
Women's Aid Federation, PO Box 391, Bristol BS99 7WS (0272-428368).
Women's Environmental Network, 287 City Road, London

EC1V 1LA (071-490 2511).

Women's International League for Peace and Freedom, 29 Great James Street, London WC1N 3ES (071-242 1521).

Women's International Resource Centre, 173 Archway Road, London N6 5BL (081-341 4403).

Working Mothers' Association, 23 Webbs Road, London SW11 (071-228 3757).

USA and Canada

Broadside (monthly feminist newspaper), PO Box 494, Station P, Toronto, Ontario M5S 2TI, Canada.

Connexions (international women's quarterly), 4228 Telegraph Avenue, Oakland, Calif. 94609, USA.

National Organization for Women, Suite 800, 1401 New York Avenue NW, Washington, DC 20005, USA.

National Women's Health Network, 45 Sutton Place South, New York, NY 10022, USA.

Off Our Backs (monthly feminist news journal), 2423 18th Street NW, Washington, DC 200090, USA.

UNIFEM (UN Development Fund for Women), Room 1106, 304 East 45th Street, New York, NY 10017, USA.

Women and Environments (network directory), c/o Centre for Urban and Community Studies, 455 Spadina Avenue, Toronto, Ontario M5S 2G8, Canada.

Women's International League for Peace and Freedom, 1102 Ironwork Passage, Vancouver, British Colombia V6H 3P1; and PO Box 4781E, Ottawa, Ontario K1S 5H9, Canada.

Women's International League for Peace and Freedom, 1213 Race Street, Philadelphia, Pa 1907, USA.

Women's International Network News (quarterly), 187 Grant Street, Lexington, Mass 02173, USA.

Australia and New Zealand

Broadsheet (feminist monthly), 288 Dominion Road, PO Box 56-147, Auckland 3, New Zealand.

Union of Australian Women, c/o Trades Hall, Goulbourne Street, Sydney, New South Wales 2001.

Women's International League for Peace and Freedom, GPO Box 2598, Sydney, New South Wales 2001, Australia.

Women's International League for Peace and Freedom, 56A Wai-iti Crescent, Lower Hutt, New Zealand.

Africa, Asia and the Caribbean (Commonwealth)

Asian and Pacific Centre for Women and Development, c/o Asia and Pacific Development Centre, PO Box 2444, Jalan Data, Kuala Lumpur, Malaysia.

Caribbean Women's Association (CARIWA), c/o The Social Centre, PO Box 16, 13 Turkey Lane, Ros'eau, Dominica.

Manushi (bi-monthly journal), C1/202 Lajpat Nagar, New Delhi 110024, India.

National Council of Women in Kenya, PO Box 67545, Moi Avenue, Nairobi, Kenya.

Self-Employed Women's Association, SEWA Reception Centre, opposite Victoria Garden, Ahmedabad 380001, India.

Sri Lanka Centre for Women's Research, 16 Elliot Place, Colombo 8, Sri Lanka.

Women Living under Muslim Law, PMB 1369, Ilorin, Nigeria.

Women's Centre, Box 185, Eket, Cross River State, Nigeria.

Women's International League for Peace and Freedom, c/o Joyce Lartey, PO Box 1949, Mamprobi, Accra, Ghana.

Women's International League for Peace and Freedom, Box 45922, Nairobi, Kenya.

5. Human and Civil Rights

"To feed and clothe a man forcibly kept in a cage offends the very essence of human dignity; but equally, what use to him is freedom of movement without food to sustain him?"

Julia Häusermann[1]

The Problem

The Universal Declaration of Human Rights was proclaimed by the United Nations General Assembly in 1948. The Declaration aims to protect freedom of speech and belief, freedom from fear of violence and persecution, the right to an adequate standard of living, the right to education and equality before the law. These are widely thought of as "natural" rights, outside and above the rule of governments. How fully do the world's inhabitants enjoy them?

Surveying human rights worldwide in the mid-1980s, the researcher Charles Humana concluded: "Only about one person in five...enjoys the security of knowing that he or she is protected by laws and constitutions that are respected by his or her government."[2] Hundreds of millions of people in the poor countries of the South suffer multiple forms of oppression, lacking democratic rule and material well-being; the armed forces are in control in many of these countries. Political rights and freedom of expression are returning in Eastern Europe, but the former centralized economies are in ruins. Most people in the Western industrialized democracies do enjoy material security and civil liberties, yet even these societies have their impoverished underclass.

The picture is troubled but not hopeless. With the world entering a period of rapid social and political change, some people believe that a major transformation in values is also taking place. If so, in the words of the social critic Murray

Bookchin, "Here, at least, is a chance for humanity to regain its sanity and rebuild this ruined planet as a world for life."[3]

Children and education

"Human rights begin with breakfast," said former President Leopold Senghor of Senegal. He might equally have said that they begin with children. These most vulnerable of people cannot secure their needs by persuasion or force. Neglect and abuse of their rights place children among the chief victims of injustice.

Most countries spend more on weapons than on education; and only about a tenth of global education spending takes place in the South, where more than three-fifths of all children live. About half of the 1.5 billion youngsters of developing countries have no school to go to. Denial of education means the loss of future rights and freedoms, because uneducated people lack the necessary knowledge and skills to secure their welfare. More than this, education is one of the essential tools of peaceful social transformation.[4]

After improvements from the 1950s to the mid-1970s, when the number of the world's children in school almost tripled, education spending fell back during the 1980s as economic conditions worsened. Literacy rates also declined. World Bank figures for the period 1972–87 show the proportion of total government expenditure reserved for education dropping by about 26 per cent in Bangladesh, 50 per cent in Tanzania, 58 per cent in Zambia, 39 per cent in Sri Lanka and 70 per cent in Argentina; even Italy halved its education budget.[5]

Early drop-outs
Family poverty may force children in the South to miss out on schooling. Fees and charges for books, equipment and uniforms are common. Long home–school travelling distances may make it impossible to attend lessons; and many children have to work from an early age. Poverty-related ill health may prevent youngsters from attending classes. Worse, many children are educationally disadvantaged *before* they reach school age, because of malnutrition, an early lack of stimulation or impaired mental development. Besides, where schooling in developing countries is too closely modelled on imported Northern approaches, or too middle class in orientation, it fails

to respond to local needs; children and their parents therefore lose interest.[6]

For all these reasons, a great many Southern children, especially girls, drop out of school after only a year or two. Less than half of Africa's population, for example, can read and write by the time they reach adulthood, as opposed to 98 per cent of people in the North.

Child labour
Child exploitation occurs throughout the South. The International Labour Organization estimates that 75 million children live as virtual slaves, deprived of liberty, play, education and their future. Among them are agricultural and industrial bonded labourers working to repay family debts, domestic servants, forced prostitutes, drug traffickers and the captives of beggar-masters. An additional 200 million are involved in dangerous or health-damaging full-time work.

Child labour is especially widespread in Asia. In Bangladesh, for example, the majority of youngsters have to work. Bought from their parents by factory owners for $130, boys of seven are put to work in carpet and textile factories for up to fourteen hours a day, seven days a week. In India children toil on tea plantations for starvation wages. Thousands of young Thais are sold annually in Bangkok to owners of industrial sweatshops; beatings and torture have been alleged. Child labour is also a feature of life in the Philippines, Portugal, Sudan, Turkey and parts of South America.[7]

Street children
The world's cities are home to an estimated 100 million street children. Many have lost all family contact. These youngsters survive by begging, collecting and selling garbage, thieving or other illegal activity. Street crime involving children's gangs is increasing in South America, and even in Europe children may be involved in organized crime, as in Italy. Brazilian vigilantes have been killing street children to make the cities "attractive" for tourists.

The sexual exploitation of children is a major industry. Child prostitution and pornography are rife in Latin America and (along with sex tourism) in South-east Asia. Corrupt police and local officials are said to collaborate. Child prostitutes also ply their trade in London, New York and other Northern cities.

The adoption trade

Babies and infants are often the victims of adoption trafficking. New-borns bought for a pittance from poor Latin Americans by dealers posing as adopters may end up in North America or Western Europe. A Bolivian lawyer was accused in 1987 of selling a boy abroad for $10,000 whose parents he had paid $40. Even unborn babies have been signed away.[8]

Victims of war

Millions of children have been orphaned, traumatized, imprisoned, forced to fight, wounded or killed in armed conflicts. The worst violations have included those committed by death squads in El Salvador and Guatemala, attacks by anti-government guerrillas in Mozambique and the unparalleled record of atrocities carried out by the Cambodian Khmer Rouge in the 1970s. In the Gulf War, Iran drafted tens of thousands of peasant boys into its army, many of them dying in human-wave attacks on Iraqi minefields and trenches. In South Africa and, to a lesser extent, the Israeli-occupied territories, children taking part in political protests or throwing stones at soldiers have been detained and ill treated or shot dead.

Indigenous peoples

The world's 200 million indigenous or tribal people make up about 4 per cent of humanity. As far as we know, all are descendants of the original inhabitants of the lands where they live. They tend to be self-sufficient, preserve the language and customs of their ancestors and have a closeness to and respect for the Earth. Most tribes are non-hierarchical.

Among the world's indigenous peoples are the Inuit ("Eskimoes") of the Arctic, the Amerindians, the Aborigines of Australia, the Maoris of New Zealand, the San bushmen of Southern Africa, the Pygmies, Chagga and other tribes of Central Africa, Asia's mountain and forest peoples and the Pacific islanders. Many of these groups still live as hunter-gatherers, trappers, fisherfolk, nomad cattle grazers or shifting cultivators.

European conquest

The oppression of indigenous peoples probably dates from the earliest city-based civilizations but continued on a massive scale during the age of European conquest. Two centuries of Spanish and Portuguese imperialism reduced the indigenous population of Central and South America from 70 million to 4 million; many of these people were worked to death in gold and silver mines. The Caribs, most Patagonian tribes and other native Americans disappeared soon after contact with the white man. Some were wiped out by disease or alcohol, others hunted to destruction. In North America many whites declared a virtual war of genocide. In Australia, the Aborigines survived – just; the first century of British domination saw their population fall from 300,000 to 60,000.[9]

Pushed into poverty

With encroachment on their land, tribal peoples invariably become the worst off of their countries' inhabitants. In the USA, Indians' per capita incomes are half the national average. In New Zealand, Maori unemployment rates are four times those of whites, with Maoris sixty times more likely than whites to go to prison. Guatemalan Indians' life expectancy is eleven years less than that of the white elite.[10]

Most indigenous groups lack legally recognized land rights. Over the years, more and more of their ancestral territories have been taken over by logging, mining, hydroelectric projects, plantation agriculture and cattle ranching. Few of the governments and commercial interests involved, including many well-known multinationals, have paid compensation.

Forest and mountain people

The forest dwellers – a million Amazonians and several million forest people in Central Africa and South-east Asia – are especially vulnerable. Neglected for decades, their worsening plight is now international news. In Brazil 87 per cent of Indian land is said to be at risk from economic development, and several tribes have been wiped out. The Brazilian government's Greater Carajas mineral project will, if completed, displace about 10,000 forest people, as will Panama's copper mine at Cerro Colorado. The forced relocation of one Brazilian forest people, the Xingu, killed a quarter of them. In Ecuador the Siona and Secoya Indians have been devastated by river pollution and other effects of industrial development.

Brazil's once-numerous Yanomami are down to less than 10,000 individuals and outnumbered four to one in their lands by gold prospectors (themselves mostly wretchedly poor). The newcomers have polluted the rivers with mercury, brought diseases, disrupted the Indians' hunting and fishing and killed them in armed clashes. In 1977 half the tribe died from measles, and the Yanomami now face extinction from malnutrition and illness. The Brazilian government has recently begun trying to remove the gold hunters from Yanomami lands, but the effort could prove too little, too late.

Land-theft (threatening the destruction of entire racial and cultural groups) is also occurring in Asia. Half a million tribal people have been forced on to marginal land in the Chittagong hills of Bangladesh because of flooding caused by the Karnaphuli hydroelectic dam; their survival chances there are not good. Mountain people in the Philippines, their landholding rights denied by Spanish and US colonizers, have been driven from their territories by commercial foresters. In Malaysia another forest people, the Penan, are waging a desperate fight against armed police to hold back the logging that is destroying their homelands, polluting their rivers, ruining their crops and desecrating their burial grounds. The Penan have set up roadblocks and formed human barricades in an attempt to protect the forests they were assigned by previous governments.

Oppression worldwide
In the industrialized countries the pattern is similar. The lands of Lubicon hunter-trappers and fisherfolk have been invaded by oil companies in Alberta, Canada. Most of the tribespeople, receiving no income or compensation from the oilmen, live off government welfare. In the USA the Arizona Hopi have been forced off reserved land to make way for mineral extraction, and the health of the New Mexico Navaho has been wrecked by uranium mining. US and French military bases and nuclear weapons tests have brought disease and dependency to half a million Pacific islanders, while at home the USA has conducted test explosions in the lands of the Shoshone. (The Communist Chinese have done the same in their country among the indigenous Nighur.) The territory of the Innu of Canada's north-east is a low-flying bombing range and the proposed site for a NATO weapons training centre.[11]

Australia's Aborigines probably have the longest continuous land occupation, going back 40,000 years. Much of their territory has been privatized by mining interests without compensation. The death rate of Aborigines in police custody during the 1980s almost equalled that of detained blacks in South Africa. Aborigines suffer abnormally high rates of suicide, alcoholism, mental illness, leprosy and venereal disease. They declared 1988, Australia's bicentenary, a year of mourning.[12]

In some cases Northerners still carry "civilization" to indigenous groups with the mindless violence of the past. The US-based Protestant fundamentalist New Tribes Mission uses spotter planes, speedboats and armed converts to hunt down Paraguayan Indians, take them to mission camps and "convert" them. Violent clashes have been reported, and many of those captured subsequently die from influenza.[13]

Genocide

Some Southern governments have come close to deliberate genocide. In Guatemala the armed forces have massacred entire Indian communities as part of a ten-year battle against "communism" during which an estimated 100,000 have died and thousands more have fled to Mexico. In South-east Asia the indigenous West Papuan culture of Irian Jaya (western New Guinea) could be doomed. The Indonesian army separates West Papuan children from their parents and has brutalized and killed thousands of adults. Sexually transmitted disease and infertility have devastated the polygamous islanders since the Indonesian government offered "hospitality" to tribal leaders on a trip to Jakarta. Thousands of West Papuans have abandoned their homelands.[14]

The cost

How much does the destruction of indigenous peoples matter? If all these tribes disappeared, our last links with humanity's ancient past would go with them. The traditional knowledge preserved by these groups may become invaluable, for example in helping researchers find medicinal plants. As the Brundtland Commission recognized: "It is a terrible irony that as formal development reaches more deeply into rain forests, deserts, and other isolated environments, it tends to destroy the only cultures that have proved able to thrive in these environments."[15]

The violent state

Human justice depends on the existence of fair legal systems and constitutions and on the even-handed application of laws by governments. Throughout Africa, Asia, the Caribbean and Latin America, however, the impact of colonialism, economic crisis, competition for resources, political conflict and inter-ethnic tension have disrupted traditional localized legal customs and prevented modern forms of genuine democracy and justice from being practised. In a great many of these countries, the state is itself the main force of oppression. Government human rights abuses range from the hidden violence of censorship and denial of other civil liberties to physical abduction, political imprisonment, torture and unlawful killing.

Political prisoners

The human rights organization Amnesty International reports that thousands of people in the South are imprisoned without being charged with any criminal offence. These "prisoners of conscience" are in gaol because of their beliefs, ethnic origin, language, religion or sex. Agents of the state in more than sixty countries routinely ill treat and torture detainees, often causing the victim's death.

Each year, too, tens of thousands of people are unlawfully killed in custody or elsewhere. Many such murders are part of a struggle between government forces and armed opposition groups. The victims may be political activists, community organizers, trade union and church leaders or students. Innocent civilians are murdered to intimidate the enemy or the population at large, such violence being blamed by one side on the other or on supposedly uncontrollable death squads.

Latin America

Extreme inequalities of wealth and power and simmering racism have brought decades of lawlessness to Latin America. The evidence indicates that government forces and paramilitary groups working alongside them are responsible for most of the bloodshed. Land rights, big business, the government and the military are controlled by a minority of the population who claim "pure" European ancestry, unlike the mass of the people. Collective attempts by the poor to improve their lives result in their being branded communists. Disappearances and killings by death squads are common.[16]

During Argentina's "dirty war" against alleged leftists between 1976 and 1983, for example, 30,000 civilians disappeared, presumably murdered, at the hands of the military; many were tortured. When the country returned to civilian rule, opposition from the armed forces blocked President Alfonsin's attempts to bring high-ranking officers to justice.[17] In 1989 Alfonsin's successor, Carlos Menem, pardoned all those involved.

Argentina's neighbour, Uruguay, underwent a military coup in 1973. For the next eleven years it had the world's highest proportion of political prisoners. Most of those detained are said to have been tortured. Civil war between government forces and Maoist guerrillas in Peru has caused the disappearance or outright murder of thousands of people. In Brazil, despite promises of land reform, the police are alleged to collaborate with landowners and their gunmen in killing peasants.

Imprisonment, torture, disappearances and murders orchestrated by the security forces were routine in Chile after the 1973 coup. More than 10,000 people were killed in the first three months of the new regime, another 20,000 subsequently. Former government figures among the 200,000 people who fled abroad were assassinated in exile.

The majority of South American countries returned to civilian rule during the 1980s, and the violence abated. There was no let-up in the killing in Colombia, however. Besides the more recent terror campaign waged by the cocaine barons, paramilitary groups have long been operating against rural workers; attempts have been made to kill all the leaders of the banana workers' union in the north of the country, for example. Colombia's death squads are reportedly financed by plantation owners (whose main customers are US fruit multinationals) and the narcotics millionaires.[18]

Violent acts carried out by state agents in Central America account for about a hundred civilian victims a day. The people of El Salvador have suffered badly. Thousands of rural Salvadorans have quit their homes and many join guerrilla bands to fight the right-wing government forces. The army has pressured the remaining villagers to form "civil defence" groups against the guerrillas. Thousands of people have been murdered by the security forces or paramilitaries, and a million Salvadorans have become refugees.

San Salvador's Archbishop Oscar Romero was a "liberation theologian" who championed the rights of the poor during the 1970s. Romero democratized his church and campaigned through the mass media against repression. He encouraged priests to help rural community organizations press for land reform and peaceful change. As El Salvador's rulers closed down most channels for popular protest, he became "the voice of those who have no voice".[19]

Early in March 1980, after attacks on newspaper offices and radio stations left twelve journalists dead, the Archbishop was murdered while saying cathedral mass. Thirty-nine more people died when soldiers opened fire after his funeral. The state-appointed investigating judge accused an army general and Robert D'Aubuisson, leader of the extreme-right Arena party that now rules the country, of being behind the crime. Then, fearing for his own life, the judge went into exile. The killers have never been brought to justice.

Asia

A similar pattern of state violence exists across the Pacific in the Philippines. Hundreds of civilians, including trade unionists, church leaders, students and community workers, have been assassinated in recent years. Even under the reformist President Aquino, official corruption, repression and unlawful murders persist. During 1987 a peaceful march by peasants demanding promised land reforms was met with army gunfire outside the presidential palace, killing nineteen demonstrators.[20]

Communist China, for all its advances in primary health care and rural industry, has shown little regard for human rights. During the 1980s the country was thought to be edging towards liberalization; but the Communist leadership stunned the world in 1989 by sending in troops to kill hundreds and possibly thousands of pro-democracy demonstrators in Beijing's Tiananmen Square. These hard-liners also stand accused of widespread political imprisonment, rigged trials, beatings, torture and murder.

China's occupation of Tibet has brought martial law to Lhasa and misery to Tibetans, who are forbidden political organization or religious practice; protesters, including Buddhist monks and nuns, have been imprisoned, tortured and killed. Even worse is the record of China's client, the infamous Pol Pot. As leader of the Khmer Rouge who ruled Cambodia in the late 1970s, he presided over the slaughter of an estimated one million Cambodians.

Middle East

State oppression is widespread in the Near and Middle East. Iran's Islamic rulers regularly execute their political opponents, sexual offenders and followers of the Baha'i religion. The Saudi Arabians publicly behead or stone to death people convicted of religious and sexual "crimes". Kurdish demands for autonomy (the Kurdish homelands are split between Iran, Iraq, Syria and Turkey) have met with imprisonment, torture and chemical weapons attack. Iraq's regime routinely tortures and kills its opponents.

For all the democratic freedoms enjoyed by its majority Jewish population, Israel's human rights record in the occupied territories is poor. Hundreds of thousands of Palestinians remain in the camps set up in Gaza in 1948 with open sewers and few medical services; water and electricity are sometimes cut off by the authorities. Since the *intifada* began on the West Bank and in Gaza in 1987, hundreds of Palestinian adults and children have been shot dead by soldiers. Thousands have been tear-gassed, subjected to ill treatment and detained without trial, and there is evidence of torture. In 1989 the Israeli government called on its forces to show more restraint.

Africa

In Africa, human rights improvements are said to have taken place in Mozambique, Nigeria, Tanzania, Uganda and Zimbabwe, but the poorest continent remains troubled with "one-party governments and military rulers...civil wars and similar strife".[21] Several million Africans are refugees. In Burundi, Ethiopia, Somalia, South Africa and Sudan the killing of civilians by government forces is relatively common. Political opponents of ruling regimes have disappeared in Chad, Guinea, Kenya and Niger. Detention without trial on political grounds – in some cases with torture – is reported from Angola, Congo, Ghana, Guinea, Kenya, Malawi, Mauritania, Mozambique, Nigeria, Zaire, Zambia and Zimbabwe.[22]

South Africa
Apartheid ("separateness") was adopted as the official race policy of the white South African regime in 1948. While whites enjoy one of the highest standards of living on Earth, blacks are allocated 13 per cent of the country's poorest land, the so-called bantustan homelands, and assigned to "townships", squatter camps and rudimentary hostels. The South African police have systematically practised arbitrary arrest and detention, intimidation, beatings, torture and killings. Under the state of emergency declared in 1986, tens of thousands of people, including children, have been detained, often in solitary confinement; many have died in custody.

South Africa has pursued an aggressive policy towards its neighbours, the front-line states. Anti-government terrorism in Mozambique, for example, has been supported by the South African state. Renamo guerrillas are said to have destroyed two-thirds of Mozambique's schools and most of its medical centres, killing, maiming and kidnapping hundreds of civilians. South Africa also violated international law by illegally occupying and controlling Namibia (formerly German South-west Africa) from 1948 until the end of 1989, and by actively supporting anti-government forces in the Angolan civil war from 1975 to 1988.

Reforms have taken place in the apartheid system since the late 1980s, especially after the state presidency changed hands in 1989. In 1990 the unbanning of the African National Congress and the release of its most respected leader, Nelson Mandela, seemed to signal a break with the past. Amid talk of reconciliation and a "new" South Africa, the government has announced its intention to desegregate health and education, end the bantustan system and dismantle apartheid. However, President De Klerk says he opposes majority rule; some black leaders remain sceptical about the whites' intentions; and the goal of "one person, one vote" still appears a long way off.

Rights in the North

Mikhail Gorbachev's reforms and the collapse of Communist rule in Eastern Europe at the end of the 1980s have produced a dramatic thaw in the cold war. For decades previously East and West criticized the injustices of each other's system while denying their own. The Western view of human rights emphasizes electoral democracy, freedom of expression and economic individualism. Communist Eastern Europe argued that such freedoms were less important than social equality and the fulfilment of basic needs. In neither case has practice lived up to theory.

Poverty and injustice in the West

The prosperous West still contains pockets of deprivation and misery. In Washington and New York the mortality rates for black children are equal to those of poor developing countries. One US child in five lives below the poverty line. Nor are civil liberties always safe; the US linguistics professor and political commentator Noam Chomsky argues: "You have about as much freedom as you can purchase...For a black teenager in the ghetto subjected to police harassment...the guarantees of civil rights often amount to little."[23]

Similar criticisms have been made in the UK – for example, about the mistreatment of suspected Irish terrorists, and with regard to the problem of homeless people. Concern has also been expressed about hardening attitudes towards refugees such as Sri Lankan Tamils and towards ethnic minorities in the European Community.

The high cost of Northern wealth

Overall, of course, the West does enjoy high material living standards. This prosperity is said to prove the superiority of democratic capitalism over communism; but in reality it comes, at least in part, at the expense of human rights in the South. How? The international economy uses the land, labour and other resources of the poor countries to produce food, luxury and convenience goods and profits for the rich. If this was not so, the South's impoverished inhabitants could spend their time producing what they need for themselves. There would then be no need for repression to keep people working for the high-income countries.

Thus, as the Australian economist Ted Trainer argues: "Very often they can be kept in the plantations, mines and sweatshops only by force...Sometimes indirect force such as censoring the press or outlawing unions is sufficient...Often, however, only physical violence is capable of keeping them in the mines on starvation wages."[24] Raising their eyes too rarely from the balance sheet, Western politicians and business leaders have overlooked many of the human rights abuses of their trading partners in the South.

Support for oppression

The West has often kept quiet about injustice in the South; sometimes it has actively encouraged it. There is a long-standing US tradition of help for violent but supposedly anti-communist regimes, such as today's rulers of El Salvador, Indonesia, South Korea and Turkey. US President Bush once congratulated Ferdinand Marcos, the late Philippines ruler whose corruption is now legendary, with the words: "We love your adherence to democratic principle and to the democratic process."[25] The USA has also obstructed the efforts of countries in its sphere of influence to bring about social and economic reform, where this was thought to endanger US interests.

Like other world powers (including France and the UK in the past, and the USSR until recently), the USA has acted as if "the equal rights of nations large and small"[26] were of little concern. The White House has frequently sent in troops or used underhand methods to destabilize uncooperative governments and to install or prop up client rulers. Investigations by the Washington, DC, inter-faith Christic Institute have revealed a CIA-based network involved in a quarter-century of corruption and terrorism in Latin America and South-east Asia in support of "anti-communism". There is evidence of drug smuggling, illegal arms shipments and thousands of assassinations.[27]

US governments usually claim that their interventions are needed to halt communist subversion and terrorism. This is baloney. "The pressure for revolution in the Third World derives from conditions which cry out for revolution, not from subversion," as Ted Trainer comments.[28]

Eastern Europe

The years 1989 and 1990 were a time of unprecedented change in Eastern Europe, with the first free elections and non-Communist governments since before the Second World War. Until these events began to redraw the political map, the situation had changed little since 1945. The centrally planned economies were inefficient and often corrupt. Few people apart from Communist Party members, their families and others of the privileged elite enjoyed the promised economic advances.

Attempted reforms in East Germany, Hungary, Czechoslovakia and Poland were crushed. Peaceful opposition to the one-party state was suppressed. There was no right to free expression or to religious practice; censorship was widespread, freedom of movement restricted. Nationalists, religious believers, human rights campaigners and independent trade unionists were victimized. Dissidents suffered police harassment and discrimination in employment and education; they were subjected to rigged trials followed by heavy sentences in labour camps, psychiatric abuse and torture in mental hospitals and prisons, internal exile and assassination.

Until the violent overthrow of the Ceausescu regime, Romania was among the worst offenders. Ruled for decades by its Stalinist President and miserably poor by European standards, the country was a police state. The Securitate's telephone tapping network reportedly covered almost half the population's calls, including most calls made by army officers and state bureaucrats. Trials opened in 1990 of accomplices of the Ceausescu regime; some were accused of genocide because of the use of troops against civilians during the regime's last days in 1989. Despite having held elections in mid-1990, the country seems unable to throw off the violence of the past.

The liberalization of the USSR and its former satellite countries is incomplete. Most of the new leaders have begun to dismantle the machinery of repression and to reform their economies. In the Soviet Union itself the Communist Party is struggling to retain its influence, while from the Baltic to Central Asia the republics are demanding independence. Hard-liners may still have power in the Red Army, and it is uncertain whether stable democracies can be established in some parts of Eastern Europe without widespread violence. Beyond unification of the two Germanies, how far the former Communist countries will succeed in adopting Western-style capitalism is impossible to foresee.

The future

Communism has been rejected in Eastern Europe because the system failed to deliver or adapt. Might not Japan, North America, Western Europe and Australasia respond to the struggle for justice taking place throughout the world, especially in developing countries, and also change their ways? As the late Barbara Ward, a leading development writer, put it: "The planet we are creating is one in which no nation, no race, no culture can escape a truly global destiny. There is no choice about this fact. The only choice available is to recognize it – and to do so in time."[29]

Action

Human rights

Many people believe that we will never see an end to injustice on a massive scale. Human beings have to saturate themselves with material wealth, it seems, before they can live peaceably together. You can't change human nature, say the pessimists – human nature being greedy, aggressive and destructive.

Making choices
Yet there is a slim chance. The thinker Erich Fromm concluded from his study of indigenous peoples and human psychology that the oppression of others is not an essential part of human nature. Fromm sums up: "It is legitimate to imagine that man will complete the full circle and construct a society in which no one is threatened: not the child by the parent; not the parent by the superior; no social class by another; no nation by a superpower... [A] real possibility exists to build such a world in a foreseeable future if the political and psychological roadblocks are removed."[30] We have a choice. We can believe that human life boils down to the accumulation of material wealth and the domination of others. Or we can try to do better.

Rights of the child
There can be no better starting-point than to put tomorrow's citizens first. In 1989 the UN General Assembly adopted the Convention on the Rights of the Child, which will commit signatory governments to safeguard children's survival, health, education and welfare and protect them from exploitation at work, physical and sexual abuse and the violations of war. The task of meeting these standards is immense, but the Convention will help and encourage everyone working for justice for children. The UN children's fund UNICEF, which has organized a World Summit for Children, hopes the Convention

will become "the standard below which any civilized nation, rich or poor, will be ashamed to fall".[31]

Community schooling
Recent decreases in national education budgets must be reversed. Investment in education is one of the best ways to improve human potential; and there have been successes. Since the 1970s Laos has doubled its number of schools, students and teachers, and during the 1980s Nicaragua raised child and adult literacy rates from 60 per cent to 87 per cent of the population.[32] Millions of rural children are sorely in need of literacy and numeracy, practical work skills, an understanding of health, welfare, legal rights and political life, environmental awareness and an ability to co-operate in the community.

How can this "minimum package" be delivered? Low-cost, community-oriented schools have been set up to tackle the problem, with promising results. The People's School in Savar, rural Bangladesh, for example, is open only to the poorest families, without fees or charges. Pupils missing classes because of household duties are not reprimanded; the school closes on market days and during harvests; no comments are made about shabby clothing; the building and furniture are of homely local materials. The curriculum centres on vegetable growing, carpentry (for both girls and boys), health education and basic literacy. Group work, not competition, is emphasized. Older students teach younger ones and once a week go outside the school to teach those who cannot attend.[33]

Bangladesh now has 2,500 rural schools providing basic education for the poor for as little as $15 per pupil per year. Parents help build the classrooms, and skilled or educated members of the local community are recruited as teachers.[34] Such schemes can help governments reach far more children than expensive Northern-style schooling. A large inflow of international funding could be one of the soundest development investments ever made.

Protection
The commercial exploitation of children results from poverty. With more public awareness, the political will can be found to tackle the problem. Where governments and development agencies give loans or economic aid, they could make it conditional on the receiving government signing or ratifying

the UN Convention on the Rights of the Child and establishing a national child-protection agency. Trade unions could also take a hand in exposing and remedying child exploitation.

Initiatives to help street children are taking place in Brazil's city slums and shanty towns. Dedicated educators come and live among the youngsters and help them organize regular meetings to discuss their problems. In São Paulo one group has set up a vegetable-growing co-operative; others have organized to demand police protection against death squads.[35]

Indigenous peoples
The threat to indigenous peoples is now widely recognized, although it may be too late for some of them to survive. Knowing that they must organize themselves to preserve their way of life, tribal peoples are campaigning for better political rights, education, housing, legal aid and health services. Regional and international groupings include the Inuit Circumpolar Conference, the Amazonian Indians' União das Nações Indígenas and the 30-million-member World Council of Indigenous Peoples. Indigenous peoples are building their organization in North America, too. Twenty-eight Canadian and US tribes have signed a joint self-defence treaty to protect their land and resources rights, and a further thirty are expected to sign.

Brazilian Amazonian tribes whose rights have not yet been fully recognized – Kayapo, Xavante, Araras and others – held a well-publicized five-day gathering in the town of Altamira early in 1989. Hundreds of journalists and observers attended to hear protests against the forest dam building that threatens the Indians' survival. Trade unions and the environmental group Friends of the Earth sent representatives; the UK MP Tam Dalyell spoke; and the Pope and the future UK Environment Secretary Chris Patten sent messages of support. As a result, Brazilian politicians, bankers and industrialists were forced to abandon at least one disruptive dam project in the region.[36]

In Indonesian Irian Jaya a major development planned by Scott Paper (makers of toilet tissues) was abandoned in 1989 after campaigning by Friends of the Earth, Survival International and the 15,000 forest people whose lives were threatened by the project. Scott had proposed to log the forest lands, plant eucalyptus and build a wood-chip and pulping factory.[37]

The outlook for the indigenous Amazonian forest dwellers of Colombia (better known for its problems with the cocaine barons) has improved in recent years owing to the enlightened policies of the government. Eighteen million hectares of the country's Amazon region – half the total and an area greater than the UK – have been handed over to the Indians as their inalienable property, never to be sold or transferred. This comprises the world's largest indigenous peoples' reservation. The Indians' right to run their own health, educational and local government programmes, using their own language and customs, has also been enshrined in law. A body of field-officers is being set up to liaise between the national government and the Indian communities and to help them achieve economic self-reliance.[38]

The Colombian model should be followed worldwide. Most indigenous peoples seek exclusive occupation of part of their original land – claims that, covering only a fraction of their former territories, deserve every support. The International Labour Organization has long recognized indigenous collective landownership rights, and several countries besides Colombia, such as Brazil, Nicaragua and the Philippines, have revised their constitutions accordingly. Results have been mixed, however. The land reserved for Brazil's Yanomami, for example, consists of a number of unconnected areas; the authorities still tolerate prospecting and industrial activity in and around them.

It is not a question of preserving indigenous groups as living museum pieces, because virtually all of them are now in contact with the outside world and affected by it; most recognize the need for income-earning activity to provide their communities with improved services. Nevertheless, their wishes to retain their culture must be respected. As in Australia, governments should publicly acknowledge past injustices against them. Educators and communicators can help eliminate racist stereotypes by giving tribal peoples the more prominent place they merit in national histories and cultural life.

If they are to survive, indigenous groups need a say in decisions that affect them; some have demanded self-government. The setting up of elected provincial or regional councils, with tribal representation, would be one solution. New laws may be needed to oblige governments and multinationals to obtain their consent before developing their lands. Beyond this, the UN General Assembly has been asked to appoint an international ombudsman for indigenous populations to monitor and report on their situation.

A change in material values

Looking at the broader problem of state violence in the South and the uneven human rights record of the North, the difficulties are daunting. How can we stop the oppression of one half of humanity by the other? Growing numbers of environmentalists, women's movement activists, human rights campaigners and Greens believe that the answer must lie in less material consumption and a change of values, especially in the Western industrialized countries, whose greed and power have dominted the world for so long.

The "American dream" of modern life as a "huge shopping mall" has to be rejected, says the writer Murray Bookchin, along with "the siren-call of material comfort and the opiates of electronic mass culture". The democratic system must be overhauled, Bookchin believes, until "every individual can feel he or she has control over the decisions that affect our society's destiny".[39]

Violent conflicts between Southern governments and their citizens will continue until Western exploitation stops. While millions of people have next to nothing, they have little to lose from upheaval and even bloodshed. So the problem of revolution and terrorism cannot be contained by brute force; "law and order" are a technical fix, not a solution.

However, when Western governments finally respond to Southern demands for a new international economic order, this will have major pay-offs. With fewer injustices, many of the South's conflicts will subside. In Latin America, for example, improved prosperity, land reform and a fairer distribution of wealth and power are the key to ending the violence.

Political will

Northern politicans will have to adopt a less hypocritical stand on human rights. Many countries refuse to condemn the injustices of others because, they say, this would be interfering in another country's internal affairs. The true reason may lie in the greater priority given to trading relationships and the wish to avoid criticism themselves. This creates a vicious circle, because neglect of human rights by one country makes similar violations easier to justify in others, on the grounds that this is how the world is.

By contrast, when countries take a strong human rights position, this gives offenders elsewhere less justification or opportunity. Good example, international persuasion and the threat of embarrassment can bring about improvements on the part of most regimes. Western governments must be prepared to withhold aid from human rights offenders and to support genuine reformers. A human-rights-oriented aid policy means a ban on the export of military and industrial equipment and know-how to oppressive regimes. Multinational corporations and banks should be pressured to disinvest from offending countries more often.

Public opinion

Many political prisoners and people who have disappeared have been released or given improved treatment as a result of international pressure, and public opinion remains one of the strongest weapons against injustice. As Amnesty International has said: "In the 1990s the impact of public opinion and the remedial action of the international community should make it more difficult for governments that aim to carry out killings which are murder by any other name."[40]

Strengthening the UN

The existing international network for human rights protection includes the International Court of Justice, the Human Rights Commission and other UN agencies, as well as the Council of Europe, the Inter-American Commission of Human Rights and similar non-UN institutions. Underfunding, internal disputes and the failure of countries to comply with decisions have limited the effectiveness of these bodies. Increased budget contributions, especially from the rich countries, and a new sense of common purpose would bring about improvements. A stronger UN would be better able to monitor, report on and intervene to prevent human rights abuses.

Better democracy

The world needs more and better democracy. When compared to the South, people in the industrialized countries enjoy civil liberties; but millions still feel powerless to affect government decisions. This way lies tyranny. As Green Party activists Sandy Irvine and Alec Ponton have argued: "Essential rights...are not safe in any society dominated by highly centralized and bureaucratic institutions."[41]

Concentrations of power, whether political or economic,

oppress the weak. When power is evenly spread, and decisions are made on a human scale, individual rights are more likely to be respected. Political and economic power must therefore be gradually decentralized. This means more grass-roots organization and self-help, with smaller groups working together to bring about democratic decision-making and change. Freedom of information is important, because people can participate in a process only when they know about it; secrecy makes human rights abuses more likely, since there is no fear of discovery. Most countries, including the UK, need a freedom of information law to guarantee accountable government.

Getting Involved

Related subjects covered elsewhere in this book include: landlessness and child malnutrition – Chapter 1; poverty and the debt crisis – Chapter 2; infant mortality, child health and the poverty factor in disease – Chapter 3; the position of women – Chapter 4; the rainforests and their peoples – Chapter 6; war and the arms race – Chapter 10. To find out more about human rights, see "Recommended Reading" (pages 324–9).

Consumer and lifestyle choices

Because so much injustice arises from economic inequalities, everyone can help improve the human rights picture by consuming no more of the planet's goods and resources than they need. This is obviously partly a matter of individual choice. But by being satisfied with moderate material comfort and rejecting luxury we are acting in solidarity with oppressed people everywhere; the next step is to become involved in campaigning work.

Buy from fair traders
Don't buy the products of slave labour. If you know of goods from Bangladesh or elsewhere made by underpaid child labour, let the retailer and other people know and write to the supplier explaining why you refuse to buy them. In general, the produce of multinationals tends to involve the exploitation of poor people in low-income countries; it is better to buy local produce or to buy through fair-trading organizations.

For more about this, see the "Getting Involved" section in Chapter 2.

Some human rights organizations have also set up fair trading links with oppressed people in particular countries and sell their goods by mail-order. The following UK organizations will send you their mail-order sales catalogue:

- Amnesty International, PO Box 10, Gateshead NE8 1LL.
- Anti-Apartheid Enterprises, PO Box 533, London N19 4SS.
- Chile Solidarity Campaign, 129 Seven Sisters Road, London N7 7QG.
- El Salvador and Guatemala Committee for Human Rights, 83 Margaret Street, London W1N 7HB.
- Nicaragua Solidarity Campaign Sales, 23 Bevenden Street, London N1 6BH.

Community and political action

Letter-writing
Some governments and parliaments have signed and ratified the UN Convention on the Rights of the Child; others say they intend to. The UK government has signed the Convention but needs to be persuaded to do more on behalf of children the world over. Write to your MP and MEP and to the Home Secretary (The Home Office, 50 Queen Anne's Gate, London SW1). Points you could make include the following:

- A major effort is needed to protect the lives and development of children everwhere; this would be the best possible investment in the world's future.
- Now that the UK has signed the Convention, it should support UNICEF's calls for a World Summit for Children.
- The European Commission should be involved in monitoring and improving the treatment of children under the Convention.
- A high-level government or EC ombudsman for children has been suggested by UNICEF.
- The rights of children could be incorporated into school and college curricula.

You could also use these points as the basis for a letter to the press or a short article in your community newspaper. For more information about the Convention on the Rights of the Child, contact your UNICEF national committee (addresses below).

In the workplace

Trade unionists, managers and employers should ensure that children are fully protected by workplace agreements. Discuss in your union or occupational association the exploitation of child labour; find out if it takes place in your industry or field of work; if it does, consider how you could stop it.

Education

Teachers, lecturers, journalists and other people involved in education or communication can try to get issues of human justice – for example, child exploitation and the rights of indigenous peoples and other minority groups – included in the school or college curriculum or featured in media campaigns. Educational and media materials are available from Amnesty International, Central America Week, Survival International and many of the other organizations listed below.

Survival International

If you are concerned about the fate of the world's indigenous peoples, join Survival International (UK and US addresses below), which works with these groups to help them secure their landownership rights, defend themselves against exploitation and run their own community services. Active in fund-raising, legal and administrative support, media campaigns and pressure for law reform, Survival International also publishes books and reports and runs a resource library, supplying schools, colleges and public meetings with videos and other material. A members' network of urgent-action letter-writers (appealing to governments, embassies and multinationals) helps indigenous peoples defend their lives, lands and culture.

Amnesty International

One of the most effective ways to help political prisoners and other victims of state violence is by joining Amnesty International, the world's leading human rights organization (addresses below; there is also a youth section, Young Amnesty). Urgent-action networks of Amnesty members are involved in letter-writing to heads of state, government ministers, prison authorities, embassies and legal bodies on behalf of political prisoners and people who have disappeared. Many of these letter-writing campaigns result in the release or improved treatment of prisoners.

Local Amnesty groups, numbering several hundred in the UK and thousands around the world, also adopt prisoners of conscience, appealing to governments on their behalf and providing practical help for them and their families. Groups produce "theme dossiers" to publicize such issues as the death penalty, take part in regional action networks and international campaigns, organize petitions, hold public meetings, write to the local press, raise funds through street collections and sales, mount local exhibitions and stalls and speak to other organizations such as religious groups, schools and colleges, trade unions and political parties.

The UK section of Amnesty is also sponsoring the replanting of native trees at Amnesty Wood at Eridge, East Sussex, as a tribute to prisoners of conscience around the world. If you want to make a donation to the project, contact the Woodland Trust, Autumn Park, Grantham, Lincs. NG31 6LL (0476-74297). The money is shared between the wood and Amnesty's other work.

Central America Week

Central America Week (address below) takes place in scores of towns and cities across the UK each year in March to commemorate the anniversary of the assassination of Archbishop Romero of El Salvador on 24 March. The Week brings together and is sponsored by development, religious, human rights and solidarity organizations concerned for the people of El Salvador, Guatemala, Honduras and Nicaragua. You can attend and participate in a variety of public events and activities during the Week, including fund-raising, video showings, meetings with speakers from Central America, music events and dances, mural painting, sponsored walks, vigils, ecumenical services, exhibitions and craft fairs.

Teachers and others involved with young people are encouraged to get involved in Central America Week. Possible educational activities include using human rights in the region as a theme for projects and assemblies, writing to young people in Central America, sending Christmas cards to families with disappeared relatives and setting up exchanges of drawings, tapes or drawing materials. Educational and audiovisual resources on

Central America are available from the National Association of Development Education Centres, 6 Endsleigh Street, London WC1H 0DX.

Broader issues
Write to your MP and MEP and to the Foreign Secretary (Foreign and Commonwealth Office, Downing Street, London SW1A 2AL) on broader human rights issues:

- Ask them to press for the government and the European Community to publicly condemn secret detention and torture, to call for the prosecution of torturers and for the abolition of the death penalty.
- Suggest that aid is given to low-income countries according to their human rights record, where necessary making aid conditional on human rights improvements.
- Request that they propose and work for the appointment by the United Nations of an ombudsman to monitor and report on the human rights of indigenous peoples.

UK democracy
In the UK, support the campaign for greater democracy: Charter 88, Panther House, 38 Mount Pleasant, London WC1X 0AP (071-278 9188). The main aims of Charter 88 are a Bill of Rights guaranteeing essential civil liberties, a Freedom of Information Act to ensure open and accountable government, electoral reform, reform of the House of Lords and the legal system, a partial devolution of power from central government to regional and local government and a written constitution.

Organizations

Organizations working to help the oppressed and for an end to injustice include:

UK and Irish Republic
Amnesty International, 99–119 Rosebery Avenue, London EC1R 4RE (071-278 6000); and (international secretariat) 1 Easton Street, London WC1X 8DJ (071-833 1771).
Amnesty International Irish Section, Sean MacBride House, 8 Shaw Street, Dublin 2, Irish Republic.

Anti-Apartheid Movement, 13 Mandela Street, London NW1 0DW (071-387 7966).

Anti-Slavery Society, 180 Brixton Road, London SW9 6AT (071-582 4040).

British Refugee Council, 3–9 Bondway, London SW8 1SJ (071-582 6922).

Central America Week, 82 Margaret Street, London W1N 8LH (071-631 5173).

Latin America Bureau, 1 Amwell Street, London EC1R 1UL (071-278 2829).

Liberty (National Council for Civil Liberties), 21 Tabard Street, London SE1 4LA (071-403 3888).

Minority Rights Group, 29 Craven Street, London WC2N 5NT (071-930 6659).

Rainforest Foundation, McCartney Estates, Marvic House, Bishops Road, London SW6 7AD.

Save the Children Fund, 17 Grove Lane, London SE5 8RD (071-703 5400).

Survival International, 310 Edgware Road, London W2 1DY (071-723 5535).

United Nations Children's Fund (UNICEF) UK, 55 Lincoln's Inn Fields, London WC2A 3NB (071-405 5592).

Women's International League for Peace and Freedom, 29 Great James Street, London WC1N 3ES (071-242 1521).

World University Service, 20 Compton Terrace, London N1 2UN (071-226 6747).

USA and Canada

Americas Watch, 739 Eighth Street SE, Washington, DC 20003, USA.

Amnesty International, 322 Eighth Avenue, New York, NY 10001, USA.

Amnesty International, Suite 900, 130 Slater Street, Ottawa, Ontario K1P 6E2, Canada.

Coalition for a New Foreign and Military Policy, 712 G Street NE, Washington, DC 20003, USA.

Foundation for the Peoples of the South Pacific, 200 West 57th Street, New York, NY 10019, USA.

Inter-Church Committee on Human Rights in Latin America, Room 201, 40 St Clair Avenue E, Toronto, Ontario M4T 1M9, Canada.

Latin American Working Group, PO Box 2207, Station P,

Toronto, Ontario M5S 2T2, Canada

Minority Rights Group, Apt 45, 35 Claremont Avenue, New York, NY 10027, USA.

Save the Children, Suite 6020, 3080 Yonge Street, Toronto, Ontario M5W 2B1, Canada.

Survival International, 2121 Decatur Place NW, Washington, DC 20008, USA.

Task Force on Latin America and the Caribbean, 515 Broadway, Santa Cruz, Calif. 95060, USA.

United Nations Children's Fund (UNICEF) USA, 866 UN Plaza, New York, NY 10017, USA.

United Nations Children's Fund (UNICEF) Canada, 443 Mount Pleasant Road, Toronto, Ontario M4S 2L8, Canada.

Women's International League for Peace and Freedom, 1102 Ironwork Passage, Vancouver, British Colombia V6H 3P1; and PO Box 4781E, Ottawa, Ontario K1S 5H9, Canada.

Women's International League for Peace and Freedom, 1213 Race Street, Philadelphia, Pa 1907, USA.

Australia and New Zealand

Amnesty International, Private Bag No. 23, Broadway, New South Wales 2007, Australia.

Amnesty International, PO Box 6647, Wellington 1, New Zealand.

Anti-Apartheid Movement, PO Box K557, Haymarket, Sydney, New South Wales 2000, and PO Box 1724P, Melbourne, Victoria 3001, Australia.

Australian Nuclear-Free and Independent Pacific Co-ordinating Committee, 56–60 Foster Street, Surry Hills, New South Wales 2010, Australia.

Latin American Information Centre, 183 Gertrude Street, Fitzroy, Victoria 3065, Australia.

National Coalition of Aboriginal Organizations, 1st Floor, 300 Sussex Street, Sydney, New South Wales 2000, Australia.

Nuclear-Free and Independent Pacific Movement, Pacific Concerns Resource Centre, PO Box 9295, Newmarket, Auckland, New Zealand.

United Nations Children's Fund (UNICEF) Australia, 14th Floor, 80 Mount Street, North Sydney, New South Wales 2060, Australia.

United Nations Children's Fund (UNICEF) New Zealand, PO Box 347, 29 Brandon Street, Wellington, New Zealand.

Women's International League for Peace and Freedom, GPO Box 2598, Sydney, New South Wales 2001, Australia.
Women's International League for Peace and Freedom, 56A Wai-iti Crescent, Lower Hutt, New Zealand.

Africa, Asia and the Caribbean (Commonwealth)
Amnesty International, PO Box 872, Bridgetown, Barbados.
Amnesty International, PO Box 1173, Koforidua, Ghana.
Amnesty International, Palm Court Building, 35 Main Street, Georgetown, Guyana.
Amnesty International, PO Bag 231, Woodbrook PO, Port of Spain, Trinidad.
Amnesty International, c/o Dateline Delhi, 21 North End Complex, Panchkuin Road, New Delhi 110001, India.
Amnesty International, PO Box 59, Agodi Post Office, Ibadan, Oyo State, Nigeria.
Amnesty International, PO Box 4904, Dar es Salaam, Tanzania.
Gandhi Peace Foundation, 221–223 Deen Dayal, Upadhyaya Marg, New Delhi 110002, India.
Planetary Citizens' Council for Peace, Development and the Environment, Robinson Road, PO Box 2753, Singapore 9047.
Sarvodaya Shramadana, 98 Damask Mandira, Rawatawatte Road, Moratuwa, Sri Lanka.
Women's International League for Peace and Freedom, c/o Joyce Lartey, PO Box 1949, Mamprobi, Accra, Ghana.
Women's International League for Peace and Freedom, Box 45922, Nairobi, Kenya.
World Rainforest Movement/Asia Pacific Peoples Environment Network, 87 Cantonment Road, 10250 Penang, Malaysia.

PART TWO

THE PLANET

6. Working the Land to Death

"The main danger to soil...not only to agriculture but to civilization as a whole, stems from the townsman's determination to apply to agriculture the principles of industry."

E. F. Schumacher[1]

The Problem

Deforestation and soil loss are occurring around the world on a scale never known before. Besides its contribution to the greenhouse effect, the stripping of trees and other vegetation leaves the earth vulnerable to flooding, erosion and desertification. Intensive farming, large-scale irrigation and the presence of too many animals also degrade vast areas of land.

These sound like technical problems, but they shape the destiny of millions of people and will probably soon affect us all. The loss of the rainforests has been called "the most crucial ecological issue of our time", while soil erosion "is at last beginning to take its rightful place in people's minds as a threat to civilization, to be ranked alongside plague and warfare".[2]

Not just technical problems, then, but human ones. And like most human problems, they have solutions, although these may be far from simple.

Disappearing forests

Trees cover more than a third of the Earth's land surface. A northern band of evergreen conifers stretches from China, through northern Russia and Scandinavia, to the USA and Canada. Further south, broad-leaved and deciduous (leaf-shedding) woodlands predominate across much of Asia, the Soviet Union, Europe and the USA. The dry savanna regions of North Africa, Asia and Latin America have a patchy covering of trees set amid grassy plains. Further south still, the warm, humid region around the equator is home to the evergreen tropical rainforests, fringed by deciduous and dry forests.

An essential resource

Fully natural "primary" forest covers about 2.8 billion hectares, 21 per cent of the world's land surface. Open woodland and regrowth on cleared forest land account for another estimated 1.7 billion or 13 per cent. Of the one billion hectares of tropical rainforest, more than half is in Latin America, the rest in West and Central Africa, South-east Asia and the Pacific.[3]

Forests make an enormous contribution to the Earth's atmosphere and climate by absorbing carbon dioxide and helping regulate temperature. Forests absorb heat and help cool the Earth. They encourage local rainfall, releasing moisture into the atmosphere and forcing water-saturated air currents to rise and produce rain. Like all vegetation, trees' "sponge" effect allows the land to absorb water and then release it slowly over time; in the tropics, where rain is infrequent and torrential, this is especially important.

Trees protect the soil from wind and water erosion. Their leaf canopy prevents the full impact of rainfall on the ground, and the roots bind soils together. Many plants will not grow easily in their absence.

River systems also depend upon the forests. Without trees local rainfall decreases in quantity and becomes more erratic, washing soil downhill to silt up streams and rivers, raising water levels and flooding river banks. The local temperature also rises, drying up water courses and contributing to drought.

The tropical rainforests are the richest of all ecosystems and the only home of about 200 million people. Forest and woodland products obtained by human communities for thousands of years include wood (for fuel, building, fencing and toolmaking), fodder for domesticated animals, fruits, nuts, honey, spices, sources of animal protein ("game"), medicinal extracts and other raw materials such as oils, fibres, resins, gums and waxes. In much of the South firewood supplies nine-tenths of domestic fuel needs.

Farmers depend on trees as windbreaks and for shade and shelter for human habitations, fields and livestock. Trees help replenish water sources, and leaf fall enriches and enhances the structure of the soil. Tree roots prevent erosion; and the roots of leguminous (bean- and pea-like) trees "fix" nitrogen in the earth and improve fertility. Woodland also provides habitats for birds and small mammals that help control insect pests.

Worldwide destruction

No forest is inexhaustible. The fringes of the Mediterranean were heavily forested until Roman times; Easter Island had trees until about 1500. The British Isles and continental Europe had large areas of thick tree cover until the Middle Ages. The agricultural and industrial revolutions of Western Europe and North America felled much of their remaining forest (some of the loss has been made good).

More than 30 per cent of the world's forest has now been destroyed, including 40 per cent of the rainforests. Most of this damage has taken place during the last forty-five years. Unlike the woodlands of the temperate North, which can regenerate relatively easily due to rich soils and mild climate, the fragile earth and harsher climate of the South make tree loss difficult – in some cases probably impossible – to reverse.

Over half of today's deforestation occurs in Latin America.[4] Roughly 10 per cent of the Amazon (currently totalling about 700 million hectares, an expanse larger than Europe) has gone. Central America has lost half its tree cover since 1960, forest accounting today for just a fifth of its land area.

In Asia 42 per cent of the original tropical forest has gone. Little more than 4 per cent of the Himalayan foothills, once covered in pine, oak and rhododendron, have primary forest left. The Philippines, four-fifths forested at the turn of the century, now have fewer trees per person than any other South-east Asian country.

Africa is the most severely deforested continent. Half of Central Africa's rainforest has been cleared. West Africa, formerly rich in tropical timber, is almost bare. Worst off are the countries of the Sahel region, bordering the southern Sahara. Ethiopia once had 40 per cent tree cover but now has barely 2 per cent, half its trees disappearing since 1940.

Each week more than 400,000 hectares of the world's forests are cleared or degraded. The annual toll includes 1.6 million hectares of Asian forest, 2 million hectares of Africa's woodlands and an area of the Amazon the size of England and Wales (15 million hectares in 1989, 30 per cent down on 1988's worst-ever total). Worldwide, trees are being felled ten times faster than planted – in Africa about thirty times faster. Only in China has the process been reversed (although less than half China's new trees are said to survive).

A UN Food and Agriculture Organization survey of 129 countries showed that by 1990 deforestation was occurring three times faster than in 1980. Burma, Ecuador, India, Madagascar, Malaysia, the Philippines, Thailand, Vietnam, most of Central America and East and West Africa are unlikely to have much forest left by the year 2000.[5]

Deforestation – the causes

What causes deforestation? Scapegoats are not hard to find. UK Prime Minister Thatcher told the UN General Assembly in November 1989: "The main threat to our environment is more and more people, and their activities: the land they cultivate ever more intensively; the forests they cut down and burn; the mountain sides they lay bare."[6]

Blaming the rural poor
Such statements help create the myth that uncontrolled population pressure among the rural poor, and their destructive way of life, are almost entirely to blame. According to critics, this approach "trivializes the...role played by dams, plantations and other development practices in the destruction of forests, and instead blames the victims of the development process...for causing deforestation".[7]

The myth nevertheless contains some superficial truth. The UN Food and Agriculture Organization estimates that at least 1.2 billion people are cutting firewood faster than nature can replace it. Rural people in the South always use dead wood for fuel if they can, but where there is no choice they cut live branches. The problem is especially acute around urban areas, due to population density and the preference for charcoal (lighter and more easily transported) over wood as fuel. Wood–charcoal conversion wastes up to half its calorific value.

In Africa shifting agriculture ("slash and burn") and nomadic livestock grazing are also major causes of tree loss. Pastoralists burn woodlands to stimulate the growth of grasses for their animals, which eat the shoots and saplings, preventing tree regrowth. Africa's traditional lifestyles were no problem while there was a relatively small population and plenty of land.

As human and livestock numbers have increased, however, and formerly common land has been privatized for export farming, the remaining open areas have come under pressure. Rural people may be the apparent problem in Africa, but the disruptions caused by colonialism and economic development are largely to blame.

Outside Africa, it is even harder to see rural people as the main problem. The World Bank/United Nations Tropical Forestry Action Plan admits: "Deforestation is a complex problem...The rural poor are often unjustly held responsible."[8] Statistically, peasant farming and firewood needs account for only 50 per cent of tree loss in tropical Asia and just 35 per cent in Latin America.

Rural defenders
Writers who have seen the situation for themselves agree that peasant farming is a subsidiary cause of deforestation and that "population pressure" is often an irrelevance. As the journalist Catherine Caufield points out, of four countries where the US State Department identified forest destruction as a major problem in the early 1980s (Brazil, Colombia, Indonesia and Malaysia), none has a high population density: "The most important issue is...how the land is distributed....Common though it is...to blame deforestation on masses of poor people searching for land, it is not the main cause."[9]

There are other factors at work and deeper underlying causes: skewed land distribution, plantation agriculture (involving the take-over of former peasant land), official policies encouraging unsustainable forest exploitation and the rich countries' greed for cheap tropical timber.

These factors are plainly recognized as enemies by the forest people themselves. In northern India local people – the Chipko activists – are the saviours, not the destroyers, of their trees: "In the mountain regions of the Himalaya, the women of Garhwal started to protect their forests from commercial exploitation even at the cost of their lives...embracing the living trees as their protectors."[10]

In the Amazon the Indians and rubber-tappers have called for international help to save the forests – but not to save them from peasant agriculture. What they oppose is "unrestrained 'development-culture' ": the huge hydro-dams, motorways and other industrial developments encouraged by the Brazilian government and the World Bank. Similarly, the Penan forest people of Sarawak, Malaysia (one of the world's largest suppliers of tropical timber), identify commercial logging as the prime agent of deforestation and the main threat to their survival.[11]

Commercial exploitation
Along with grossly uneven land distribution, Catherine Caufield cites big business as the chief culprit in forest destruction. In Brazil cattle ranching was the leading factor in deforestation between 1966 and 1975, official figures show. In parts of South-east Asia, Africa and the Pacific, forestry destroys more trees than peasant agriculture does; in Indonesia, four times more land is logged annually than encroached on by rural people.[12]

High-level mismanagement and corruption are often to blame. In Brazil, journalists Susanna Hecht and Alexander Cockburn report, the forest crisis is mainly the creation of the country's military and industrial elite. Brazil's military rulers announced their intention to "inundate the Amazon forest with civilization" in 1964. Huge government grants and tax subsidies have been used ever since to destroy Amazonia.[13] The pattern is familiar. Malaysian politicians allegedly own most of the logging rights in Sarawak, and Thailand's military was said to have a large financial interest in the now defunct Nam Choan forest hydroelectric project.

The disastrous effect of logging, ranching, mining, dam construction and other forms of development on forests is under-reported. While the commercial timber industry claims to "selectively" harvest only 5 per cent or so of the trees in some forests, it destroys up to 60 per cent of the unwanted trees and is often followed by complete clearance.[14] Shoots, saplings and unwanted species are crushed by heavy machinery, obliterated by road building and track-laying or damaged during felling. Accessible by road, logged-over forest becomes the target for landless people, who carry on felling and burning where the loggers left off.

Japan imports more tropical timber than the rest of the world combined, although over half its own land is forested (a proportion exceeded only in Scandinavia). With its traditional hardwood sources in South-east Asia running out, Japan plans to finance a "timber road" from Acre in Brazil across the Andes to the Pacific coast.[15]

Two-thirds of Central America's deforestation has been

caused by beef ranching, mainly for US markets. A 53 per cent rise in the region's area of pasture between 1961 and 1978 took place alongside a 39 per cent decline in forests and woodlands. European Community cattle are fed on soya grown as a cash crop in Central America on land taken from peasants, who then migrate to forest areas to clear them.[16] In the Amazon hundreds of big cattle ranches were established between 1965 and 1983, causing probably 30 per cent of the region's deforestation.

Dams and mining
The damage caused by the construction of large hydroelectric dams has also been underestimated. Forest and woodland areas are flooded by new reservoirs, cleared for roads and industrial buildings and, in some cases, felled for the resettlement of people displaced by the dammed waters. The Kabini Dam in India, for example, involved the felling of 12,000 hectares of virgin forest in the reservoir's catchment area so that displaced villagers could be resettled. Had it gone ahead, Thailand's Nam Choan Dam threatened to destroy South-east Asia's largest remaining zone of protected primary tropical forest.[17]

Another badly misjudged industrial cause of deforestation is mineral extraction. Brazil's Greater Carajas project (funded by the World Bank, the European Community and Japan) could eventually lay waste to 90 million hectares, 13 per cent of the Amazon. The project aims to extract iron ore, gold and copper and to produce pig-iron fuelled by charcoal smelting that will alone deforest 1.5 million hectares.[18]

Migration programmes
Dams, mines and industries cannot be built and developed without roads, and roads attract settlers, hunters, loggers and speculators. The Brazilian and Indonesian governments have also used road building to actively *promote* migration into the forests, where landless people clear patches of land, burn the felled wood and plant crops. Brazil's programme was launched with the slogan "For men without land, the land without owner is the Amazon." One sector (Polonoreste) has involved constructing a 1,500 kilometre road along which hundreds of thousands of migrants have set up farmsteads; 75,000 more people were encouraged to clear rainforest and settle in Rondonia, to the west, every year. Most have had to keep on the move, as the forest soils become virtually barren after one or two seasons.[19]

The World Bank has withdrawn funding from the Brazilian transmigration scheme but still supports the Indonesian programme. The peasants, many of whom were previously driven off tenant farms by landowners, know they are destroying a priceless resource in the struggle to survive. In Brazil the land they painstakingly clear is often taken over by ranchers and speculators once they have abandoned it.

Who is responsible? The settlers? Or the governments, landowners and bankers who push impoverished people off into the jungle instead of redistributing existing farmland? As the development writer Teresa Hayter concludes: "The poor continue to be the enemy, misunderstood and blamed for circumstances beyond their control."[20]

Deforestation – the real costs

Who benefits?
Deforestation produces few economic gains for the countries where it takes place and none for the poor. Despite management plans, royalties, taxes and fees, activity in the forests still benefits wealthy elites at the expense of the poor. Catherine Caufield writes: "The permanent, widely distributed benefits of the intact forest – the protection of wildlife, water catchments, and soil, and the provision of food, medicines and building materials – are turned into immediate, short-term profits for a small group of investors and consumers." Or the forests are destroyed by destitute people with no alternative.[21]

The tropical timber industry supplies mahogany, teak and other hardwoods to the North for building, floor panelling, furniture and boat making; it ruins several million hectares of rainforest a year. Demand is said to have multiplied sixteen times in forty years and could double again by the end of the century, by which time, the World Bank estimates, only ten of the thirty-three main tropical timber exporters may have wood left to exploit.[22] Only a fraction of the trade's annual turnover (estimated as $8 billion in 1985) goes to countries supplying the wood.

In the 1980s timber firms paid about $1,000 per hardwood tree. Once the wood was processed, the value could rise to $17,000. Using transfer pricing, the logging subsidiary of a multinational will sell the timber to the Northern parent company at a low price. The subsidiary makes little profit or runs a loss, avoiding tax or investment dividend payments to the producer country.[23]

Job creation? The plum jobs go to a few skilled company men, and the capital-intensive operation gives little unskilled work to locals, as economist Robert Repetto confirms: "In some countries, including the Philippines, annual revenues...from forest exploitation have not covered even the administrative and infrastructure costs incurred...The timber sectors in tropical wood-exporting nations have typically provided jobs for less than one per cent of the labour force."[24]

Logging operations by Japan's Jat corporation have cost the Papua New Guinea government an estimated $11 million a year in subsidies. Unilever's forestry in the Solomon Isles is said to have had a comparable effect there, depriving the once self-reliant islanders of sources of food.[25] Timber multinationals have as yet rarely been obliged to finance the expensive regeneration programmes that offer the only hope of rehabilitating logged-over forest. Even when followed by plantation reforestation, however, logging worsens the plight of the rural poor. "A permanent asset, the benefits of which are broadly distributed among many people, is converted to a short-lived one that profits the few with the money to exploit it," comments Catherine Caufield.[26]

Financial gains from export beef ranching on former forest land have been similarly one-sided. Central American beef is cheaper for North Americans than home-grown meat largely because the producer country makes relatively little from the trade.

The Brazilian government used to encourage cattle ranching with tax credits that have been virtually the only source of "profit" for the Amazonian livestock industry. Why the failure? The cleared tropical soils can support relatively few cattle; under the hoof the land soon becomes almost useless; Brazilian cattle are prone to foot-and-mouth disease; and the long distances to railheads and ports can be prohibitively costly. Ranching has cost Brazil billions of dollars, and at least half the 16 million hectares of Amazonia deforested for cattle ranching or (along similar lines) for large-scale plantation farming have since been abandoned.[27] Brazilian speculators have remained involved, however, because clearing forest is a way of establishing landownership so as to profit from spiralling land values in an inflation-dominated economy.

With heavy industry, too, the financial outcome is rarely satisfactory. Rather than providing electricity to improve the lives of ordinary people, most giant hydroelectric schemes are harnessed to produce goods for export – to earn the necessary foreign currency to pay interest on the money borrowed to build the dams in the first place! Mineral exploitation tends to work the same way; the Greater Carajas project is unlikely to benefit Brazil for years, because 26 million tonnes of high-grade iron ore have been promised at knock-down prices to Japan and the European Community.[28]

Environmental damage

What of the environmental impact? Deforestation is one of the primary causes of global warming, and rainforest destruction is the number-one threat to biological diversity. Locally, where tree cover is reduced, climates become hotter and drier, water sources less dependable. Plants die off. Soils are exposed to extremes of wind, rainfall and sunshine, drying out and baking or crumbling and eroding. The earth loses productivity and may change to desert.

Eroded soil is washed into waterways. The silting of reservoirs, along with diminished rainfall, reduces the power of hydroelectric dams and shortens their working life. Loss of vegetation's "sponge" effect means that deforested land cannot retain or release water steadily. In treeless parts of West Africa the bare earth has been found to absorb only a twentieth of the rainwater that tree- and plant-covered land soaks up; the rest runs off the surface.

Forest clearance in Central America has jeopardized the future of the Panama Canal. Two-thirds of the canal's watershed has been denuded of trees, and the steady water flow needed to raise and lower ships through its locks has fallen, while silting has reduced the canal's depth. During dry periods vessels have to offload their cargoes for transportation by rail. The canal could become useless before long.[29]

Combined with the commonly increased intensity of rainfall when it is sporadic, the sedimentation of waterways raises the risk of floods. Silting and flooding of China's Yellow River (named after the colour of its silt) may have begun as early as the third century BC; and deforestation and erosion have caused the river Arno to overflow its banks and threaten

Florence since medieval times. Floods and flood-related land-slides are on the increase all around the world, and the number of people affected is said to have almost tripled between 1960 and 1980. The stripping of tree cover is probably the main factor.

Less rainfall / more drought
Deforestation also contributes to drought, which is only partly caused by too little rain. In the Sahel rainfall became increasingly erratic and declined by about 5 per cent during the 1970s and 1980s. Each year the rain comes during a short spell, if at all. For this to benefit people, crops and animals, the water must be retained in the ground. Without vegetation, however, most African soils lose their water-holding capacity almost completely; rainwater just flows away. The result in the Sahel has been a sustained water shortage, beginning in 1968, producing a death toll from famine of up to 100,000 in 1973 and a second tragic crisis in 1984–5; the killer drought returned in 1989–90.[30]

Deforestation has led to similar if less severe water crises throughout northern India and in Bolivia, north-east Brazil and Peru. Southern Europe and the southern USA have also been affected.

Firewood crisis
A further result of deforestation is the firewood crisis. The shortage of wood limits many Southern rural families to one cooked meal a day, increasing the risk of disease, malnutrition and premature death. The only available fuel may be crop residues and animal manure, organic waste needed to restore the earth's structure and fertility. As one African farmer described it: "When there were trees, we burned wood. Then, when there were still a lot of animals, we burned dung. When the animals died, we burned millet stalks."[31]

Forest peoples
Unless it is halted, deforestation will destroy the lives of indigenous forest peoples of the Amazon, Central Africa and South-east Asia along with millions of other traditional forest users. Awareness of this common threat has brought together the Indians of the Amazon and their former enemies: the rubber tappers, nut gatherers and fisherfolk. All are now united in the struggle to save the rainforest.

Until his murder in 1988, the charismatic Francisco "Chico" Mendes was a prominent figure in this Forest Peoples' Alliance. A rubber-tappers' union organizer in Acre state, near the Brazil–Bolivia border, Mendes helped lead an increasingly effective campaign. The Alliance set up a network of co-operatives, schools and health posts. Its spokespeople demanded an end to trans-Amazonia road building and denounced the timber multinationals and Northerners' purchases of hardwood furniture. In 1987 Mendes, who had received repeated death threats, was awarded the UN Environment Programme's "Global 500" prize. A year later, on 22 December 1988, he was gunned down at night behind his house, despite a police guard. A wealthy landowner was charged with the murder and awaits trial.

Death of the soil

Soil loss ancient and modern
Land degradation and food shortages are thought to have contributed to the fall of Crete's Minoan civilization, Rome's Mediterranean power and the Mayan culture in Central America. The Gobi and Iranian deserts were once fertile; and waterlogging and soil sterility probably hastened the end of Mesopotamian civilization. Much later, in the 1930s, millions of tonnes of topsoil were lost and entire farming communities devastated during the USA's Dust Bowl catastrophe.[32]

Never before, however, has land been eroded or degraded as much as now. Billions of tonnes of earth are worn away by wind and rain every year, going to the bottom of rivers, lakes and seas and rendering millions of hectares of farmland unusable. Soils take hundreds of years to form from rock and decayed organic matter. Lost topsoil is therefore, in practical terms, irreplaceable.

Asia loses perhaps as much as 25 billion tonnes of soil annually. Vast quantities of silt are washed down India's rivers to form new islands in the Bay of Bengal. China's spring ploughing season raises a cloud of wind-blown dust detectable in Hawaii. Every year in Africa rainwater washes about a billion tonnes of Ethiopia's soil off the central highlands, and the wind blows another half-billion tonnes of soil west over the Atlantic. The North's annual soil losses caused by erosion are said to include 1.7 billion tonnes in the USA and a billion in Europe. "The topsoil of the Eastern Great Plains of North America is eroding down to the great rivers so fast that nobody knows what to do about it," John Seymour recently found.[33]

The deserts advance

In hot, dry climates, soil erosion and loss of fertility produce desertification, with deserts spreading across and developing in formerly productive areas. In the world's dryland regions – North and Southern Africa, the Middle East, Central Asia, the US south-west, western South America and Australia – the livelihoods and survival of more than 200 million people are threatened. During the 1990s hundreds of millions of hectares of useful land could turn to desert.

Desertification is most severe in the Sahel, where the Sahara has advanced 350 kilometres southwards into Mali in the past two decades and more than 100 kilometres into Sudan. Here "the connection between the expansion of the area devoted to the cultivation of annual export crops and the desertification process is obvious...Africa cannot afford any further adoption of unsuitable foreign farming methods," writes agricultural adviser R. D. Mann.[34]

Destructive farming

The farming of marginal land has helped produce a large increase in world food output but is a leading cause of soil loss and therefore unsustainable in the long term. Unequal land distribution, population pressures, rural poverty and a thirst for profits have conspired to bring into cultivation or under hoof land that is not fit for either purpose.

In the South the establishment of export plantations has denied millions of peasants access to good-quality land. Such people have little option but to move on to steep hillsides and other places where soils, once disturbed, are easily washed or blown away. Even wealthy farmers in the North have steadily increased the proportion of marginal land in production in response to US federal and European Community price guarantees (a trend at last going into reverse). By 1976 US farmers were said to be losing 6 tonnes of topsoil through erosion for every tonne of grain they grew.

Overgrazing is widespread, with livestock stripping vegetation and churning up the earth. Beef ranching has dramatically increased world cattle numbers beyond the land's carrying capacity. Southern Africa is said to have twice as many cattle as the grasslands can properly support, and US ranchlands are also badly eroded. In the Sahel, nomad populations have grown, as have herd sizes (prompted by economic insecurity), while the area of open grazing land has shrunk.

Mechanized and chemical-based farming can damage even the deep, rich earth of the temperate North; in the South they are the soil's mortal enemy. Africa has especially dry, thin soil, low in humus (decayed plant and animal matter), that is easily eroded by mechanized ploughing and sowing. As Lloyd Timberlake remarks: "Africa's soil cannot be bullied into submission by Northern technology."[35]

Under modern agribusiness conditions, the earth is not fed with organic matter. Chemical fertilizers such as phosphates, nitrates and potassium, which showed impressive short-term gains when first introduced, are used instead. The damage that agrochemicals cause by failing to maintain the soil's physical structure has been discovered only gradually. The less crop residues and animal manure are put back into heavily farmed land, the faster the soil loses its ability to retain water and withstand erosion. In the Punjab, after several bumper harvests with chemical fertilizer, increased doses failed to halt a decline in productivity; local farmers resorted to organic manures.[36]

Today's monocrops tend to be grown on large fields. So greater expanses of the ground are exposed to wind, rain and sun for longer periods than is the case with traditional rotational polyculture. The grubbing up of hedgerows and trees in and around fields increases the vulnerable area, and failure to observe fallow periods gives the land little chance to recover. Monoculture and modern high yield cereal varieties in any case absorb more of the earth's nutrients (such as trace elements of iron, manganese and zinc) and moisture than traditional strains do. This hastens the drying out, exhaustion and erosion of the soil.

Mismanaged irrigation

Waterlogging, salinization (the build-up of salt in the soil) and alkalinization, resulting from poorly managed irrigation, also threaten the land. They occur when irrigation water is channelled into badly drained fields or when groundwater tables are so high that the irrigation water inundates the soil and cannot sink away underground.

Waterlogged soil, unlike well-drained land, loses most of

its moisture through evaporation, especially in dry climates. Salts formerly dissolved in the water are left on and near the surface of the soil in concentrated form. Where water tables are high, irrigation may cause them to rise through the earth; with evaporation, salt attacks the roots of plants. Salt eventually makes land completely sterile.

Alkalinization occurs where irrigation water is heavily laden with sodium or sodium bicarbonate salts of volcanic origin, causing the earth to turn rock hard. Irrigated regions of Australia and the USSR are most affected.

The amount of arable land under irrigation has increased enormously as the world has doubled its food production since 1945. Up to 55 per cent of the crops grown in Chile, Peru and India are produced on irrigated land, 70 per cent in China, 80 per cent in Pakistan and 95 per cent in Egypt.[37] Other countries relying heavily on irrigation include the USA, Iraq and Argentina. Developers of modern irrigation have, however, paid insufficient attention to drainage needs and groundwater levels, attempting to cut costs.

About a billion hectares worldwide were found to be affected by salinization in the 1970s, and up to 80 per cent of the world's irrigated land may be waterlogged, salinized or alkalinized to some degree today. Pakistan loses an estimated 100 hectares of farmland daily from this cause, and the south-western US San Joaquin Valley alone could lose 400,000 hectares over the next century.[38]

In the 1980s, angered by waterlogging, some Indian farmers refused to pay the tax levied as a contribution to the costs of state-subsidized irrigation. In India's Narmada Valley a "save the soil" campaign has built up among those whose livelihoods have been badly hit by waterlogging caused by the region's giant and still incomplete dam and irrigation complex.[39]

Action

Deforestation and soil loss

Can deforested land recover? Small slash-and-burn sites regenerate relatively fast, although rainforest trees need decades to mature. Where there has been soil erosion, regrowth is problematic. Large expanses of bulldozer-cleared rainforest may take a thousand years to recover or not recover at all.

Problems with "sustainability"

In 1985 the main tropical timber importers (Japan, the European Community and the USA) and producer countries set up the International Tropical Timber Organization (ITTO), with seemingly contradictory goals: to assist forest conservation and to promote "the expansion and diversification of the international trade in tropical timber".[40] Responding to public concern, the organization funds research into reforestation and has announced a scheme to promote more careful forest management.

This is progress of a kind. But the ITTO's idea, shared by the World Bank/UN Tropical Forestry Action Plan (also launched in 1985), that logging can be "sustainably" managed is unproven. Few rainforest logging operations are even remotely sustainable, according to research commissioned by the ITTO itself. *At most* about 800,000 hectares of tropical rainforest are being logged slowly enough for the trees to regenerate – out of an estimated 828 million productive hectares remaining in 1985. Commercial forestry, then, is managed "sustainably" in less than 0.1 per cent of the rainforests.[41]

It is also wrong to think that there are areas of totally unused rainforest where logging harms nobody. In fact, "virtually all rainforest lands are managed by and provide for local cultures".[42]

Damage limitation

Logging could nevertheless be made far less destructive, and improvements have taken place. In the Philippines animals are used instead of heavy machinery to haul timber out of the forests, and the wood is sawn up before removal, reducing damage and creating jobs for local people. A potentially important local project has been set up with World Wide Fund for Nature support in Peru; here logging is said to be entirely managed by an indigenous group of forest dwellers, the Yanesha Forestry Co-operative, whose landownership rights have official recognition. Entirely new hardwood species are being harvested "by mimicking the processes by which a forest regenerates itself naturally". Production is "strictly controlled and kept within the regrowth capacity of the forest". The timber, already being imported into the UK, costs about 15 per cent more than the average market price for tropical hardwoods.[43]

In favour of such locally managed schemes, ex-Friends of the Earth campaigner Koy Thomson says: "What is needed is a bottom-up approach; entrusting the forests to those increasingly organized people whose survival has depended for generations on environmental knowledge...Sustainable development is fundamentally a moral concept, based on...justice and equality."[44]

Problems remain, however, because the interests of indigenous communities in managing their own resources rarely coincide with those of the multinationals. It is possible, too, that forest dwellers could use their lands in better ways to generate income than by exporting timber (see below). Only time will tell whether the Peruvian approach can work on a wide scale, because such delicately managed operations need careful consultations between forest peoples, governments and NGOs before they can start up; also, verification problems may arise similar to the difficulties of distinguishing between legally and illegally traded wildlife products (see Chapter 9).

International bans and campaigns
For the present, very little forestry is under the control of the forest dwellers themselves. With the rapid rate of deforestation by commercial loggers, the fast approaching exhaustion of so many rainforest lands and the lack of benefits for ordinary people in low-income countries, the wisest course is surely to reduce drastically our consumption of tropical hardwoods. The logging of virgin rainforest should stop altogether.

Local councils in the Netherlands and West Germany, as well as the West German building ministry, have taken a lead by announcing a total ban on the use of tropical timber. Rainforest campaigner Patrick Anderson agrees with this approach: "Banning the import of rainforest timbers [from primary forests]...into our countries is a small sacrifice we can make to reduce our consumer pressure...[Then] we will be in a much better position to assist with the essential work of funding the protection and rehabilitation of rainforest lands and [helping] local peoples." Anderson suggests financial compensation for producer communities and countries for lost sales.[45]

Supporting such measures, many of the world's environmental groups are backing the Save the Forests – Save the

Planet campaign launched in 1987. The campaign, which in 1989 delivered a petition carrying 3.3 million signatures to UN Secretary-General Perez de Cuellar, calls for: an emergency General Assembly debate on the rainforests and their peoples; a halt to logging and all industrial development of the rainforests; a ban on tropical timber imports from primary forests; an end to the wasteful consumption of hardwoods; and a programme for forest regeneration based on local needs. The campaign intends to collect millions more signatures.

Alternatives
Treated softwoods (such as pine) can be used instead of tropical hardwoods, while some former rainforest land may be convertible to commercial secondary-forest plantations (but not if people live on it). "All of the world's tropical timber could be supplied from plantations established on already degraded land, or from properly managed secondary forest," says former FOE director Jonathon Porritt, quoting Brazil's new environment secretary José Lutzenberger. "Logging of virgin rainforest should therefore be completely prohibited."[46] Those timber companies permitted to continue plantation logging should pay a "depletion tax" to help fund reforestation. Exporting countries might process more of the wood, earning a larger share of the profits and so be better able to conserve their resources. Debt relief will also ease producers' need to export timber to earn foreign currency. All this requires progress towards a new international economic order (see Chapter 2).

A pilot scheme investigating alternative forms of income generation in the rainforests is under way in Korup, Cameroun, backed by the WWF. The project hopes to produce food and medicines, develop small industries and establish tree nurseries for reforestation. A core area of rainforest park will receive total protection. Local people will be provided with roads, clinics and access to markets and schools, and there will be facilities for researchers.

Extractive reserves
Even with agreement to curb deforestation, enforcement problems remain. The Brazilian government has withdrawn former tax subsidies for forest clearance and imposes hefty fines for illegal forest burning; but can the fines be collected? In 1989 the national forest protection agency had only 500 guards and some

helicopters to protect the whole Amazon region. Resources were increased in 1990 with the launch of "Operation Amazonia", involving 300 new inspectors drafted in to stop illegal activity by ranchers, prospectors, loggers, factory fishers and charcoal smelters.

Brazil is at last beginning to implement a zoning protection system. In 1990 the first legally constituted "extractive reserve" – 500,000 hectares of state-owned land in Acre – was set aside for the benefit of the forest people, as "Chico" Mendes had demanded. The Forest Peoples' Alliance hopes that it can build up markets for new forest products and wants to join the reserve to neighbouring Indian and national park lands.

Such extractive reserves, excluding big business, are the only truly sustainable forest use. Their economic potential is surprisingly good. The market price of timber or beef may be only a fraction of the value of the forests' renewable resources. Environmentalist José Lutzenberger (appointed by President Collor to the Brazilian government in 1990) believes that, left intact, rainforest can produce ten times more food (nuts, fruits, game and fish) than the same area converted to ranchland.[47]

The Colombian government has established in the Amazon the world's largest single forest reserve (see Chapter 5) and is working with the indigenous forest dwellers to develop sustainable income-earning activities. Now in the forefront of rainforest conservation, the Colombians are said to regard recognition of forest peoples' rights as the key to protecting the rainforest itself.

No more big developments
Large-scale developments, having destroyed so much forest for so little benefit, can no longer be justified. The World Bank has withdrawn loans for some of the worst schemes, and the heyday of ranching has passed; but some governments still appear to favour giant dams, mining and similar mega-projects.

Brazil, India and other countries with major hydroelectric plans must be persuaded to switch to a sustainable energy path, including the use of small-scale hydropower, biogas, solar energy and wind power (see Chapter 8). A 1977 study by the US Department of Energy concluded that it was more cost-effective to build six small dams than one large one. Small dams can usually be built using local know-how and materials, enabling the developing country to save its foreign currency and avoid borrowing abroad. Costs of upkeep and maintenance are also lower and more easily managed.

International pressure has helped change the priorities of governments, development advisers and multinationals. Environmental campaigning persuaded Coca Cola to cancel plans to clear rainforest in Belize for citrus trees; nationwide protests in Malaysia halted the commercial exploitation of a proposed national park; and a coalition of forest people, conservationists and trade unionists stopped Thailand's Nam Choan Dam.

New trees
An estimated 150 million hectares of new trees are needed by the year 2000, costing perhaps $60 billion, to solve the world's firewood shortage, enhance atmospheric humidity, provide shade and windbreaks, stabilize and enrich the soil and supply rural needs. During the 1980s only a fifth of this target was reached; forestry received less than 1 per cent of development banks' aid in the early 1980s and a tinier fraction of Southern government spending.[48]

The global community must radically increase the resources it provides for reforestation, switching the emphasis from commercially oriented and state-controlled plantations to grass-roots management. Large-scale single-species plantations are usually unsuccessful. Rubber and fruit trees introduced on logged forest land in Thailand, for example, had poor soil-anchoring characteristics and failed to prevent a fatal landslide in 1988. Angry Indian villagers often uproot the government's saplings of fast-growing eucalyptus, a water-greedy tree providing few of the benefits of traditional woodland.

Southern villagers need trees that give fruit, animal fodder, shade for crops and wood for poles and building materials, as well as firewood. African villagers tend to neglect trees planted only for fuel, whereas when consulted or involved in planting programmes, and given a choice of species, they ensure the new trees' survival. In India trees planted by local women were found to have three times better survival rates after ten years than government reforestation efforts, and similar success has been reported from China, El Salvador, Honduras and Kenya. A single tree used sustainably over time, through coppicing and pollarding, can yield up to ten times the volume of firewood it gives when felled.

One hardy tree, the balantine, has been identified by the

UN Industrial Development Organization as of major potential. Among the balantine's products are livestock fodder, edible oil, nuts, soap, fuel, natural pesticides and medicines, plus diosgenin, which can be used in the manufacure of contraceptives.[49]

Local control

The only people able and numerous enough to make reforestation work are local communities. Worldwide, hundreds of thousands of village seed banks of multi-purposes species, managed by trained foresters, could sell seeds to women's groups, schools and community associations, to be cultivated along roads, rivers and boundaries, on farms and around buildings, not just in forests or plantations. This massive tree-planting programme needs to be part rural economic regeneration, helping reduce migration to the towns, create employment and enhance self-reliance. Changes in landownership or land use rights will be necessary to give rural people full use and control of the trees.

In Nepal the control of government forest land has been transferred to villagers, who are paid to plant trees and grasses. In India public funds for tree-planting are distributed directly to village organizations. The West Bengal state government handed over bare land to landless people, supplying seedlings, fertilizer and technical and financial help. The peasants grew the trees for cash, using the dead wood for fuel. On selling the trees at maturity they used the proceeds to buy their own farmland. Cape Verde has handed over state-owned land to local co-operatives to encourage them to build terraces and plant trees; the government provides seeds and marketing centres to help islanders diversify from sugarcane cash crops into mixed fruit and vegetables.[50]

Local solutions

Improved firewood-burning efficiency, more efficient stoves and fuel substitution (for example, using biogas and wind power) can ease the wood shortage. China, India and South Korea have hundreds of thousands of village biogas plants, turning organic waste matter into gas fuel and fertilizer.

Shelterbelts of trees can reportedly improved crop yields by up to 40 per cent. Other low-cost soil conservation and rehabilitation techniques include: the use of stone-built "bunds" to obstruct water flow and encourage moisture retention; small channels to direct rainfall to individual trees ("micro-catchments"); organic manuring of the topsoil, said to reduce erosion by up to 97 per cent; changes in crops, such as a switch from cereals to fruit trees and a return to traditional varieties; the cultivation of leguminous grasses for livestock fodder and to enrich the earth; the planting of marginal lands with bushes, shrubs and hardy trees to halt desertification; and a reintroduction of fallow periods, impossible where there are severe local food shortages, but feasible with land redistribution and a return to rotational and polycrop farming for local consumption.

Soil management

Terracing of sloping land, where so much erosion occurs, is essential. Forestation along contours slows runoff and erosion; soil collects above the trees to form natural terraces. Other low-cost techniques include the Kenyan "work-up terrace"; a narrow trench is dug along the contour and the extracted earth thrown uphill to form a ridge, then planted with grasses or trees to hold it in place. The flow of rainwater gradually levels off each terrace, and the soil is conserved.[51]

Soil conservation can reportedly increase yields by up to 200 per cent, but few countries have so far achieved much success. In the industrialized countries, vested agribusiness interests tend to oppose the all-important change from chemical-based to organic farming. The Worldwatch Institute says that about $24 billion a year is needed to reverse the decline in natural soil fertility, less than the USA spends annually to support domestic farm prices.[52]

Livestock

Reductions in livestock numbers and improvements in quality are needed to halt overgrazing. In poor countries fatter and better-quality sheep and goats use their food more efficiently than scrawny animals, causing less damage because herders get better prices and need fewer animals. Carefully located new wells can improve geographical distribution among nomadic pastoralists, and an internationally financed insurance system has been suggested to protect their livelihoods. In the Americas and Western Europe, especially in the USA where huge beef herds have caused severe damage to drylands, a reduction in meat consumption is essential.

Irrigation
Waterlogging and salinization can be tackled by improving field drainage and, once again, changing from high- to low-input farming, reducing the reliance on irrigation. Saline-tolerant trees have been grown in India to soak up water, while (in an impressive display of lateral thinking) their foliage is used to feed silkworms. According to zoologist and conservationist Lee Durrell, hundreds of species of salt-tolerant trees and plants can be grown on heavily salinized land; many are potential sources of food, medicines and industrial materials.[53]

Getting Involved

Related subjects covered elsewhere in this book include: food and land use – Chapter 1; poverty, debt and maldevelopment – Chapter 2; poisons on the land – Chapter 3; forest peoples – Chapter 5; dams and floods – Chapter 7; global warming and renewable energy – Chapter 8; endangered habitats and species – Chapter 9. To find out more about deforestation and soil loss, see "Recommended Reading" (pages 324–9).

Consumer and lifestyle choices

Avoid hardwoods
Few people really need new furniture, doors or window frames made out of tropical hardwoods. Wherever possible, buy second-hand or reclaimed items or items made from treated softwoods or alternative materials. If you are involved in the building industry, furnishing or local government, see what you can do to reduce the amount of new hardwood timber that your organization uses.

If you have to buy hardwood items, find out about the best-managed sources through *The Good Wood Guide*, available in the UK from Friends of the Earth (1990 edn, £4.50 incl. post and packing; address below); for architects and builders, FOE publishes *The Good Wood Manual*. In UK shops look for the FOE Good Wood seal of approval.

Tell them what you think
If you are considering travel to a forested tropical country, write to their tourist office and their ambassador expressing

your concern about forest preservation. Points you could raise include:

- Less than 0.1 per cent of the world's rainforests are being sustainably logged; most are disappearing fast.
- All the world's rainforests are inhabited by indigenous peoples and other long-term forest dwellers, who should be consulted about how their lands are used and managed.
- Few of the financial benefits of commercial logging go to the deforested country, least of all to forest peoples themselves.
- Far more benefits to rural communities and to countries as a whole result when forests and woodlands are used sustainably as a source of fruits, nuts, meat, fish, animal fodder, firewood and other goods (as well as for income-generating scientific research and wildlife tourism) than when trees are felled for cash.

Food choices

Eat less beef. Central America's tropical forest is being destroyed to provide soya feed for European cattle, and beef production everywhere is a threat to soils. More vegetarianism means increased food self-sufficiency in the North, allowing people in the South use of their better land to grow food for home consumption, avoiding the damage to soils caused by cash cropping and marginal land use. Eat organic produce and reject chemical fertilizers for gardening or food growing. A steady build-up in the organic movement is essential to save the planet's soils. (There is more on vegetarianism, organic food and organic gardening and farming in the "Getting Involved" section in Chapter 1.)

Recycling paper and card

Recycling paper and packaging materials won't do much to help save the rainforests – because softwood conifers grown on Northern plantations, not hardwoods, are used for card- and papermaking. However, paper and card recycling is important for water conservation and energy saving (see Chapters 7 and 8) and means that less land has to be planted with conifers (which may destroy natural habitats, as in parts of the UK; see Chapter 9).

Plant trees
More trees are needed everywhere. The industrialized countries lose traditional woodland through development and neglect, and their soils are being eroded. Plant trees in your garden, at your local school, community or social centre, on farmland and patches of waste ground. Encourage others to do the same. Trees make good birthday presents. Plant mixed native species, and in suitable places; young trees need care and protection (such as weed clearance and dry-weather watering) to help them survive. If you need advice on tree planting and tree care, ask at a reliable garden centre or, in the UK, try:

- Common Ground, 45 Shelton Street, London WC2H 9HJ (071-379 3109).
- *The Dendrologist*, PO Box 341, Chesham, Bucks HP5 2RD.
- Men of the Trees, Crawley Down, Crawley, West Sussex RH10 4HL (0342-712536).

The Dendrologist will also put you in touch with a local tree-interest group. (For more about tree planting, see below.)

Community and political action

Join campaigns
Add your signature to the international Save the Forests – Save the Planet campaign described earlier in this chapter. Become a collector of signatures in your community or at your workplace and a campaign letter-writer, too. For petition forms and more details, write to Ecoropa (European Group for Ecological Action), Crickhowell, Powys NP8 1TA, Wales.

In the UK Friends of the Earth's local group network is working to persuade companies and local government to scale down their use of tropical timber and to buy only from the best managed sources. More help with this campaign is needed.

Join the Woodland Trust's campaign (address below) to replant the UK countryside with native broad-leaved species. The Trust buys up degraded land that comes on the market and arranges long-term agreements with some landowners.

National Tree Week
As part of the UK's National Tree Week in 1989, Kirklees Council in Scotland invited local residents to "buy a tree

and save a forest". The council sold people locally produced saplings and donated the money to a reforestation project in Nepal assisted by Action Aid.[54] Why not persuade your local council or community group to take part in such a scheme, perhaps in conjunction with one of the organizations listed below, during the next National Tree Week? The Week takes place every November and is organized by the Tree Council, 35 Belgrave Square, London SW1 (071-235 8854).

Reforest the Earth
Reforest the Earth (address below) is a newly launched campaign in the UK with the aim of promoting awareness of the problems caused by deforestation, publicizing the connection between deforestation and the debt crisis and involving people in tree-planting and other campaigns. Write for your Reforest the Earth information and action pack, which includes post-cards to deliver to local branches or to send to the chairmen of the leading commercial banks. The postcard politely points out the links between the debt burden of low-income countries, forest destruction, banks' profits and Southern poverty, asking banks to take responsibility for the results of their actions by writing off the debts and diverting some of their profits to environmental protection and human welfare in poor countries.

Make the connections
Write to your MP and MEP and to the press, or contribute to radio phone-ins, about the connection between the debt crisis, high levels of tropical hardwood consumption in rich countries and deforestation. You could raise some of the points suggested above for letters to tropical countries' tourist offices and ambassadors and also suggest that:

- The UK government and the European Community could do much more to promote debt/conservation swaps to save the rainforests and other natural resources and to reduce the economic pressures that lead poor countries to abuse their soils for the sake of agricultural exports.
- We do not really need the vast quantities of tropical hardwoods we consume; there are alternatives.

These points could also be raised in letters to the Minister for

Overseas Development (Foreign and Commonwealth Office, Downing Street, London SW1A 2AL).

Letter-writing
You could also write to your MP and MEP and to the Minister of State for Agriculture (Ministry of Agriculture, Fisheries and Food, Whitehall Place, London SW1A 2AH) about the problem of soil erosion. Important points are:

- If it goes on unchecked around the world, soil erosion – resulting from the over-reliance on chemical inputs and from the overcultivation of land – is likely to result in wide-scale famine.
- Besides tree-planting, careful organic-based farming has been shown to be the best way of slowing and preventing soil erosion.
- Positive financial incentives need to be provided by government to help farmers change from chemical-based to organic farming and save our soils.

Organizations

Among the organizations working to protect the world's trees and soils are:

UK and Irish Republic
Friends of the Earth, 26–28 Underwood Street, London N1 7JQ (071-490 1555).
Friends of the Earth Scotland, Bonnington Mill, 70–72 Newhaven Road, Edinburgh EH6 5QG (031-554 9977).
Gaia Foundation, 18 Well Walk, London NW3 1LD (071-435 5000).
Green Alliance, 5a Fownes Street, off Dame Street, Dublin 2, Irish Republic.
Green Deserts, Rougham, Bury St Edmunds, Suffolk IP30 9LY (0359-70768).
Reforest the Earth, 48 Bethel Street, Norwich, Norfolk NR2 1NR (0603-631007).
Soil Association, 86 Colston Street, Bristol BS1 5BB (0272-290661).
SOS Sahel, 1 Tolpuddle Street, London N1 0XT (071-837 9129).

Survival International, 310 Edgware Road, London W2 1DY
(071-723 5535).
Women's Environmental Network, 287 City Road, London
EC1V 1LA (071-490 2511).
Woodland Trust, Westgate, Grantham, Lincs. NG31 6LL
(0476-74297).
World Rainforest Movement, 8 Chapel Row, Chadlington,
Oxon. OX7 3NA (060876-743).
World Wide Fund for Nature, Panda House, Weyside Park,
Godalming, Surrey GU7 1XR (0483-426444).

USA and Canada
Canadians for Conservation of Tropical Nature, Faculty of
Environmental Studies, York University, 4700 Keele Street,
Toronto, Ontario M3J 1P6, Canada.
Environmental Defense Fund, 257 Park Avenue South, New
York, NY 10010, and 1616 P Street NW, Washington, DC
20036, USA.
Friends of the Earth, Suite 701, 251 Laurier Avenue W, Ottawa,
Ontario K1P 5J6, Canada.
Friends of the Earth, 218 D Street SE, Washington, DC 20003,
USA.
National Resources Defense Council, 122 East 42nd Street,
New York, NY 10168, USA.
Rainforest Action Network, Suite A, 301 Broadway, San
Francisco, Calif. 94133, USA.
Sierra Club, 730 Polk Street, San Francisco, Calif. 94109,
USA.
Survival International, 2121 Decatur Place NW, Washington,
DC 20008, USA.
World Wide Fund for Nature, Suite 201, 60 St Clair Avenue
East, Toronto, Ontario M4T 1N5, Canada.
World Wide Fund for Nature, 1250 24th Street NW, Washington DC 20037, USA.

Australia and New Zealand
Australian Conservation Foundation, 672B Glenferrie Road,
Hawthorne, Melbourne, Victoria 3122, Australia.
Friends of the Earth, PO Box 530E, Melbourne, Victoria
3001, and GPO Box 1875, Canberra, New South Wales,
Australia.

Friends of the Earth, PO Box 39-065, Auckland West, New Zealand.

Native Trees Coalition, PO Box 756, Nelson, New Zealand.

Pacific Concerns Resource Centre, PO Box 9295, Newmarket, Auckland, New Zealand.

Rainforest Information Centre, PO Box 368, Lismore, New South Wales 2480, Australia.

Tasmanian Conservation Trust, 102 Bathurst Street, Hobart, Tasmania, Australia.

Wilderness Society, 362 PH Street, Sydney 2000, Australia.

World Wide Fund for Nature, PO Box 6237, Wellington, New Zealand.

World Wide Fund for Nature, Level 17, St Martin's Tower, 31 Market Street, GPO Box 528, Sydney, New South Wales, Australia.

Africa and Asia (Commonwealth)

Chipko Information Centre, PO Silyara, via Ghansali, Tehri-Garhwal, Uttar Pradesh 249155, India.

Friends of the Earth Bangladesh, PO Box 4222, Ramna Dhaka 1000, Bangladesh.

Friends of the Earth, PO Box 3794, Ghana.

Friends of the Earth/Sahabat Alam Malaysia, 43 Salween Road, 10050 Penang, Malaysia.

Friends of the Earth, PO Box 4028, Boroko, Papua New Guinea.

Friends of the Earth, PM Bag 950, 33 Robert Town, Freetown, Sierra Leone.

Green Belt Movement, c/o National Council of Women of Kenya, PO Box 67545, Moi Avenue, Nairobi, Kenya.

International Council for Research in Agroforestry, PO Box 30677, Nairobi, Kenya.

Research Foundation for Science, Technology and Natural Resources Policy, 105 Rajpur Road, Dehradun 248001, India.

Tanzania Environmental Society, PO Box 1309, Dar es Salaam, Tanzania.

World Rainforest Movement, 87 Cantonment Road, 10250 Penang, Malaysia.

7. Water – the Most Precious Resource

"Of all our natural resources water has become the most precious...In an age when man has forgotten his origins and is blind even to his most essential needs for survival, water along with other resources has become the victim of his indifference."

Rachel Carson[1]

The Problem

Water covers more than two-thirds of the planet's surface, and every living thing owes its existence to it. Life formed in the seas before it emerged on land; half the world's oxygen is produced by the floating microscopic plankton that also support the marine food chain; and water comprises about 70 per cent of the human body. Together with the sun, the oceans are the source of air pressure, clouds, rain and wind. Massive quantities of marine saltwater are evaporated by the sun's heat every day, turned into freshwater and released as rain to nourish and cleanse the Earth.

The vastness of the seas promises an infinite supply of pure, life-sustaining water. But no natural resource is inexhaustible, and human activity is overloading water systems everywhere. It is time to call a halt.

Water rich and water poor

As with many of the world's natural resources, freshwater is often least available where most needed. It is most abundant where rainfall is plentiful and regular and temperatures are moderate. Year-round shortages occur in regions of light rainfall and fast evaporation, such as the Middle East and North Africa, and seasonal droughts where there are severe variations between wet and dry seasons, as in South Asia. Seven-tenths of

India's rains, for example, fall during just 100 days each year. Monsoon rainfall is largely uncontrollable and cannot be stored to meet dry-season shortages.

Overall, some countries have 1,000 times more freshwater per hectare of land than others, but population also makes a difference. Canada and China receive comparable amounts of rain, but China's huge population means that on average each Chinese enjoys only one-fortieth of the freshwater available to each Canadian. Other water-poor countries, because of climatic and population factors, include Egypt, India, Kenya, the Netherlands, Peru, Poland, Saudi Arabia, Singapore and South Africa.[2]

Heavy water users
The industrialized countries use much more water than the poor countries do. The USA is the world's heaviest water consumer; its combined domestic, industrial and agricultural use works out at about 800 litres per person per day. Next in order of high water demand come Canada, Australia, the Netherlands, Italy, Spain and Japan. In the North as a whole, people use on average about 200 litres of water daily. When flushed, a conventional modern lavatory in the West uses about 20 litres of water – water cleaner than that usually drunk in poor countries – and transforms it into sewage.[3]

Industries that consume large quantities of freshwater include woodpulp and papermaking, chemicals, foods, metal manufacturing, plastics, power generation and irrigated agriculture. In the 1970s the manufacture of a tonne of paper was said to require 500,000 litres of water, a tonne of aluminium almost a million litres and a tonne of synthetic rubber up to 2 million.[4] Northern industry has in recent years improved its water efficiency but remains recklessly thirsty.

Exhausting supplies
Human communities around the world have been pumping up groundwater for industry, irrigation and domestic use faster than these stores naturally recharge. Nobody can be sure how soon underground supplies will be exhausted, but the fast-growing US city of Phoenix, Arizona, is purchasing farmland for the water mining rights. As underground reserves are depleted, the aquifers (layers of rock that hold the water) compact, and land subsidence sets in. London has subsided 2 metres over

three centuries due to aquifer depletion, and Las Vegas has dropped a metre or more in the last twenty years. Some parts of Mexico City are said to have sunk by up to 9 metres. In Bangkok and Jakarta, also subsiding, water wells are becoming unusable because of marine saltwater infiltration.[5]

Water is naturally scarce in many parts of the South. Combined with the disruption of traditional lifestyles, industrial and agribusiness development, declining rainfall and growing populations, this has produced severe water shortages for millions of the Southern poor. More than half the inhabitants of some non-industrialized countries cannot obtain the daily 5 litres of clean water (half a bucketful) that everybody needs.

Access to water
Rural people are generally worse off than town and city dwellers, with clean water often far from their homes. In 1980 only 29 per cent of the rural population of the South was judged to have fair access to safe water. By 1987 the proportion had risen, but the overall figure remained low, with less than 10 per cent of rural people provided for in Cambodia, Congo, Ethiopia, Mozambique, Paraguay and Sierra Leone. One report has commented: "It is shameful for a world advanced in science and technology to allow tens of millions of women and children to struggle for hours every day to haul home a basic necessity of life."[6]

Urban water availability is often little better. Between a third and a half of the inhabitants of Bangkok, Calcutta, Colombo, Dar es Salaam, Jakarta, Kinshasa and other Southern cities have no access to piped water. Millions have to buy water from private vendors at exorbitant prices. Where there are local standpipes, these may flow only intermittently and be shared by hundreds of people, making users queue for hours. Not surprisingly, the urban poor use far less water than the rich.[7]

Increasing demand
As consumption levels increase, the world's water demand could double by the end of the century. Between thirty and eighty countries are thought likely to suffer major shortages by then. In the Middle East, for example, several Gulf states now have to import or expensively desalinize much of their water. Saudi Arabia has almost exhausted its underground reserves. The Israelis, West Bank Palestinians and Jordanians

are in dispute over control of the River Jordan. Egypt, which relies totally on the Nile, may come into conflict with Ethiopia, where the river headwaters rise. When Turkey completes its planned Ataturk Dam on the Tigris/Euphrates in the 1990s, this is likely to reduce the downriver flow to water-poor Syria and Iraq.[8]

Flooding
Regions suffering drought for much of the year can be flood-prone at times of peak rainfall – the drought–flood cycle. Flooding is a natural occurrence made worse by deforestation and soil erosion. Anders Wijkman and Lloyd Timberlake write: "Floods are increasing more rapidly than any other type of disaster."[9] In the 1980s there were significant floods in Argentina, Bangladesh, Bolivia, Brazil, Canada, China, Colombia, Cuba, Ecuador, Gabon, India, Nepal, Papua New Guinea, Paraguay, Peru, the Philippines, Sudan and Thailand. More than the inconvenience of water everywhere, flooding causes skin rashes and disease epidemics as cess pits, latrines and industrial sewers overflow.

Damage from annual floods in India mounts steadily. The government spends about $1 billion a year raising river embankments. One in twenty of the country's population is threatened, and hundreds were killed by the 1978 and 1980 floods. Millions of Bangladeshis live less than 3 metres above sea level in the Brahmaputra/Ganges delta, where flooding is aggravated by rainstorms swept inland from the Bay of Bengal. The inundation of a million hectares of East Pakistan (as it was) in 1970 caused the death of 300,000 people; most of the country was under water again in 1987 and 1988, with further major loss of life, disease epidemics and destruction.[10]

China's Yellow River, flowing on levees above the surrounding plain, floods about 800,000 hectares a year. The river may have killed more people than any other physical feature of the planet: up to 2 million in 1887, possibly 3 million in 1931 and half a million when a levee was breached to hold back the Japanese in 1938. Ten million people were evacuated from floods in 1954.[11]

Floods are worsening in the industrialized countries, too. The building of roads and urban areas reduces the area of land capable of absorbing water, increasing the amount of surface runoff entering streams and rivers and raising peak water levels.

Irrigation and large dams – hidden costs

Irrigation
The world's area of irrigated farmland has almost tripled since 1950 and now produces about a third of the world's food. Intensive irrigation may account for 70 per cent of global water consumption, and 20 per cent more land could be irrigated by the year 2000. Yet large-scale irrigation is usually inefficient. As much as two-thirds of the water is lost through evaporation or wasted through overwatering.[12]

The money needed to invest in canal building, pumping equipment and water supplies is beyond the reach of most farmers. Governments usually provide loans or a subsidized irrigation service to richer landowners and agribusiness farmers, with the intention of recouping their costs by selling produce abroad. This leads to a concentration on water-greedy export commodities such as coffee, cotton, tobacco and modern cereals, to the detriment of local staple foods. In India's Maharashtra state, for example, wealthy landowners have profited from World Bank loans used to set up mechanized irrigation schemes to grow sugarcane, while thousands of small farmers have a water shortage.[13]

The prodigal consumption of water for irrigation has heavily drained water reserves. California, where much of the USA's fresh fruit and vegetables are grown, Texas and northern Mexico are running out of water because irrigation has tapped underground sources too fast; a second Dust Bowl disaster is predicted. Saudi Arabia's recent grain surpluses have been achieved at the expense of most of its non-renewable groundwater. Irrigation on private farms in India has led to water tables falling by as much as 90 metres, and thousands of village wells have run dry. Similar problems are reported from China. In the USSR the Aral Sea has dried up and split into two because of the diversion of water to irrigate cotton fields.[14]

The cost of keeping irrigation schemes working is high. Heavy siltation, low water availability, reduced reservoir storage capacity and waterlogging have inflicted heavy financial losses on India's public irrigation operators. The degradation of land through salinization is an additional problem.

How dams go wrong
Much of the world's irrigated land is supplied by water from giant modern dams. Such dams are also intended to store rainy-season floods and to generate hydroelectricity. Their economic and environmental consequences are often disastrous. Women environmentalists argue that large dams are the work of men more concerned with displaying their technological and economic power than with the well-being of ordinary people. Vandana Shiva comments: "Every major new dam in India has displaced people from fertile river valleys...The masculinist mind, by wanting to tame and control every river in ignorance of nature's ways, is in fact sowing the seeds of large-scale desertification and famine...Dams create dead rivers, and dead rivers cannot support life."[15]

The still incomplete Narmada River dam project in India has been called the world's largest planned disaster. Up to a million people may be dispossessed of their homes and farmland, while big business interests and landowners gain from this massive 3,000-dam scheme that will provide irrigation and hydroelectricity by way of the world's largest artificial lake. The reservoir is likely to flood as much land as it brings under irrigation, causing massive deforestation, the destruction of rare animals and a rise in water-borne disease. Project costs have risen tenfold since the late 1970s. The Narmada complex may also increase the local risk of landslides and earthquakes, since seismic activity has been found to increase around dams higher than 150 metres, probably the result of the massive weight of water in the reservoir. The Indian government has ignored widespread protests against the project.

Construction of another giant dam is under way in China on the Yangtze River. The Three Gorges project, due for completion in the mid-1990s, has enormous associated cost and risks. Ten cities and a huge area of farmland will be drowned by the reservoir, and critics say that the danger of floods and landslides has not been properly assessed.

Silting is a major problem with giant dams, caused by deforestation, soil erosion and overgrazing in the watersheds. Along with decreasing local rainfall, this lowers the depth and reduces the volume of reservoir water; there is then less water power to drive the generator turbines. Worldwide average reservoir sedimentation rates are about five times faster than projected. Hydroelectricity generation by the Sanman Gorge Dam on

China's Yellow River has been reduced by three-quarters; similar problems have caused power cuts in Colombo, Sri Lanka; the Ambuklao Dam in the Philippines, said to need sixty years' operation to pay for itself, is expected to seize up after thirty-two; siltation of Cost Rica's Cachi reservoir has so far cost about $200 million.

Further trouble arises when vegetation is badly cleared from the reservoir site. Acidification caused by rotting trees and plants caused $12 million of turbine damage at Surinam's Lake Brokopondo in the 1960s and $5 million worth at Brazil's Curva Una Dam in the 1970s. Acidification can destroy prospects for reservoir fishing, too, which may be a serious blow for local people. Dams also harm freshwater fisheries downstream by reducing the river's flow of water and nutrients and allowing saltwater to enter too far upstream from the sea.

Dirty inland waters

Deteriorating quality and declining freshwater reserves are a mounting threat to human well-being. As Rachel Carson wrote: "It is not possible to add [pollution] to water anywhere without threatening the purity of water everywhere."[16]

What are the main enemies of water purity? First, agents of disease (bacteria, viruses and worms), thriving in stationary or slow-flowing waters; second, biodegradable organic wastes (such as sewage and agricultural runoff), which can exhaust water-borne oxygen, leaving lakes and rivers dead; third, non-biodegradable organic compounds (notably modern pesticides); fourth, minerals, heavy metals, petrochemicals, solvents and other non-biodegradable industrial by-products; fifth, nuclear radiation.

Disease and waste
In the South sanitation and pollution laws are weak or non-existent, and waterways carry multiple forms of contamination. On its seaward journey past scores of Indian cities of over 50,000 inhabitants, for example, the River Ganges picks up sediment from the mountains, toxins from factories (where woodpulp, paper, DDT, fertilizer and petrochemicals are produced), untreated sewage, disease and even human corpses.[17]

The Ganges is not unusual. Malaysia's rivers are dangerously polluted with raw domestic sewage and effluent from mining, tanneries, textile works, food processing, rubber factories, electronics and electroplating plants and various chemical processing industries. The Suzhou Creek and Huangpu River are the main sewers for Shanghai's 13 million inhabitants and collect between them an estimated 3.4 million cubic metres of industrial and domestic waste daily. The dead and stinking Huangpu may be the world's most heavily polluted river. In Brazil, São Paulo's two major rivers are filthy and lifeless. The River Bogotá, flowing through Colombia's capital, is "the most polluted river in the world for its size". Market gardening downriver of La Paz, Bolivia, has been halted because of water contamination.[18]

Urban water pollution in the South affects the poor more than the rich. In urban areas wealthier people tend to live upstream and on higher ground, with the poor further downstream in lower-lying neighbourhoods.

Waters of the North

Are the waters of the North any cleaner? After the 1989 reforms in Eastern Europe startling facts emerged about the extent of water pollution there. Beaches are closed, fish stocks have declined, and drinking water is dangerous along most rivers and in and around the Baltic and Black seas. The Vistula is now too contaminated even for industrial uses. Seventy per cent of Czechoslovakia's rivers are poisoned with industrial and farm wastes and oil, 66 per cent of East Germany's overloaded with farm waste and untreated sewage. Hundreds of Hungarian towns use dangerously contaminated water. Few of Romania's rivers carry drinkable water.[19]

In the Rhine, Western Europe's most contaminated waterway way, phenol, mercury, nickel, zinc, copper, chromium, lead, manganese, arsenic, ammonia and other potential toxins have been found in significant quantities. Twenty per cent of the world's industrial chemicals are produced along the river, and in 1986 more than 30 tonnes of pesticides were released into it after a fire at the Sandoz factory in Basel, Switzerland. The Rhine is nevertheless expected to supply millions of Europeans with their drinking water. Some chemicals used to make the water supposedly safer, such as chlorine, are themselves potentially dangerous. As early as the 1950s Dutch cities depending on the Rhine for drinking water were found to have higher cancer rates than those using wells.[20]

With their stiller waters, lakes are especially prone to pollution. The world's largest freshwater lake is the USSR's Lake Baikal. Once renowned for its purity, Baikal has been degraded by industrial and agrochemical contamination, including effluent from two notorious pulp and paper mills. Just one river flows out of the lake; if all sources of pollution were stopped, it would take about 400 years for the contaminated water to drain away.[21]

The Great Lakes of the USA and Canada are said to be irreversibly degraded, despite an embargo on the discharge of untreated sewage into them since the 1960s. Phosphate fertilizers are washed into this huge freshwater reservoir in huge quantities, and the fish are contaminated with PCBs.[22]

Chemical and nuclear contamination
Nitrate and phosphate, the mineral fertilizers used in agriculture, are washed into waterways in areas of intensive farming. Nitrate is also present in the liquid animal manure or slurry produced by factory farms; phosphate is a common washing agent in household detergents; and human excrement contains plenty of both. Used by farmers to encourage plant growth, nitrate and phosphate unfortunately have the same effect in water, resulting in eutrophication, the uncontrolled growth of oxygen-consuming algae. Algae suffocate aquatic plant and animal life, producing dead water, and may be poisonous.

The enormous volume of domestic and industrial waste dumped on landfill sites sooner or later contaminates groundwater supplies, because toxic particles are leached down by rainwater. Thousands of waste dumps in Western Europe and North America have been identified as posing some threat to underground drinking supplies. Even domestic wastes can poison aquifers; but where household refuse is indiscriminately dumped with toxic waste – as in the UK, one of the few industrialized countries where "co-disposal" remains legal – the risk is greater.[23]

Then there is radioactive waste. A report by the US government in 1986 found that eight out of nine plants producing nuclear weapons materials were contaminating groundwater, including drinking water supplies. Between 1945 and 1973 storage tanks at the USA's main dump for liquid radioactive waste at Hanford are said to have leaked 1.8 million litres, leading to the detection of radioactive isotopes in aquifers and rivers.[24]

The contamination of water by many different chemicals is alarming because it brings together substances that "no responsible chemist would think of combining in his laboratory" and whose hazards may multiply many times when they are combined. In the USA 129 dangerous substances, and in the UK more than 350 chemicals (some no doubt harmless), have been detected in drinking water. The presence of radioactivity increases the risk of unpredictable and dangerous chemical reactions.[25]

Many of the agrochemicals applied to the soil and the toxic substances leaching down from landfill dumps are only slowly entering water systems. Water pollution will worsen as this cocktail becomes stronger. It could take decades for groundwater to receive the full impact and *centuries* for it to be cleansed with uncontaminated rainfall – assuming that the sources of pollution have been stopped by then.

Filthy seas

Hundreds of millions of tonnes of untreated municipal sewage, industrial effluent, agrochemical runoff, toxic waste and pollution from shipping and offshore drilling are pumped and dumped into the world's seas each year. Poisonous sediments carried by the world's rivers can be traced 2,000 kilometres out to sea. Heavy metals from coal burning and factory fumes are borne on the winds and deposited on the ocean surface, where concentrations of non-biodegradable pesticide residue and petrochemicals have also been found. The marine environment has been invaded by nuclear radiation, too, from power-station effluent, waste dumping and fallout from atmosp�ె weapons tests.[26]

The effects of dumping
How much refuse can the marine environm▒▒ not know. Much of the non-biodegradab▒ taken up by plankton, either falling to the se▒ ton excrete and die, or entering the food chai▒ is a region of complex physical, chemical, and bi▒

where microbial processes play a major role," observes the Brundtland Commission. Nobody can tell what the long-term effects will be. As for the food chain, the cancer/radiation scientist Rosalie Bertell points out that any waste absorbed by plankton, which forms the diet of fish, "eventually . . . arrives back on the human dinner table".[27]

Continental shelves and coastal waters are the seas' most biologically productive and most contaminated region. Declining populations of fish, marine mammals and seabirds may be an indication of the damage that awaits us if present trends continue. Ultimately, in Dr Bertell's words, "The death of the oceans would...lead to the death of most higher life forms on earth."[28]

About 3.5 million tonnes of oil are discharged annually into the sea, of which a million are released deliberately by shipping. Major tanker routes in the Baltic, Caribbean, Mediterranean and Red seas and the Persian Gulf are among the worst affected zones. Oil biodegrades slowly, some of its components persisting for long periods. With increasing oil exploitation in the Arctic, serious damage to ships and pipelines by icebergs and consequent oil spills seem likely; oil takes longer to break down in colder temperatures.

Plastic is probably a worse polluter than oil. It never decomposes. More than half a million plastic items – sheeting, pellets, fishing nets, bags and packaging – are discarded into the sea *each day* by the world's merchant ships.[29] As the ocean currents gather this garbage around coasts and islands where marine life is concentrated, large numbers of seabirds and whales, turtles and other sea mammals die through ingesting or becoming tangled in the plastic.

Nuclear waste

About 90,000 tonnes of radioactive waste were dumped in the North Atlantic and Pacific oceans, the Irish Sea and the North Sea from the 1940s until the practice was halted in 1983, as well as a lot of nuclear hardware. Some of this disposal was secret but has since been revealed. Regular barge and plane disposal f US waste in east and west coast fishing waters took place, ometimes with damaged and leaking containers. Very high bed radiation levels have been found near some of these ing grounds. Greenpeace has reported that fifty nuclear ads and nine nuclear reactors have gone to the bottom following accidents since 1945. One obsolete US nuclear submarine was deliberately sunk in the North Atlantic, complete with its reactor.[30]

Once thought to be stationary, the deepest ocean waters are unsuitable for radioactive waste disposal and nuclear dumping because they are subject to slow currents and eventually mix with shallower seas. As containers rust in the corrosive saltwater, leaks of radioactivity will spread. The ultimate impact of all this nuclear material on the marine environment and human health is impossible to tell.

Despite the suspension of nuclear sea dumping, the discharge of radioactive effluent into coastal waters continues from reprocessing plants at Sellafield (UK) and La Hague (France). Each year during the 1970s Sellafield emitted about 18 kilos of water-borne plutonium, making the Irish Sea the world's most radioactively contaminated waterway. Discharges from Sellafield were partly (not entirely) reduced during the 1980s; by this time some of the effects had been washed around the Scottish coast to the North Sea.[31]

No escape route

Among the most polluted seas are slower-moving, semi-landlocked waters. In summer 1989 along the Adriatic coastline there was an outbreak of algal scum and foam up to 10 metres thick that carried dangerous viruses. The cause was factory and agricultural wastes washed down from northern Italy by the River Po, which discharges 230 tonnes of arsenic, 18,000 tonnes of phosphate and 135,000 tonnes of nitrate into the sea each year. The Adriatic's troubles are likely to recur every summer, and a clean-up could take ten years. The annual cost in lost tourism and fishing is put at $1 billion.[32]

With its dense coastal population, the seemingly tranquil Mediterranean receives huge volumes of untreated sewage. The regional incidence of illnesses carried by unclean water is high, and many Mediterranean beaches are dangerously filthy. In the narrow Persian Gulf oil pollution, largely from tanker deballasting and tank washing, combined with urban sewage and industrial wastes, is having a damaging impact. Further enclosed still, the Black Sea could be lifeless by the end of the century, while damage to the Aral Sea is said to be out of control. The Sea of Japan is also badly contaminated.

Another semi-enclosed sea, the Baltic, has lost much of

its oxygen. Close by, the North Sea is also heavily contaminated, largely because of the amount of waste released into it; currents and winds tend to carry North Sea pollution from west to east.

Vast amounts of liquid and semi-solid waste have entered the Baltic and North seas over the years, steadily increasing in quantity and toxicity until recently. During the 1980s the annual payload included more than 20 million cubic metres of river-borne domestic and industrial effluent and an estimated 15 million cubic metres of directly discharged factory waste contaminated with as many as 140,000 chemicals. The UK has contributed millions of tonnes of (sometimes contaminated) sewage sludge. With the burning of toxic waste on incinerator ships (due to end in 1992), escaping unburned residues have probably entered the marine food chain.[33]

Damage to fishing
Sedimentation, pollution and waste dumping are causing more and more problems for the world's fishing communities. Even non-toxic silt clouds the water, reduces aquatic plant growth, smothers corals and shellfish beds and reduces fish populations. Fish and seafood catches around the world have decreased markedly because of pollution, among them those of the North Sea, the Barents Sea, the USA's north-east coast, Brazil's Sepetiba Bay, the Bay of Dhaka, India's Hooghly River and Indus delta, Manila Bay, the Malacca Straits, South Korea's Han River and China's Li Jiang River and Hangzhou Bay.[34]

Action

Water use and abuse

"Our water reserves...must be used with the utmost economy and treated with the utmost respect. If they are not, the availability of clean and unpolluted water in the next decades will decrease, with the most serious consequences for our health and the health of living things in general," write biologists Armin Maywald, Barbara Zeschmar-Lahl and Uwe Lahl.[35]

Conservation

Water metering and realistic cost pricing will provide the main financial incentive for water conservation. Water-saving technology already exists. For example, water cleansing and recycling can cut industrial freshwater consumption by two-thirds or more, and low-consumption lavatory cisterns use relatively little water.[36]

Dual solution

In industrialized countries most piped water is taken from underground or is expensively processed to ensure purity. Yet water for lavatory flushing, clothes washing, car cleaning, industrial production and farm irrigation does not need to be of this quality. Homes and factories could largely make do with recycled water from sewage plants or partially treated river water (some factories in Italy and Japan already do). Recycled water could be cheap or free; purer drinking-quality supplies for kitchens and laboratories, say, would be metered and paid for. This dual approach is recommended by environment writers John Seymour and Herbert Girardet: "The drinking water (a tiny proportion of the total) would come from deep boreholes, which provide the purest untreated water, or else from thoroughly filtered surface water...The much greater quantity needed for industrial use, washing cars and so on...would not need elaborate and expensive treatment."[37]

Most countries' water mains, many of them dating from the nineteenth century, will have to be replaced eventually. Then could be the time to install two-tier systems. Tokyo and Hong Kong already use waste water and seawater for lavatory flushing.

Seymour and Girardet suggest similar dual treatment for domestic liquid waste, as practised in Sweden. Most household drainwater from kitchen and bathroom would be piped to treatment plants, cleaned and discharged into rivers. Lavatory wastes, however, containing valuable nitrate, phosphate and potash (nutrients usually released to pollute waterways), can be sterilized separately and used as fertilizer and to improve soil quality. Greenpeace estimates the value of this use of sewage sludge as $24 million annually in the UK. Human excrement could even go to methane digesters, as in some Asian countries, to produce fuel gas and farm compost. This again is a long-term solution.[38]

Political action

Many of the water and sanitation problems of the South, and their solutions, are considered in Chapter 3. While the North controls the global economy, and millions have few democratic rights, few Southern governments will provide their citizens with the facilities that rich countries take for granted. Political solutions can be effective, however; in Valle state, Colombia, landowners lost their water monopoly in the 1970s when a nationalized corporation, answerable to the local community, was given ownership of groundwater and control over the digging of new wells. A water-conservation campaign was launched simultaneously. The number of violent disputes over water declined dramatically.[39]

In the towns and cities of low-income countries, a redistribution of water charges could bring about increased access to water for the poor. Why should almost unlimited quantities of water be cheap or free for urban elites, landowners and big business (as well as for people in the North), while the urban poor have to pay heavily for inadequate supplies? Metering could be accompanied by a progressive scale of charges, so that users pay at higher rates the more water they demand.

Flood and irrigation controls

The problem of flooding requires reforestation and soil conservation on a massive scale (see Chapter 6). Floods nevertheless have a natural place in tropical seasonal cycles that should be accepted up to a point. It is poverty, which prevents people from moving away from flood-prone areas and stops Southern governments from taking appropriate measures, that needs to be challenged.

Can the squandering of irrigation water be reduced? The use of sophisticated flow-control technology is beyond the means of most farmers. More effective would be a switch from capital- and chemical-intensive to labour-intensive agriculture, along with a change from export-oriented production back to food cultivation for local needs.

Why would this work? Water flows can be controlled and waste reduced by employing people to monitor and regulate the irrigation of individual fields (thus also easing rural unemployment). Thirsty cash crops would be replaced by traditional water-thrifty varieties, while the reintroduction of organic fertilizers and time-honoured water-conservation techniques would enhance the soil's water-holding capacity. Much less irrigation would be needed.

Could it happen? Yes, with financial incentives. Many governments, believing that bigger is better, heavily subsidize giant irrigation schemes, sometimes bearing up to 80 per cent of the cost and charging farmers according to the area of land irrigated not the amount of water consumed. This encourages waste and obliges taxpayers to pay for bad farming. By changing to cost pricing, governments can encourage water saving. This is happening in the USA, where farmers will increasingly have to bear a realistic price for irrigation construction and use.[40]

Another approach would be to recycle treated waste water for irrigation. This is done in Israel, in market gardens around Paris and in parts of the USA. "Soil itself is the safest, cheapest and most useful purifier," wrote Barbara Ward, advocating waste-water irrigation in the 1970s.[41]

These solutions, alongside growing awareness of the doubtful benefits of giant dams, could make the large irrigation dam obsolete. Small dams, however, can be valuable. The people of India and China have built small earthen irrigation dams for two thousand years. Japanese farmers now use inflatable and collapsible rubber barrages, bolted to the river floor, to store water during rainy seasons for dry-season farming.[42]

Recovery time
Water conservation, water recycling and labour-intensive organic farming will reduce the discharge of harmful substances into rivers, lakes, seas and groundwater, too. Assuming that pollution can be halted, can waterways and underground reserves recover? Most river systems will gradually cleanse themselves; inland seas will take longer to recover, and slow-moving lakes and aquifers longer still, perhaps hundreds of years. As for the oceans, they can digest vast quantities of organic waste; but non-biodegradable pollution such as pesticide residues and radioactivity could remain in circulation for thousands of years.

We must do what we can. With enough funding, an operation could be mounted to remove water-borne plastic garbage from coastal waters for safe disposal or re-use. (Plastic can be recycled.) Above all, we must prevent dangerous substances from entering the water cycle in the first place.

Industry and agriculture

"Industry must disconnect from the sewage system and deal with its own waste," says Greenpeace. This will be costly, but a global arms spending cut could probably meet the bill. Some governments have started to take action: India has begun to control effluent discharges into the Ganges; the Rhine's contamination has been reduced through better monitoring, enhanced purification and greater regulation; and London's Thames has been partially restored through improved waste treatment.

Worldwide, stricter controls on potentially harmful chemicals in industry and agriculture must be established, with procedures for more stringent health testing, a ban on the discharge of dangerous liquids into waterways and more research into alternative treatments for toxic waste. Advances will be needed in pollution laws and the enforcement of taxes and fines. Water pollution taxes already operate in Japan and in Colombia, where they have helped bring about major reductions in effluent from paper and sugar factories. Grants could be provided to encourage the installation of anti-pollution equipment, especially in poor countries, perhaps from an internationally financed world environment fund.

A phase-out of factory farming will eliminate the problem of liquid slurry, and the establishment of environmental protection zones, banning agrochemical use, could help pave the way towards low-input farming. The legally enforced recycling of household and industrial waste will leave only small amounts of dangerous refuse for careful storage and monitoring. In the USA the land disposal of liquid toxics is now prohibited, and landfilling with untreated solid wastes is to be phased out. Drinking water will have to be tested more frequently, better treatment systems introduced and, where necessary, badly contaminated water supplies discontinued.

According to UK Friends of the Earth, manufacturing processes and products need to be redesigned to minimize waste and maximize the recycling of materials; industries should be legally obliged to take "cradle-to-grave" responsibility for their wastes and to draw up programmes to reduce pollution. FOE also argues the need for company waste registers, open to public inspection, as well as regional public registers of waste disposal and monitoring and national registers of contaminated land.[43]

Recycling

Much more can be done to promote materials recycling. In parts of the USA and many European countries, household batteries, glass, paper and tins have to be separated for collection. Denmark requires beer and soft drinks to be sold in re-usable containers and, more important, has trebled the tax on landfilling to make it relatively far cheaper to recycle than to dump. West German industry is obliged to pay a refund on returned plastic bottles.

Meeting the cost

All these measures to protect and conserve our water are, of course, a tall order. The expense will be compensated for by job creation, savings through recycling and the avoidance of far greater long-term problems if we fail to act.

Eastern Europe, Africa, Asia and Latin America can do little while they are dogged by poverty. The European Community has begun to set aside funding for a clean-up in Eastern Europe. Sooner or later, however, the international community must accept the need for a world environment fund to provide interest-free loans or grants as needed.

Enforcement of standards

Some progress has been made with regard to cleaning up the seas, but enforcement is as usual a problem. Despite being banned by the International Maritime Organization (IMO), the disposal of plastics at sea continues. The IMO has also negotiated liability and compensation arrangements for coastal oil spills, but few countries have so far ratified them. In 1990, 134 IMO member countries agreed a draft international convention that, if implemented, will provide for the setting up of national centres in every country to cope with oil pollution, mandatory spillage contingency plans for tanker crews, international standardization of spillage combat equipment and the pooling of information on the handling of oil spills.

The 1975 London Dumping Convention prohibits the disposal of heavy metals, petrochemicals and weapons materials at sea and has halted radioactive waste dumping (although the UK, the USA and several other countries reserve the right to dump). A European Community committee has called for a halt to all discharges of liquid nuclear waste into the sea; many people are convinced that there can be no truly safe disposal of nuclear waste, the best option being to stop producing it.

The 1982 UN Convention on the Law of the Sea established the principle of 320 kilometre Exclusive Economic Zones around countries' coastlines. This gives some protection to vulnerable coastal waters and fisheries, yet few countries have so far ratified the Law of the Sea. Under the UN Environment Programme, regional agreements for reducing sea pollution have been reached in the Mediterranean and elsewhere, but these programmes have run short of funds. Greater international co-operation is essential if we are to protect the marine environment, and the industrialized countries must be prepared to contribute realistic sums to support this work.

Getting Involved

Related subjects covered elsewhere in this book include: agribusiness and sustainable farming – Chapter 1; poverty, development and large dams – Chapter 2; water-borne disease and sanitation – Chapter 3; soil conservation – Chapter 6; climate change – Chapter 8; threatened habitats – Chapter 9; the "peace dividend" – Chapter 10. For more information about water use and abuse, see "Recommended Reading" (pages 324–9).

Consumer and lifestyle choices

Use water sparingly
In the home, showers use far less water than baths. Don't leave tapwater running unnecessarily. Recycle your cooking and washing-up water by using it to water garden or house plants. Install a water-butt in your garden, connected by plastic piping to the gutters, to collect rainwater from the roof; use this water for plants, garden vegetables, car washing (if you have one) and so on.

Washing-machines and dishwashers waste a lot of water if used half-empty. You can probably wash-up in a bowl using far less water than any dishwasher does. When you have to replace washing-machine, find out which are the most water-efficient appliances by consulting *The Green Consumer Guide* by John Elkington and Julia Hailes (London: Gollancz, 1988).

Dual-flush lavatory cisterns are commercially available that can be set to flush with either 10 litres or 5 litres (conventional lavatories use 10 litres); there are also 7-litre cisterns on the market. An even more waste-saving approach, suitable for people in rural areas, that is being pioneered in the UK at the Centre for Alternative Technology (CAT; address below) is to use composting latrines; this both avoids the heavy consumption of water in flushing and ensures that nutrient-rich human waste goes back on the land. You can buy composting latrines from the CAT or send for a resource list that includes books about how to construct your own.

Buy wisely

Reduce your contribution to water pollution. Avoid factory-farmed meat, which produces slurry. Buy organic fruit and vegetables, and do your own gardening and cultivation organically; this way there will be less water pollution from chemical fertilizers and pesticides on your account. (For more about organic food and cultivation, see the "Getting Involved" section in Chapter 1.) Switch to phosphate-free and totally biodegradable household detergents and cleaning agents such as the UK brands Ecover, Earthcare and Sainsbury's Greencare; reduce the amount of detergent you use.

Fewer chemicals and batteries

Use as few potentially dangerous household chemicals as possible. Avoid silicone- or solvent-based furniture polish and reduce your use of white spririt, paintstripper and other dangerous substances. It is illegal to dump waste oil down drains or into rivers. For more information on garden and household chemicals, see *The Green Consumer Guide*.

Use as few batteries as possible, because of the dangers of heavy metal contamination when they are discarded (batteries are energy wasteful, too). In the UK rechargeable batteries, preferable to disposable ones, are available with mains rechargers from electrical wholesalers, some retailers and by mail order from the Centre for Alternative Technology, which also sells solar-powered rechargers. "Green" cadmium- and mercury-free disposable batteries are widely available and less polluting than conventional ones, although they still contain other caustic chemicals.

Recycle paper and other products
Paper and card recycling saves water in the manufacturing process (as much as two-thirds), and recycled paper is not usually so heavily bleached as new paper so it causes less water pollution. (Paper recycling also cuts down on greenhouse-gas methane emissions and saves energy; see Chapter 8.) Buy non-chlorine-bleached recycled paper products, whose whitening does not contaminate water with dioxins, for home and workplace. Persuade your organization to start using recycled-paper stationery and photocopy, computer and printing paper; the quality is steadily improving. UK Friends of the Earth (address below) publish a *Recycled Paper Directory*, listing wholesalers and retailers of recycled paper and card.

Recycle your household wastepaper and set up a workplace paper recycling scheme. You can get a leaflet about how to run workplace schemes from Friends of the Earth.

Paper recycling is not going as well in the UK as it could, mainly because not enough people and organizations are using recycled supplies and because too few products are made from low-grade recycled newsprint. You can help by asking for and buying Nature brand recycled toilet tissue and any other brand that comes on the market made from genuinely low-grade wastepaper. We also need to persuade newspapers and magazines to use a higher percentage of low-grade recycled paper in their newsprint.

Recycle as much other waste as you can so that less has to go for landfilling, with all the risks that involves to water purity (or for incineration, another potentially unsafe process). Compost your vegetable leftovers and plant waste; recycle glass, metal and fabrics. The use of recycled glass and metal reduces the amount of water needed and polluted when new glass and metal products are made.

Friends of the Earth and the *Daily Telegraph* have published recycling directories for fifty-one regions of the UK, giving details of the location of council recycling facilities and of collection schemes run by voluntary groups. The guides are available from booksellers W. H. Smith and direct from FOE. Details about local collection and recycling schemes in the UK are also available from Waste Watch (address below). Some local FOE groups regularly tidy up around neighbourhood bottle and can banks and wastepaper containers (complaints about the mess is a frequent public objection); why not join or help start a local FOE group doing this?

Plastics
Use as few non-biodegradable products as possible. Buy clothing and soft furnishings (such as carpets and curtains) made of natural fibres, not synthetics. Reduce your consumption of plastics for disposable items. Try not to buy fresh food that is needlessly pre-packed in plastic; buy fruit and vegetables loose. Buy in bulk to cut down on the packaging used, where possible in returnable containers. Reject unnecessary packaging and explain to retailers why you are doing so. Re-use plastic bags over and over again.

Many plastics can be recycled to make packaging, fencing and traffic cones, for example. Bags and bin liners made from recycled waste plastic are coming on to the market. PET plastic, used for drinks bottles, is quite easily recycled. In the UK Sainsbury and Tesco are starting pilot plastic collection schemes in conjunction with the vinyl manufacturer EVC to find out the commercial potential.[44]

As for biodegradable plastics, made from carbohydrates (instead of petroleum), there is some disagreement about how long these take to decompose, what they leave behind and whether they are a good idea. Follow the newspaper reports before deciding whether you want to try biodegradable plastic bags.

Boat users
If you use a boat, ensure that you dispose of all your waste properly on land, not in the water.

Community and political action

Water metering
UK water companies have until the year 2000 to decide whether to introduce water metering or apply a flat-rate charge; trials are under way. The main objection to metering is the cost of installing meters and of reading them regularly, but this is labour-intensive work and will create jobs, as well as preparing us for the higher cost of clean water in the future. Metering

is surely essential in the long term. Campaign for the introduction of water metering and consumption-related charges by
writing to your regional water company and to Water Services
(the renamed Water Authorities' Association), 1 Queen Anne's
Gate, London SW1. You could point out that:

- The UK already experiences serious water shortages during
  dry summers.
- Water conservation is likely to become a priority in the
  future as aquifers are depleted and the cost of keeping
  waterways pollution-free increases.
- Dual-system water supplies and sewage treatment have
  long-term cost benefits and environmental advantages and
  should be considered when sewage systems need replacing.

Recycling schemes
In the UK, major local-authority recycling schemes have been
launched in Leeds, the London borough of Richmond, Sheffield and Cardiff (Dundee is next, in 1991). Sheffield and Cardiff
now operate the "blue box scheme": door-to-door household
collections as pioneered in Canada and the USA. If you want
your local council to investigate setting up its own door-to-door
operation, get them to write for information to Recycling City
Ltd, 140 Devonshire Street, Sheffield S3 7FF.

Most towns and cities in the UK still need more and better
recycling facilities and greater public involvement. Write to
your local council, suggesting suitable sites; ask local supermarket managers if they will set up bottle and glass banks on
their premises.

Many people don't bother to recycle because the income and
savings that recycling can generate for local councils tend to
disappear from public view. Why not lobby your council to
set up a special recycling fund so that all money raised can
be used to buy books or equipment for local schools or to pay
for educational visits? Schools with a suitable nearby site for a
bottle or can bank or paper bin could be asked to "adopt" the
facility for a slightly larger share of the proceeds; the children
could be involved in tidying up the site regularly.

Limiting landfill
The Danish government has sharply raised its tax on landfilling
(giving a greater financial incentive to recycling), has made it

obligatory for some drinks to be sold in re-usable bottles and is about to start a subsidized household collection scheme for recycling. Other governments oblige manufacturers to pay a refund on returnable bottles. If you would like to see the UK government do some of these things, write to your MP, to the Secretary of State for the Environment (Department of the Environment, 2 Marsham Street, London SW1P 3EB) and to the press, or raise the subject on radio phone-in programmes. Points you could make include:

- Landfilling even with household rubbish alone can cause dangerous long-term water pollution.
- As time goes on, it will become harder to find suitable dumping sites for our growing mountains of domestic and other solid waste.
- Recycling saved about 7 million cubic metres of landfill space in the UK in 1989.
- By imposing a sizeable tax on landfilling and by subsidizing door-to-door recycling collections, the government would create the financial incentive for recycling, raise revenue to finance collections and to deal with problem sites, reduce water pollution, save energy and materials and create jobs.
- Re-use of glass containers is more environment-friendly than recyling glass; it saves more water and energy and helps keep public areas free of broken glass.
- Labels on glass and metal containers and other packaging should include information about re-use and recycling.

Report pollution incidents
Report any serious pollution of waterways you come across – for example, large blooms of algae, lots of plastic or other waste dumping (including oil on beaches or in inshore waters). In the UK, the bodies to contact are:

National Rivers Authority, 30 Albert Embankment, London SW1.
Advisory Comittee on Pollution of the Sea, 3 Endsleigh Street, London WC1H 0DD.

Alternatively, if beaches or the sea are polluted in your area, ask your local council to test for contamination and take up the matter with your water company, which has a legal obligation to keep the amount of sewage released into the sea to European Community standards

Organizations

Organizations offering advice, information and a focus for action on water supply in low-income countries, water pollution and recycling include:

UK and Irish Republic
Centre for Alternative Technology, Llangwern Quarry, Machynlleth, Powys SY20 9A2, Wales (0654-702400).
Friends of the Earth, 26–28 Underwood Street, London N1 7JQ (071-490 1555).
Friends of the Earth Scotland, Bonnington Mill, 70–72 Newhaven Road, Edinburgh EH6 5QG (031-554 9977).
Greenpeace, 30–31 Islington Green, London N1 8XE (071-354 5100).
Greenpeace Ireland, 44 Upper Mount Street, Dublin 2, Irish Republic.
Intermediate Technology Development Group, Myson House, Railway Terrace, Rugby CV21 3BR (0788-60631).
Oxfam, 274 Banbury Road, Oxford OX2 7DZ (0865-56777).
Pesticides Trust, 258 Pentonville Road, London N1 9JY (071-354 3860).
Waste Watch, National Council for Voluntary Organizations, 26 Bedford Square, London WC1B 3HU (071-636 4066).
Water Aid, 1 Queen Anne's Gate, London SW1H 9BT (071-222 8111).
World Wide Fund for Nature, Panda House, Weyside Park, Godalming, Surrey GU7 1XR (0483-426444).

USA and Canada
Coordinating Committee on Pesticides, #505, 942 Market, San Francisco, Calif. 94102, USA.
Environmental Defense Fund, 257 Park Avenue South, New York, NY 10010, and 1616 P Street NW, Washington, DC 20036, USA.
Greenpeace, 1436 U Street NW, Washington, DC 20009, USA.
Greenpeace, 578 Bloor Street W, Toronto, Ontario M6G 1K1, Canada.

National Resources Defense Council, 122 East 42nd Street, New York, NY 10168, USA.

Pollution Probe, 12 Madison Avenue, Toronto, Ontario M5R 2S1, Canada.

Rachel Carson Trust, 8940 Jones Mill Road, Chevy Chase, Mass 20815, USA.

Recycling Council of Ontario, PO Box 310 Station P, Toronto, Ontario M8S Canada.

Society for the Promotion of Environment Conservation, 2150 Maple Street, Vancouver, British Columbia V6J 3T3, Canada.

Australia and New Zealand

Australian Conservation Foundation, 672B Glenferrie Road, Hawthorne, Melbourne, Victoria 3122, Australia.

Campaign against Nuclear Power, PO Box 238, North Quay, Brisbane, Queensland 4000, Australia.

Friends of the Earth, PO Box 530E, Melbourne, Victoria 3001, and GPO Box 1875, Canberra, New South Wales, Australia.

Friends of the Earth, PO Box 39-065, Auckland West, New Zealand.

Greenpeace, Private Bag No. 6, 134 Broadway, Sydney, New South Wales 2007, Australia.

Greenpeace, Private Bag, Wellesley Street PO, Auckland 1, New Zealand.

Pacific Concerns Resource Centre, PO Box 9295, Newmarket, Auckland, New Zealand.

World Wide Fund for Nature, PO Box 6237, Wellington, New Zealand.

World Wide Fund for Nature, Level 17, St Martin's Tower, 31 Market Street, GPO Box 528, Sydney, New South Wales, Australia.

Africa and Asia (Commonwealth)

Friends of the Earth, PO Box 3794, Ghana.

Friends of the Earth/Sahabat Alam Malaysia, 43 Salween Road, 10050 Penang, Malaysia.

Friends of the Earth, PO Box 4028, Boroko, Papua New Guinea.

Friends of the Earth, PM Bag 950, 33 Robert Town, Freetown, Sierra Leone.

Institute for Environment and Development Studies/Friends of the Earth Bangladesh, PO Box 4222, Ramna Dhaka 1000, Bangladesh.

Kenya Water for Health Organization, PO BOX 61470, Nairobi, Kenya.

Pesticide Action Network, PO Box 1045, 10830 Penang, Malaysia.

Planetary Citizens' Council for Peace, Development and the Environment, Robinson Road, PO Box 2753, Singapore 9047.

Research Foundation for Science, Technology and Natural Resources Policy, 105 Rajpur Road, Dehradun 248001, India.

Tanzania Environmental Society, PO Box 1309, Dar es Salaam, Tanzania.

8. The Atmosphere – the Sky's the Limit

"Without improved energy efficiency, it is only a question of which will collapse first: the global economy or its ecological support systems. With greater energy efficiency, we stand at least a fighting chance."

Worldwatch Institute[1]

The Problem

The Earth's atmosphere is the natural resource we take most for granted. We notice the air only by its absence or when it is polluted, and we have generally assumed that it will deal with any gases released into it. Today, of course, most people in the industrialized countries know about global warming and the ozone layer and have heard of acid rain. We know that they result from high levels of energy consumption and aerosol use. Some damage has certainly already been caused, but nobody can be sure how much worse the problems will get or how effective any preventive action will be.

The wisest course is to assume that serious environmental damage is likely and that future atmospheric changes could make the planet an uncomfortable and dangerous place. By taking the problem seriously, using available technologies and acting in time to adjust our consumption habits, there is much we can do to prevent the crisis turning into a disaster.

Global warming

The stratosphere
Global warming results from chemical changes in the stratosphere, the atmospheric layer 12 to 50 kilometres above the Earth's surface. Like the rest of the atmosphere, the

stratosphere is mostly nitrogen, oxygen and argon, with small proportions of carbon dioxide, water vapour and other gases as well as a thin layer of ozone. All these gases have a natural "greenhouse effect" that has kept the world warm for many thousands of years. Like the windows of a greenhouse, they allow the sun's rays through to the planet's surface, then trap the heat by absorbing or reflecting back to Earth the outgoing radiation.

Since the Industrial Revolution, however, and perhaps before, human activity has been altering the chemical make-up of the stratosphere – slowly at first but now increasingly fast. We have added to the quantities of carbon dioxide (CO_2), nitrous oxide (N_2O) and methane in the air and introduced new chemicals, the chlorofluorocarbons (CFCs) and halons. The atmosphere's effectiveness as a heat trap is thought to have already increased as a result, and a larger warming is likely. Accumulating waste heat from fuel burning probably adds to the effect.

Rising temperatures

Average temperatures around the world are believed to have increased by about O.5° centigrade in the last century. This may not sound much, but parts of the Arctic tundra have warmed up by 3.9° centigrade, and worldwide the 1980s were the hottest decade on record, with several of the most blistering summers and the worst droughts this century.[2] Grain-growing regions of India, the USA, the USSR and much of Europe suffered water shortages, while the Sahel was devastated by desertification and famine. Depleted rainfall and river flows left water levels low in countless lakes and reservoirs.

Scientists agree that sea levels have risen by 10 to 25 centimetres because of the expansion of the water as it warms up. Storms appear to be becoming fiercer as higher temperatures result in greater amounts of evaporated water combining with stronger updraughts of air. Hurricane Hugo, which struck the Caribbean and the south-east USA in 1989, was seen as a sign of increasingly violent weather to come. Scientists working on behalf of the UN-appointed Intergovernmental Panel on Climate Change (IPCC) believe that these changes are happening faster than predicted, and climatologists are now certain that warming is taking place.

Greenhouse gases

CO_2 is the largest contributor to global warming, responsible for about 50 per cent of the effect.[3] During the last ice age, about 18,000 years ago, the atmospheric concentration of CO_2 (known today through examinations of air pockets in the polar ice) was 210 parts per million (ppm). The concentration rose to between 265 and 310 ppm by the mid-nineteenth century and has now reached 350 ppm. The atmosphere therefore contains about one and a half times the CO_2 it held in 1800, and there could be nearly twice as much again by the mid-twenty-first century.

More than two-thirds of global CO_2 emissions (5.4 billion tonnes each year) results from the burning of fossil fuels (coal, oil and gas) in electricity generation and industry, as a heating and cooking fuel and in motor vehicles. The remainder (between 1 and 2.6 billion tonnes) is due to deforestation. Most fossil fuel combustion takes place in the industrialized countries. The USA and USSR each contribute a fifth of the world's fuel-burning CO_2 emissions, followed by China, Japan and West Germany. Both fossil fuel consumption and world CO_2 emissions are rising by between 1 and 2 per cent a year, and the increase is likely to accelerate as more developing countries with large populations become major CO_2 emitters.

The destruction of the world's forests and woodlands has a double impact on atmospheric CO_2. First, each tree cut down means less living plant tissue available to absorb CO_2 in photosynthesis. (Forests and oceans are the main "sink" in which CO_2 is absorbed and stored.) Second, when trees are burned for forest clearance or firewood, this releases stored-up carbon into the atmosphere. Deforestation of an area of the Amazon the size of Austria in 1988 is said to have released 600 million tonnes of carbon compounds. "The forests of the world no longer absorb carbon dioxide, they actually release it," remarks the environment writer Herbert Girardet.[4]

Methane (marsh gas) accounts for about a fifth of the warming effect. Although there is less methane than CO_2 in the atmosphere, methane molecules are stronger as greenhouse gases, and methane emissions are increasing faster. The expansion of the world's livestock herds is a major contributor, methane resulting from the bacterial breakdown of organic matter in the gut of cattle and sheep (as well as in other animals, including humans and insects). Other sources of the gas are swamps, ricefields, coal mining, gas leaks, refuse burning and refuse dumps (especially decomposing wastepaper).

CFCs and halons, like methane, are potent greenhouse gases although present in relatively small quantities. Better known for depleting the ozone layer, they account for perhaps 15 per cent of the greenhouse effect. Production of these industrial gases has been increasing by about 6 per cent a year.

The fourth main greenhouse gas (about 12 per cent of the effect) is lower-atmosphere ozone, a component of smog and not to be confused with the stratospheric ozone layer. Low-level ozone results from the chemical reaction in sunlight of such polluting gases as carbon monoxide, nitrogen oxides and hydrocarbons. Nitrous oxide (N_2O), the fifth main component (6 per cent) of the greenhouse effect, is released by fossil fuel and wood combustion and by the use of nitrate fertilizer.

Too hot to handle

How hot will it get? IPCC scientists now estimate an average temperature rise around the world of between 1.4°C and 2.8°C by the year 2030 and between 2.6°C and 5.8°C over the next century. A sea level rise of perhaps 65 cm, or possibly even 96 cm, by the end of the century has been predicted, caused by thermal expansion and by the melting of glaciers and the polar ice. (Water takes longer to change temperature than land does.) A 4°C rise would mean as much difference between today's temperatures and those in sixty years' time as between temperatures at the end of the last ice age and those today. This time, however, in terms of the planet's history, the change would take place at breakneck speed. The world could become hotter than at any time in human history or, with a 5°C warming, hotter than at any time in the last 2 million years.[5]

Among the uncertainties, it is not known how fast the polar ice will melt. The large quantities of methane trapped in the frozen Arctic will be released as the tundras melt, probably adding to the greenhouse effect. Then there is the albedo effect – the way lighter areas of the planet's surface reflect back more of the sun's rays than darker areas, which absorb more heat. The melting of the icecaps to expose darker sea is likely to mean less albedo and more heat absorbed, accelerating warming. Loss of forests, by contrast, may work the other way by reducing the dark tree cover and exposing lighter-coloured and more reflective soil and grass. As warming causes the evaporation of greater quantities of water, the extra vapour is likely to trap more heat inside the "greenhouse", accelerating the process.

With more evaporation from oceans and transpiration from plants, some experts have predicted an increase in rainfall. Yet most studies indicate a decline in rainfall in the tropics, with airborne moisture having to be carried further than before towards the poles to cool, condense and fall as rain. As the rainbelts move polewards, continuing loss of vegetation is likely to reduce tropical rainfall further. Changes to prevailing winds and ocean currents could complicate the picture. An IPCC report produced in mid-1990 predicts that the Northern hemisphere's rainfall will become more irregular, falling in brief, intense bursts rather than all year round; this may hasten soil erosion and cause the rapid depletion of underground water supplies, producing regular water shortages. Rivers and lakes may shrink or dry up.[6]

The rise in temperature will probably be uneven, with a relatively small change near the Equator and major increases of up to 7°C at the poles. Temperate winters could become shorter, wetter and warmer, summers hotter, longer and drier. In the tropics, dry areas are likely to become more arid, with humid areas more prone to storms. Where there are already water shortages, a change of as little as 1°C could have a devastating effect, disrupting rains and causing crop failures. Grain-producing regions of the USA, the USSR and Central Europe could suffer serious droughts (although there may be increases in food productivity in Canada and Siberia due to warmer temperatures). Africa could lose its remaining tree cover and be devastated by desertification. Widespread food shortages and famines are possible, and tropical diseases may become common in formerly temperate lands.

Rising seas and refugees

The result of any sea level rise will be felt soonest in the coastal regions and islands where more than a third of the world's people live. Low-lying land is likely to be vulnerable to flooding and storms. Beaches, cliffs and headlands may be eroded or washed away, mangroves and wetlands flooded, and cities, ports and coastal property destroyed unless protected by engineering works. Coastal roads, bridges, railway lines, power plants and nuclear power stations could all be at risk from flooding, coastal erosion, storm surges and wave attack. Saltwater from the seas could invade ricefields, river systems, irrigation networks, underground aquifers and urban sewage and drainage systems.

Low-lying regions of the globe are already said to suffer up to 20,000 deaths and $7 billion in damage each year through climate-related causes. Millions of seaboard-dwelling people may have to migrate, but "areas to which they flee are likely to have insufficient health and other services...Epidemics may sweep through refugee camps and settlements, spilling over to surrounding communities," says the IPCC. Widespread psychological problems and social tensions could result.[7]

Many islands, such as the Maldives in the Indian Ocean and hundreds of Pacific atolls, will be badly affected by a 1 metre sea level increase and could be completely submerged by a larger rise, especially if cyclones become more severe. A 1 metre rise would be enough to flood the homes of 15 million Bangladeshis and 8 million Egyptians. Other low-lying coastal regions at risk include the Netherlands, eastern England, India's east coast, Guyana, parts of the south-east USA and several European river deltas.[8] Cities and ports such as Buenos Aires, Calcutta, Istanbul, Jakarta, London, Manila, New York, Tokyo and Venice could be badly flooded.

Disappearing habitats
Animal and plant species, including the forests themselves, have responded to previous climate changes by migrating. Because of the likely speed of global warming, however, this may be impossible. Built-up areas, cleared farmland and roads may prevent forests moving from warmer regions towards cooler ones, especially where trees suffer from acid rain damage. The lack of suitable habitats may then prevent animals from migrating successfully, resulting in species extinction.[9] Loss of forests through the failure to migrate will itself accelerate climate change. As for aquatic species, warm water contains less oxygen than cold; so marine plants and animals may need to migrate. Those unable to respond quickly enough could die out. The consequences of such a loss of biological diversity are impossible to foresee.

The hole in the ozone layer

A thin layer of ozone, forming part of the stratosphere, helps filter out ultra-violet (UV) radiation from the sun before it reaches the Earth's surface. In the 1970s indications from weather satellites that gaps were appearing in the ozone shield reached the US National Aeronautics and Space Administration (NASA). This information was rejected by NASA computers as impossible. Ten years later, research scientists in Antarctica repeated the discovery. Each winter the ozone hole over the Antarctic becomes detectable, seeming to close up in the warmer months.

What causes it?
Ozone destruction is caused mainly by chlorofluorocarbons (CFCs) and, to a lesser extent, halons, two groups of synthetic gases. (The metal cleaning agent methyl chloroform is also a factor.) CFCs are used as aerosol propellant, a cooling agent in refrigerators and air conditioners, a medical sterilant, a micro-chip solvent and a blowing agent in the manufacture of poly-styrene insulation for buildings and packaging for eggs and burgers. Halons are used in fire extinguishers. Atmospheric CFC emissions increased from 100 tonnes in 1931 to over 600,000 tonnes in 1985.[10]

Once synthesized by chemists and released into the air, CFCs take a hundred years or more to split back into separate atoms of carbon, chlorine and fluorine. They float upwards in the atmosphere until they come into contact with enough UV light to trigger the separation of one chlorine atom from each molecule; this occurs at the ozone level. Each split-off chlorine atom destroys thousands of ozone molecules in the process. Halons act similarly, and the reaction takes place most readily in cold conditions.

Depletion rate
The size of the ozone hole over the Antarctic has been growing. In winter 1987 and again in 1989 it was twice the size of the USA. Fifty per cent of the ozone over the South Pole is said to have disappeared, a deficit likely to last at least fifty years. As the wind disperses the depleted patches of the ozone layer, Australasia and South America are affected; average Southern hemisphere ozone levels have decreased by 5 per cent since 1979.[11]

Depletions have also been registered over the Northern hemisphere. A 1988 study found a 3 per cent loss of ozone during the last twenty years. Ozone thinning is greatest over

Alaska, Scandinavia and northern Siberia but also occurs over China, Japan, North America, the Soviet Union and Western Europe.[12]

The effects

Loss of stratospheric ozone allows more UV solar radiation to reach the planet. What are the dangers? The main impacts on human health are a heightened risk of skin cancer, especially for people with fair skin, and eye disease. According to the US Environmental Protection Agency, each 2.5 per cent increase in CFC use results in a million extra cases of skin cancer and 20,000 cancer deaths in the USA. Every 1 per cent decrease in ozone is thought to blind 100,000 people through cataracts.[13] UV radiation may also impair disease immunity.

Environmental effects of stronger UV radiation include the killing off of the microscopic plant-plankton that support the marine food chain, which the World Wide Fund for Nature says is already taking place.[14] Anchovy, crab and shrimp larvae, some young fish and other small sea creatures are also considered vulnerable. The elimination of plankton could mean that less CO_2 is absorbed by the oceans and aggravate global warming. (Ozone depletion probably contributes to warming in any case, by allowing more solar heat to penetrate the stratosphere.) On land, increased UV radiation restricts photosynthesis and weakens plant and tree growth by reducing leaf size. Food crops may decline and become more vulnerable to weeds, pests and diseases, and genetic mutations are possible.[15]

Despite recent reductions in their use in the industrialized countries, the world is still releasing CFCs into the air five times faster than the biosphere can absorb them, and ozone depletion rates could double over the next decade. Future problems are likely to arise from the fast increasing manufacture and use of refrigerators in Brazil, China, India, Mexico and other developing countries. By the end of the century China could equal current US levels of CFC production.[16]

Airborne acid

Acid precipitation, as it is correctly called, does not always fall as rain but can take the form of snow, mist, sleet, cloud and solid particles. It is not a new problem. Fish have been killed by the acidification of waterways, and poisonous acid fogs such as the London smogs have occurred, since the nineteenth century.[17]

The causes

Acid pollution arises from airborne sulphur dioxide (SO_2) and nitrogen oxides (NO_x, including nitric oxide, NO, and nitrous oxide, N_2O). These gases are emitted by coal- and oil-fired power stations, industrial fossil fuel burning, metal smelting and motor vehicle exhausts (the main sources), also by household coal and firewood burning and the use of nitrate fertilizers (much of the nitrate evaporates). Where coal has a high sulphur content, as in China, Czechoslovakia, East Germany and Poland, more sulphur is released.

When the SO_2 and NO_x combine with moisture in the air, they form sulphuric and nitric acids, the key ingredient in acid precipitation. They may also combine with other exhaust gases, such as carbon monoxide and hydrocarbons, producing an ozone-rich photochemical smog. The quantities of SO_2 and NO_x involved are huge. In 1980 about 120 million tonnes of SO_2 and perhaps 56 million tonnes of NO_x were released into the air worldwide. A single nickle smelter in Ontario is said to have emitted more SO_2 during the 1970s than all the volcanoes in the planet's history.[18]

Widely travelled pollution

Where does the acid pollution go? Some of it remains as urban smog in and around the area where it is generated. The SO_2 and NO_x may split into solid particles and gases, the particles being deposited on nearby vegetation, inland waters and buildings. Much of the pollution, especially from high smokestacks, is carried away on the wind. (Taller chimneys were built in industrialized countries after the 1950s to disperse emissions away from population centres.) These windborne gases are often blown hundreds of kilometres before combining with water vapour to fall as rain, sleet, snow or mist.

Acid precipitation has been most thoroughly studied in the Western industrialized countries, although evidence of its effects is also being gathered in Brazil, China and Eastern Europe. In the Western hemisphere it is carried by the prevailing winds in a north-easterly direction from its emission points; emissions from Western Europe usually end up in the Nordic countries, those from the USA in Canada. Eighty per cent of Sweden's acid pollution and 90 per cent of Norway's are believed to come from abroad. Along with Canada, Finland and Switzerland, these countries are net importers of acid pollution; Belgium, Denmark, France, the UK, the USA and West Germany are net exporters. Traces of acid precipitation have, however, been discovered in the remote polar snows.[19]

How serious?

How acid is the rain and how bad the damage? Europe's rains may be as much as eighty times more acidic today as in 1950, Pennsylvania's a thousand times more acidic than natural rain. The US Office of Technology Assessment rates acid pollution as a significant threat to human health and lives, causing a national death toll of between 50,000 and 200,000 a year. Acid rain in Canada, says environment minister Tom McMillan, is "destroying our lakes, killing our fish, undermining our tourism, retarding our forests, harming our agriculture, devastating our built heritage, and threatening our health".[20]

"Forest death"

Forest destruction can be severe. More than a fifth of Europe's trees in fifteen countries are said to be affected, with many forests regularly receiving rain thirty times more acid than non-affected areas.[21]

When acid precipitation settles on leaves and conifer needles it damages their cells and chlorophyl systems. Falling on forest soils, it displaces the nutrients on which tree growth depends and reduces trees' take-up of moisture through their roots. (Alkaline soils may give trees a better chance of survival.) Conifers are more vulnerable than broad-leaved trees; and the effects tend to be worse at higher altitudes, because clouds, fog and mists are usually more acidic than rain.

"Crown dieback" is the chief symptom in conifer forests, with the foliage turning yellow from the top down and falling off. Other signs include stunted growth, misshapen leaves, damaged bark and a loss of resistance to storm stress, insects, disease and fungi. The presence of other pollutants aggravates these effects.

When the first signs of tree damage were noted in West Germany, suggestions of a pollution link were dismissed. But by the late 1980s, when almost 90 per cent of the country's fir trees showed similar effects, the evidence was conclusive.

Other countries especially badly affected include the UK (two-thirds of its conifers damaged according to a 1987 UN study), the Netherlands and Switzerland (half their forests affected), Czechoslovakia (former forest soils virtually incapable of supporting trees), East Germany (possibly 83 per cent forest damage) and Poland (75 per cent forest damage estimated).[22]

The evidence of severe forest deterioration in West Germany gave rise to a new term, *Waldsterben* ("forest death"). Monitoring showed the number of affected trees nearly doubling between 1983 and 1986, and the annual cost to the country's timber industry is now put at about $800 million. The price eventually paid in Switzerland could be higher; walls and barriers may have to be built to hold back landslides on mountain slopes where trees whose roots once anchored the soils have died.[23]

Waterways and fish
Lakes, rivers and streams suffer, too, as rainfall and runoff from the land acidify waterways; there may be sudden surges during the spring snow melt. As the water becomes more acidic, aquatic ecosystems and food chains are destroyed. Floating plant life and insects, crustaceans and snails die off, while the decomposition of dead matter in the water slows down (the reason why acidified lakes appear so clear).

The effect on fish? Besides wiping out their food sources, acidification interferes with their body-salt systems and, by washing impurities and toxins (including aluminium and heavy metals) into the water from surrounding soils, damages their respiration and metabolism and kills their eggs. "The fish quietly go extinct...They simply fail to reproduce and become less abundant, and older and older, until they die out," one researcher remarks.[24]

The gradual sequence by which acid pollution attacks lake ecosystems means that the effects are often worse than they appear. Adult fish may show few signs of damage, but these creatures are often the last to succumb after their young and their food have all but disappeared.[25] Some eels seem able to survive in badly acidified waters, as can mosses and algae, which often form a thick carpet on lake and river beds.

Twenty thousand of Sweden's 85,000 lakes are acidified, and 5,000 are without fish. Four-fifths of the lakes in southern Norway are biologically dead or listed as critical, and half the freshwater fish in the region have died. Fish in up to a third of northern UK lakes and rivers have been badly affected. Fifty thousand Canadian lakes are threatened, and many thousands in the eastern USA have been called virtual "fish graveyards".[26] Other countries hit by the acidification of inland waters are Belgium, Finland, the Netherlands and West Germany.

Other damage

Acidic clouds that cling to hillsides are wiping out communities of dragonflies and frogs, and acid precipitation also has destructive impacts on food crops, human health and the built environment. Crops suffer in a similar way to trees. With other airborne pollution, acidification attacks leaf cells, reducing photosynthesis and plant growth. Destroying micro-organisms in the soil, it deprives crops of nutrients and may make some more prone to pest damage. Tomatoes, potatoes, barley and beans are all vulnerable, and agricultural damage due to air pollution costs hundreds of millions of dollars a year in Europe and up to \$3 billion in the USA.[27]

As for human health, acid smogs have been linked to the aggravation of heart, lung and respiratory diseases. SO_2 poisoning can cause gastrointestinal disorders, conjunctivitis and anaemia; large doses can asphyxiate and kill. Atmospheric nitrogen oxides combine with oxygen to produce nitrogen dioxide (NO_2), a poison that attacks lung tissue and increases susceptibility to viral infection. Acid rain increases the levels of toxic metals in edible fish and drinking water, and acidified water can dissolve copper and lead from piping, a source of diarrhoea and poisoning. Where all these effects combine, as in the badly polluted heavy-industry areas of Eastern Europe, they may cause circulatory and respiratory illness, cancers and child deformities.[28]

Damage to the built environment can be severe. In Athens the stonework of the Parthenon is said to have been corroded more by air pollution in the last twenty-five years than during the previous two thousand. The face on Egypt's Sphinx is being eaten away, as are the facade of the Taj Mahal, the ornamentation on historic Krakow's walls and roofs and upper stonework on St Paul's Cathedral. Modern concrete-and-metal structures are affected, too; forty-six people were killed when a sulphur-corroded steel road-bridge collapsed in the USA in 1967. Water and sewage systems, telecommunications and electricity networks and the contents of libraries and archives also suffer damage connected to atmospheric pollution.[29]

In poor countries the poisonous and corrosive atmosphere is all the worse because of the use of heavily leaded petrol in inefficient vehicles, the widespread burning of low-grade coal and charcoal, the concentration of industry in a few regions and the lack of pollution controls. Energy consumption is growing rapidly in the South; world fossil fuel consumption could increase threefold before the year 2050, doubling annual sulphur emissions.[30]

Action

Atmosphere and climate

If all greenhouse gas emissions ceased today, global warming would still probably continue irreversibly for years. "Once the earth gets warmer," the Worldwatch Institute tells us, "there will be no practical way of cooling it." Likewise with acid rain: "Europe may be experiencing an immense change to irreversible acidification, the remedial costs of which could be beyond economic reach." Only ozone depletion, it seems, is not permanent; scientists say that the ozone layer could probably restore itself after about a hundred years once all ozone-destroying gas emissions were halted.[31]

The outlook is indeed worrying. The IPCC has forecast that climate changes over the next sixty years will probably be so fast that "nature will be unable to adapt, and man will not be able to control them". Dr Mick Kelly of the University of East Anglia believes that "If global warming is to be dealt with, it requires the same commitment that reached the moon."[32]

Preventive measures
The UN Environment Programme has called for more research into rising seas and for international planning of coastal defences. The Netherlands and the south-eastern US states are already strengthening their sea defences. The Dutch spend 6 per cent of their GNP on sea dikes, but few countries in the South will be able to finance such work. Will action be taken in time?

Worldwide it could cost trillions of dollars to protect the land from rising seas and storms, to relocate vulnerable coastal and island communities and to cope with food shortages caused by climate change and flooding. More food self-sufficiency will give countries a better chance. "Migration corridors" (preserved wilderness zones leading towards cooler latitudes, encouraged with tree planting) may be of some help in allowing ecosystems to move in response to warmer temperatures.

The worst effects of global warming may be avoidable if we can hold down the temperature increase to less than 2°C over the next century; this will require a 60 to 80 per cent cut in all greenhouse gas emissions. Atmospheric CO_2 emissions will have to be reduced by 1 or 2 per cent each year until 2075 by halting deforestation, limiting coal and oil burning, promoting energy efficiency and using renewable energy. This is no small task in view of predictions that atmospheric CO_2 levels will more than double by then if nothing is done. Speed is essential; smaller CO_2 emission reductions now will have greater effect than larger ones later.[33]

Planting new trees

Deforestation and reforestation have already been considered (see Chapter 6). Forestation of an area the size of the USA would absorb perhaps half the world's annual fuel-burning CO_2 emissions. European Community environment commissioner Carlo Ripa di Meana believes that this could be funded from a fossil fuel tax or by levies on forest clearing. However, few large continuous areas of land are available; instead, tree planting must take place wherever possible – in regional forests, roadside and wasteground woodlands, fields, parks and gardens.[34]

Curbing CO_2

An agreement signed in 1988 committed countries to curb CO_2 emissions by a fifth by the year 2005; but Japan, the Soviet Union, the UK and the USA would not commit themselves to reductions, calling for more scientific evidence. "We know enough right now to begin action," commented UN Environment Programme director Dr Mostafa Tolba, criticizing this refusal to face facts. By mid-1990 the UK government had at last accepted that global warming was proven, leaving the USA (the world's biggest CO_2 producer) and Japan as the only major industrialized countries rejecting the need for firm action on greenhouse gas emissions.[35]

What greenhouse-gas-curbing measures can we take? First

there is simple fuel substitution. Natural gas releases 25 per cent less CO_2 and N_2O when burned than oil and 40 per cent less than coal. With at least eighty years of supplies worldwide even with rising consumption, gas should be substituted for coal and oil where possible. Advanced gas turbines are efficient and suitable for small power stations.[36]

The main approach to cutting down CO_2 and N_2O fuel-burning emissions, however, must be to burn less fuel. Since the oil price rises of the 1970s, energy efficiency in industrialized countries has improved by about a fifth – with the result, says the Worldwatch Institute, that "The world has saved far more energy than it has gained from all new sources of supply combined." Technology is available to increase efficiency by at least 50 per cent more, because Japanese industry is twice as energy efficient as its Western competitors.[37]

Energy efficiency
Energy efficiency is said to be up to seven times more cost-effective in reducing CO_2 emissions than building a nuclear power station. Studies in the UK have found that cuts in energy consumption of as much as 60 per cent could be made without lowering living standards, by reducing heat losses from buildings, using more efficient appliances, enhancing motor fuel performance, improving public transport and increasing power generation efficiency. Up to three-quarters of the fuel burned in most power stations is wasted, accounting in the UK for a fifth of all CO_2 released. Combined heat and power ("CHP") systems – already used in many cities around the world – utilize most of this waste heat for space heating in buildings, reducing the gas emissions.[38]

Better insulation and double glazing can halve heating bills and mean significant CO_2 savings. Swedish triple-glazed homes are said to be warmer and to use less winter fuel than double-glazed homes in the milder UK climate. The US Department of Energy has developed one-way window coatings for offices that allow light and heat to penetrate but retain heat in the building.[39]

Among electrical appliances, fluorescent lightbulbs last ten times longer than conventional incandescent bulbs and use under a third of the electricity (the higher price is recouped during their lifetime). Introduced worldwide, these bulbs could curb CO_2 emissions by an estimated 500 million tonnes a year.

The best mass-produced refrigerators and other appliances are five times more energy efficient than the average. The UN Environment Programme believes that energy-efficient refrigeration could save the USA the electricity produced by eighteen coal-fired power stations. The US government has banned the sale of low-efficiency household appliances after 1992.[40]

Recycling

Recycling is both energy- and cost-effective, as Japan has proved, where almost half of all industrial materials are recycled. The industrial use of recycled steel, copper and aluminium can produce fuel savings of 50, 90 and 95 per cent respectively. Even the smaller energy gains from recycling glass and paper help.[41]

Government action

Market forces will not be enough to bring about an energy-efficient future. "Japan...the world's third largest economy, is one of the most efficient simply because both government and industry have emphasized energy efficiency to make their resource-poor country more competitive," argues the Worldwatch Institute.[42] Governments can do a great deal: tax fossil fuels according to their CO_2 emissions (a "carbon tax"); set higher efficiency standards for lighting, electrical appliances, vehicles and buildings; legislate to encourage energy conservation programmes; eliminate financial incentives that encourage fuel burning by large consumers; give tax incentives for energy-saving investment; offer free energy audits for buildings; promote recycling with loans and grants; set up information-labelling schemes; price-subsidize energy-saving appliances; and run relevant public information campaigns.

Restoring a balance

There is a moral argument, too. The billion or so inhabitants of the industrialized countries use four-fifths of the planet's commercial energy. While average electricity consumption worldwide is about 2 kilowatts per person, North Americans use an average of 10 kW and people in China just 0.8 kW each. According to research in Brazil, however, a healthy person needs the equivalent of just over a kilowatt of energy (depending on climate) to provide themselves with heating, lighting, hygiene, food and leisure activities. Produced and used efficiently, this much power could be available to all without harmful consequences.[43]

For two centuries the rich countries have spewed out greenhouse gases while their poor neighbours have not. Now the situation is turning critical, change must start in the rich countries. An international fund giving interest-free loans (perhaps financed from Northern carbon taxes) may be needed to help poor countries switch to the "low energy path" that the Brundtland Commission, among others, has accepted as crucial.[44]

Nuclear power

Great hopes were once pinned on nuclear power. Yet despite all the money poured into nuclear research and development for the last half-century, the risks remain large and the benefits few. Nuclear power is the most expensive form of mass electricity generation. Its enormous "back-end" costs are only just emerging. When reactors finish their working lives they must be dismantled or encased in concrete-and-steel tombs; the radioactive material needs careful storage for thousands of years. The construction, maintenance, transportation, uranium mining and waste storage that nuclear power involves themselves consume energy and cause CO_2 emissions. Besides, it would take thousands more nuclear power stations to meet the world's energy needs, producing vast mountains of long-lived radioactive waste.

In addition to the health dangers of nuclear power, political problems arise. One is the question of international proliferation, another the sort of overcentralized and security-obsessed social arrangements that the industry tends to require. The Brundtland Commission was surely right to conclude: "The generation of nuclear power is only justifiable if there are solid solutions to the presently unsolved problems to which it gives rise." Friends of the Earth's view is that using nuclear power to solve global warming would be like "replacing a migraine with a gastric ulcer".[45]

Alternative energy

Renewable energy has great potential as a substitute for fossil fuels, although policy-makers and big business have generally been dismissive. Given a reasonable level of research and development funding, renewables would be cheap, reliable and widely used.

Solar panels are effective even in relatively cool climates (such as Milton Keynes in the UK), where they can be fitted to walls and roofs to supplement conventional heating. Solar collectors provide domestic water heating in Cyprus, Israel and Japan; low-cost solar lighting is being introduced in the Dominican Republic. National building regulations should specify that homes and offices are designed to include panels for supplementary solar heating.

Electricity-generating wind turbines are used in more than ninety countries, many of which are developing new "wind farms". Especially suitable for coastal locations, 400,000 potential wind farm sites have been listed by the European Commission. Denmark is the world leader, but wind generators are now manufactured as far afield as Egypt and India. Wave and tidal power also have potential, although wave power has been badly neglected in the UK since the government withdrew research funding in 1982 on the basis of misleading costings. In fact, wave power is significantly cheaper than nuclear energy.[46]

Small-dam hydroelectricity is increasingly turned to in the South for local energy needs and may come back into favour in the North. Cheap and simple to construct, with few environmental ill effects, "micro-hydros" are suitable for generating power close to where it is needed in rural areas. France and West Germany now have thousands of small dams. China, which has 90,000, reportedly produces 40 per cent of its electricity with them, the equivalent of the output of several nuclear power stations. Many other countries use this technology.

Then there is biomass – energy from organic matter. The burning of methane (from fermented organic wastes) as a domestic and industrial fuel is well established in the South. Methane is often also tapped from landfill dumps and burned in the North. Brazil successfully runs many of its motor vehicles on ethanol, made from fermented sugarcane; a similar fuel, methanol, looks set for introduction in California.[47]

Renewable sources could provide an estimated 13 billion kilowatts of energy a year, about as much as the world's present total demand. Governments and the international community should set up and fund more agencies to promote renewables. Energy substitution may appear expensive but can generate wealth. Brazil's ethanol programme has created nearly half a million jobs, and the US energy conservation industry has an annual turnover of $10 billion.[48]

Less motor car use

Motor vehicles waste a great deal of fuel, producing close to four times their own weight in CO_2 each year and contributing 15 per cent of world CO_2 emissions. The faster they go, the more wasteful they are. Lightweight ceramic engine parts and plastic body components improve fuel efficiency, but there is no technology to stop vehicle CO_2 emissions without a change of fuel. (Catalytic converters, which reduce acid pollution, may actually increase vehicles' CO_2 output through higher fuel consumption.) Although biomass fuels may help, motor vehicle use as a whole must be discouraged.

Governments can contribute by improving and promoting public transport, phasing out road-building programmes, eliminating free city-centre car parking (except for people with disabilities and residents), park-and-ride schemes, imposing a fuel tax to discourage wasteful driving and to promote smaller-engined fuel-efficient vehicles and car sharing, eliminating subsidies for business car use, setting lower speed limits, developing waterways (rivers, canals and coastal waters) for goods transportation, running public education campaigns, encouraging cycling and walking and fostering the inter-siting of workplaces and homes to reduce commuting.

These measures will work. In the USA following the 1973 oil crisis, lowering of the speed limit to 55 mph and the increased use of smaller, more fuel-efficient cars reduced petrol consumption by 20 per cent between 1978 and 1984.[49] (Oil has since become cheaper, speed limits have eased, cars are bigger, and gas-guzzling is back.)

Anti-pollution traffic laws recently enacted by California (said to consume more petrol than every country in the world except the USA and the USSR) may be the shape of things to come. Large firms will have to reduce car journeys made by employees by setting up car pools and encouraging people to work four-day weeks or telecommute from home. Car-pool lanes and car-free zones are to be designated; and many of the state's buses, cars and trucks will switch to methanol or natural gas fuels.[50]

CFCs
Emissions of the four other main greenhouse gases also need
to be cut. Falling fossil fuel consumption and the introduction
of clean-burning technologies to combat acid rain will help
reduce the production of N_2O and low-level ozone. Less
chemical-intensive farming and more organic cultivation will
cut N_2O evaporation from chemical fertilizers.

To reduce methane emissions, livestock numbers will have to
decrease. Large commercial ranches rather than the small herds
of low-income pastoralists should make the sacrifice. Northern
governments have yet to recognize the need for a low- meat diet.
Methane generated by decomposing paper and other refuse in
landfill sites can be extracted and burned as fuel. Better still
would be to waste less paper in packaging and recycle more.

The rapid phasing out of CFCs is necessary to ease global
warming and to save the ozone layer. A halt to CFC manufacture by the end of the century would produce an estimated 15
per cent decrease in the greenhouse effect. Eighty-one countries
are committed to ending CFC use by the year 2000. In addition,
use of the other ozone destroyers – halons and some CFC
substitutes – should also be halted.[51] CFC aerosols were
banned in the USA in 1978 and are being eliminated in Western
Europe. Fast food chains use fewer CFC-blown burger cartons,
and the world's largest CFC maker, DuPont, is terminating
production. There are plenty of alternative packaging and
building insulation materials but as yet few substitutes for CFC
coolant; ammonia and propane are possibilities. Atmospheric
leaks can be reduced by CFC recovery and recycling from old
refrigerators and air conditioning into new units. Increasing
numbers of manufacturers recycle CFC coolant.

CFC use is predicted to grow in the South unless firm action
is taken. The 1990 London ozone conference agreed to provide
China, India and other Southern countries with funds and
technology to produce CFC substitutes. Yet even a worldwide
phase-out by 2000 will probably be too late to save another
fifth of the ozone layer.

Acid pollution
As for acid pollution: energy efficiency and conservation, more
use of gas, a switch to renewables and reductions in motor
vehicle traffic will all help slow the damage, but additional
measures are needed.

A short-term answer to acidity is to spray forests and inland waters with powdered calcium, limestone, magnesium and other alkalies. This deals with symptons rather than causes, however; it needs to be done repeatedly and cannot reverse "forest death". About 3,000 Swedish lakes have been limed at a cost of over $20 million, and similar work has been done elsewhere in Europe and in Canada.

In 1987 the Thirty Per Cent Club agreement on acid rain came into force; countries committed themselves to SO_2 emission cutbacks of at least 30 per cent by 1993. (The UK and the USA, major sulphur emitters, would not sign.) Austria, Belgium, France, Luxembourg, Sweden and Switzerland have already reduced SO_2 emissions by up to 50 per cent since 1980. The European Community has since agreed on overall cuts of 57 per cent for SO_2 by 2003 and 30 per cent for NO_x by 1998 – both targets criticized as too little and too late by the Worldwatch Institute, which wants 90 per cent curbs for both chemicals.[52]

Cleaner power stations

"Scrubbers" (flue-gas desulphurization equipment) reduce the airbone sulphur emitted by coal- and oil-fired power stations. New electricity generating plants should be built with this technology, and existing plants can be converted. After undertaking to fit scrubbers at its main coal-fired power plants, the UK government has backed out of the commitment and will instead import low-sulphur South African coal, a less effective way of cutting SO_2 emissions.

Fluid bed combustion is said to be the most complete and cleanest way of burning coal, suitable even for low-grade, polluting coal. The coal is ground into a fine powder, combustion taking place over a bed of ash or sand through which an airstream is blown, making the burning more complete. The addition of powdered limestone absorbs sulphur and reduces emissions further. The technology is being introduced in a number of countries.

Industrial emission controls have sometimes been opposed on grounds of cost, but the price of not doing enough could be far greater. "It is difficult to put a precise monetary value on acidified forests and lakes, dead animals and plants, reduced rural vistas, corroded buildings, or impaired human health," comments the writer John McCormick.[53]

Catalytic converters

The fitting of catalytic converters to motor vehicles is essential in the battle against acid pollution. The "cat", a cylinder containing a ceramic honeycomb coated with precious metals, eliminates up to 90 per cent of the emitted nitrogen oxides, hydrocarbons and carbon monoxide, triggering the conversion of NO_x to water and nitrogen.

Converters have been compulsory for new cars in the USA since the early 1980s; the EC follows suit after 1992. Many manufacturers now fit them automatically. Costing $100 or so each (too much at present for poor countries), they cannot be used with leaded fuel, which governments must ensure is taxed heavily enough to encourage the speedy change to unleaded. "Cats" have to be replaced after about ten years; nobody knows how long supplies of platinum and palladium will last. Given these drawbacks, the adoption of converters worldwide is hard to envisage. Less motor vehicle use is what we must aim for.

Getting Involved

Related subjects covered elsewhere in this book include: development needs in poor countries – Chapter 2; the health risks of nuclear power and air pollution – Chapter 3; deforestation and community forestry – Chapter 6; drought – Chapter 7. To find out more about the greenhouse effect, the ozone layer, acid rain and how we can deal with them, see "Recommended Reading" (pages 324–9).

Consumer and lifestyle choices

Where fuel and energy resources are concerned, think of yourself as a *conserver*, not a consumer. In the home and workplace, make sure your building is properly insulated (without CFCs). Draught excluders and self-assembly secondary double glazing are the easiest-to-fit and lowest-cost way of improving domestic energy efficiency; if you pay for full double glazing to be fitted, it will take between ten and sixty years to recoup the outlay. Use as few electrical appliances in the home as possible. In the UK, larger gas and electricity showrooms and the government Energy Efficiency Office (Room 1312, Thames House South,

Millbank, London SW1P 4QJ) can advise on energy savings.

Conserve energy and heat
Use gas heating rather than coal or oil. Use heating only when it is really necessary, and set temperature controls and thermostats as low as possible. Wash at lower temperatures and dry clothes in the open air. Avoid energy-wasteful fan and convection heaters. Fit thermostats to central heating radiators. Consider installing a heat pump such as the warm air circulator made by the Centre for Alternative Technology (address below) in the UK; the pump extracts warm air from up near the ceiling and recirculates it to lower levels.

Find out about installing supplementary solar heating panels. There are a number of solar heat collectors on the market. In the UK, information and advice are available from the Solar Trade Association, Brackenhurst, Greenham Common South, Newbury RG15 8HH. To see solar heating at work in the UK, visit the Centre for Alternative Technology.

Buy energy-efficient domestic electrical appliances. *The Green Comsumer Guide* by John Elkington and Julia Hailes (London: Gollancz, 1988) and the UK consumers' magazine *Which?* compare brands for energy consumption. Energy-saving fluorescent lightbulbs are ideal for places where lights are left on for long periods, such as stairways; they cost more to buy than conventional lightbulbs do but have lower running costs and last much longer. These bulbs are available in the UK by mail order from the Centre for Alternative Technology, from Chalkline Energy, White Cottage, Canalside, Harefield, Middx UB9 6JA, and from First Light, 28 Eastwood Road, Birmingham B12 9NB.

Try to avoid using electric batteries, even rechargeable or "green" ones. Batteries use up to fifty times more energy to produce than they give back in use.

Recycling schemes
Support metal, glass and paper recycling schemes, all of which can produce major energy savings. Paper recycling and the composting of vegetable waste matter also reduce the quantity of greenhouse-gas methane produced by rotting garbage. Ask your local council and supermarkets to provide more recycling facilities. The use of returnable glass containers would provide far greater energy savings than recycled glass. See the "Getting Involved" section in Chapter 7 for more about recycling and re-use.

Organic foods
Eat more organic foods (no chemical fertilizers, fewer N_2O emissions) and less meat (fewer livestock, less methane). Try to buy local produce where possible (less energy consumed in transportation). Plant trees (to absorb CO_2) and support reforestation efforts overseas (see Chapter 6).

Avoid CFCs
Many manufacturers now produce refrigerators and air-conditioning units using less CFC insulation and coolant, and some retailers will take in your appliance to recycle the CFCs. Use CFC-free aerosols, packaging and building insulation in your home and at your workplace. For information and advice on CFCs in the UK, contact Friends of the Earth or see *The Green Consumer Guide*.

Less driving/more cycling
To reduce your contribution to CO_2 emissions further, cut down on your private motor travel. Reduce the total amount of travelling you do, by taking care of as many needs as possible locally; this will save fossil fuel energy and pollution and save you money, as well as allowing you a more relaxed and healthy life. Try to work as close as you can to your home.

Walk, cycle, car-share or use public transport rather than driving. Car ownership is expensive; and over-reliance on cars is unhealthy and, in urban areas, time-wasting. Many people find it better not to own a car but to hire or borrow one or take a cab when they really need one. (If you must use a car, choose a smaller, fuel-efficient vehicle; drive reasonably slowly; use unleaded petrol and a catalytic converter; respect the rights of cyclists and pedestrians.) If your employer pays a mileage allowance to car users, ask for a mileage allowance for cyclists, too. In the UK, cyclists can obtain advice, information and road insurance (in the first two cases) from:

London Cycling Campaign, 3 Stamford Street, London SE1 9NT (071-928 7220).
National Bike Club, ROSPA, Cannon House, The Priory Queensway, Birmingham B4 6BS (021-200 2461).

New Cyclist magazine, The Lees Stables, Berwickshire, Scotland TD12 4BR.

Environmental Transport Association
In 1990 a new UK transport campaign was launched with World
Wide Fund for Nature backing to encourage environment-
friendly transport: the Environmental Transport Association
(address below). This Association offers: low-premium motor
insurance for private car owners who drive less than 8,000 miles
a year, whose cars are fitted with catalytic converters and who
have passed the advanced driving test; full insurance for cyclists
including a bicycle recovery service; and a 24-hour helpline
giving journey-planning advice. The Association also intends
to campaign for improved government investment in rail and
bus transport.

Community and political action

For youngsters
WWF in the UK has produced an imaginative Energy Education Pack for secondary schoolteachers, focusing on energy
consumption in industry, the home and transport, energy
waste and the environmental and other costs involved. The
pack costs £14.50 including p&p and is available from WWF-
UK Education Distribution, PO Box 963, Slough SL2 3RS.
Youngsters who want to become involved in campaigning for
energy conservation and safe energy sources can join Earth
Action, the youth section of FOE (address below).

UK government
To find out more about what the government could do in the
UK to set energy efficiency standards, you can obtain the booklet
Setting Standards for Energy Efficiency for £1 from Friends of
the Earth. Join in FOE UK's energy campaign: when you next
go into an electrical shop, ask why they don't have a labelling
system for appliances; write to your MP, the Secretary of State
for Energy (Department of Energy, Thames House South,
Millbank, London SW1P 4QJ) and the government's Energy
Efficiency Office (Room 1312 at Thames House South); raising
points like these:

• Immediate action is needed to tackle global warming.

- Energy efficiency is a cost-effective and simple way to reduce CO_2 emissions.
- The USA already has a comprehensive system of appliance efficiency standard laws.
- People want to buy energy-efficient appliances but need more information; a national product-labelling system should be introduced.
- Manufacturers should be persuaded to produce and advertise low-energy lightbulbs.
- Funding of the Energy Efficiency Office should be increased.
- Grants for home insulation should be reintroduced.
- The government should subsidize energy audits for homes and workplaces.

Write to your area electricity company (address in the phone book) and ask what they are doing to promote the development of renewable energy sources.

Campaign against nuclear power
Nuclear power may become a thing of the past in the UK but not yet. The more taxpayers' money is spent on it, the less there seems to be available to develop renewable energy sources. The Central Electricity Generating Board and the new state-owned company Nuclear Electric still want the go-ahead for a new nuclear power station at Hinkley, Somerset. To help prevent this, join the Stop Hinkley Expansion campaign, Hockpitt Farm, Nether Stowey, Bridgwater, Somerset TA5 1EX.

Campaign against nuclear power (on economic, environmental, health, safety and political grounds) and for greater investment in renewables. Send your letters to your MP, your MEP, the Secretary of State for Energy at the Department of Energy (address above) and the press, or raise the subject on radio phone-ins. Point out:

- how much money has been invested in nuclear reaeach and development;
- how many problems – cost, health, safety, environmental damage, long-term waste-storage, political unacceptability – remain;
- how little money has been invested in renewable energy research and development up till now and how great the potential could be;

- the UK has Europe's best potential for wind power, which could produce up to a fifth of our energy needs.

To find out more about renewable energy, contact Friends of the Earth for their Energy Resources List or write for information about the Ideal Energy Exhibition to Stop Hinkley Expansion (address above).

Environment-friendly transport
Campaign for environment-friendly transport. In the UK find out about FOE's or the WWF's transport campaigns or join Transport 2000 (address below) or a local public transport users' group. Lobby your local council for cycle lanes and traffic calming in residential streets; ask for mileage allowances for council employees who use bicycles as well as for those who drive cars.

Little has been done to halt the expansion of motor traffic. The growing number of vehicles in the UK could emit as much CO_2 as all the country's power stations in sixty years' time. If you agree that this is the wrong direction for our transport systems, write to your MP and MEP, to the Secretary of State for Transport (Department of Transport, 2 Marsham Street, London SW1P 3EB) and to the press, or raise the subject on radio phone-ins. Points you could make include:

- It will be impossible to cut CO_2 emissions as long as the amount of motor traffic keeps increasing.
- Delays caused by traffic congestion cost a great deal of money.
- New roadbuilding tends just to increase the number of vehicles on the road.
- More urban pedestrian precincts and cycle lanes will make towns and cities safer and more pleasant and help reduce crime.
- Other countries are starting to develop light railways and tramways as an alternative to road traffic, as well as investing more generously in rail transport.
- There should be tax concessions for company bicycles and season ticket users rather than for company cars.
- Tax concessions should also be given for the purchase of cars fitted with catalytic converters.
- Other useful measures would be stricter parking controls

(including more wheel-clamping, fines and licence endorse-
ments), more bus lanes and new traffic rules giving buses
priority over other traffic.
- It is cheaper in the long run and far more energy-efficient to
transport goods by rail and waterways than by road.

Organizations

Organizations involved in the battle against global warming,
ozone depletion and acid rain and campaigning for safe energy
include:

UK and Irish Republic
Association for the Conservation of Energy, 9 Sherlock Mews,
London W1M 3RH (071-935 1495).
British Wind Energy Association, Climatic Research Unit,
University of East Anglia, Norwich NR4 7JT.
Centre for Alternative Technology, Llangwern Quarry, Mach-
ynlleth, Powys SY20 9A2, Wales (0654-702400).
Environmental Transport Association, 15A George Street,
Croydon CR0 1LA (081-666 0445).
Friends of the Earth, 26–28 Underwood Street, London N1
7JQ (071-490 1555).
Friends of the Earth Scotland, Bonnington Mill, 70–72
Newhaven Road, Edinburgh, EH6 5QG (031-554 9977).
Greenpeace, 30–31 Islington Green, London N1 8XE
(071-354 5100).
Greenpeace Ireland, 44 Upper Mount Street, Dublin 2, Irish
Republic.
Transport 2000, Walkden House, 10 Melton Street, London
NW1 2EJ (071-388 8386).
Women's Environmental Network, 287 City Road, London
EC1V 1LA (071-490 2511).
World Wide Fund for Nature, Panda House, Weyside Park,
Godalming, Surrey GU7 1XR (0483-426444).

USA and Canada
American Council for an Energy Efficient Economy, 1001
Connecticut Avenue NW, Washington, DC 20036, USA.
Atmospheric Environment Service, 4905 Dufferin Street,
Downsview, Ontario M3H 5T4.

Canadian Coalition for Nuclear Responsibility, PO Box 236, Snowden, Montreal, Quebec H3X 3T4, Canada.

Canadian Coalition on Acid Rain, Suite 504, 112 St Clair Avenue West, Toronto, Ontario M4V 2Y3, Canada.

Climate Action Network, c/o Friends of the Earth, Suite 701, 251 Laurier Avenue W, Ottawa, Ontario K1P 5J6, Canada.

Energy Probe, 100 College Street, Toronto, Ontario M5G 1L5, Canada.

Environment Action, 1525 New Hampshire Avenue NW, Washington, DC 20036, USA.

Environmental Defense Fund, 257 Park Avenue South, New York, NY 10010, USA.

Global Greenhouse Network, Suite 630, 1130 17th Street NW, Washington, DC 20036, USA.

Greenpeace, 1436 U Street NW, Washington, DC 20009, USA.

Greenpeace, 578 Bloor Street W, Toronto, Ontario M6G 1K1, Canada.

Nuclear Information and Resource Service, Suite 601, 1424 16th Street NW, Washington, DC 20036, USA.

World Wide Fund for Nature, Suite 201, 60 St Clair Avenue East, Toronto, Ontario M4T 1N5, Canada.

World Wide Fund for Nature, 1250 24th Street NW, Washington, DC 20037, USA.

Australia and New Zealand

Australian Conservation Society, 340 Gore Street, Fitzroy, Victoria, Australia.

Campaign against Nuclear Power, PO Box 238, North Quay, Brisbane, Queensland 4000, Australia.

Climate for Change, 42 Waitohu Road, York Bay, Eastbourne, Wellington, New Zealand.

Friends of the Earth, PO Box 530E, Melbourne, Victoria 3001, and GPO Box 1875, Canberra, New South Wales, Australia.

Friends of the Earth, PO Box 39-065, Auckland West, New Zealand.

Greenpeace, Private Bag No. 6, 134 Broadway, Sydney, New South Wales 2007, Australia.

Greenpeace, Private Bag, Wellesley Street PO, Auckland 1, New Zealand.

Rainforest Information Centre, PO Box 368, Lismore, New South Wales 2480, Australia.

Total Environment Centre, 18 Argyle Street, Sydney, New South Wales 2000, Australia.

World Wide Fund for Nature, PO Box 6237, Wellington, New Zealand.

World Wide Fund for Nature, Level 17, St Martin's Tower, 31 Market Street, GPO Box 528, Sydney, New South Wales, Australia.

Africa and Asia (Commonwealth)

Centre for Science and Environment, 807 Vishal Bhavan, 95 Nehru Place, New Delhi 110019, India.

Friends of the Earth, PO Box 3794, Ghana.

Friends of the Earth/Sahabat Alam Malaysia, 43 Salween Road, 10050 Penang, Malaysia.

Friends of the Earth, PO Box 4028, Boroko, Papua New Guinea.

Friends of the Earth, PM Bag 950, 33 Robert Town, Freetown, Sierra Leone.

Institute for Environment and Development Studies/Friends of the Earth Bangladesh, PO Box 4222, Ramna Dhaka 1000, Bangladesh.

Kenya Energy Non-Governmental Organizations, PO Box 48197, Nairobi, Kenya.

Planetary Citizens' Council for Peace, Development and the Environment, Robinson Road, PO Box 2753, Singapore 9047.

Research Foundation for Science, Technology and Natural Resources Policy, 105 Rajpur Road, Dehradun 248001, India.

Tanzania Environmental Society, PO Box 1309, Dar es Salaam, Tanzania.

TATA Energy Research Institute, 7 Jor Bagh, New Delhi 110003, India.

9. Habitats and Species – Nature under Siege

"No generation in the past has faced the prospect of mass extinction within its lifetime...No generation in the future will ever face a similar challenge; if this present generation fails to get to grips with the task, the damage will have been done, and there will be no 'second try'."

Norman Myers[1]

The Problem

The Earth is billions of years old. Human beings are relative newcomers, with a history of less than 100,000 years. Yet human activity over the next half-century could cause the destruction of a quarter of the planet's plant and animal species, including many that have never been named or studied. This will be almost certainly the greatest extinction of life since the advent of *Homo sapiens* and perhaps the most epoch-making since the dinosaurs died out 65 million years ago. What can we do to prevent the worst predictions from being fulfilled?

The importance of biological diversity

It was once thought that there were fewer than 5 million living species, but tropical rainforest research suggests that there could be as many as 30 million, the majority of them insects. Would it matter much if we destroyed a tenth or even a quarter of all these animal and plant forms? It could matter a great deal.

Species co-operation
Species develop their characteristics over thousands of generations in response to the environment. With each species seeking out a "niche" where it is as free as possible from

competition with others, nature makes the maximum use of its opportunities. Plants and animals survive through a network of relationships with each other and with the environment; in fact, living species *are* much of the environment. Separate a species from its essential surroundings and its days are probably numbered. The habitat may also suffer, because of the species' crucial role in the ecosystem.

Contradicting the nineteenth-century concept of the law of the jungle, according to which living things battle mercilessly for supremacy, evolution is today increasingly thought of in terms of co-operation. The more the natural world is investigated, the more the pattern of interdependence emerges. Some writers, such as the former NASA scientist James Lovelock with his Gaia hypothesis, consider the planet and its species to be a sort of super-life-form in its own right.[2]

Animals depend directly on plants for energy and oxygen and indirectly on the way plants maintain and anchor the soils, modify extremes of climate, recycle water and help control pests and diseases. In return, many plants, including some rainforest trees, depend on animals in order to reproduce. Insects, attracted by petals, scent and nectar, carry the pollen of most flowering plants from flower to flower; birds and other animals eat the fleshy fruits of some plants and scatter the seeds with their droppings; salt-marsh grasses rely on mussels to recycle the nutrients they feed on. In some cases a single insect species may be essential to a plant's reproduction.

Even relationships between predator and prey are a two-way affair. In return for its source of food, the predator helps maintain the health of the prey species by killing off old, weak or sick individuals and preventing the population from outstripping its food supply. Apparent pests usually have a function – in the case of Central Africa's tsetse fly, keeping the region free of the livestock that would overgraze and erode the soils.

To appreciate the damage done by the loss of a single species, consider the South Asian frog. In great demand as a luxury food in some countries but a predator of insects in its native habitat, the frog's numbers are now in decline. This has meant increased insect damage to rice crops, causing Bangladeshi and Indian farmers to use more DDT and other insecticides. Greater numbers of people now suffer from pesticide poisoning and, equally as bad, from malaria, carried by the mosquitoes the frogs would have controlled.[3] The elimination of coyotes from several canyons in the US west had a similarly unexpected but logical result: a decline in local bird populations, because the coyotes had kept in check the foxes and house cats that preyed on the birds.

Disrupting the system

Human technology looks pretty limited when contrasted with the vast diversity of nature's life-supporting network, but the web of life also has its limits. The more species are depleted in numbers or lost for good, the more their ecosystem relationships are vulnerable to disruption; and an accumulation of local disruptions eventually produces major ecological change. As the Worldwatch Institute observes: "Any development that depletes the world's resource base without providing for its replenishment cannot be sustained for long." The Indian physicist Vandana Shiva supports this view: "Diversity of living resources...is critical to soil and water conservation, it is critical for satisfying the diversity of needs of people...and the diversity of nature's needs in reproducing herself."[4]

Nature's wealth

We have only just begun to tap nature's potential. Over half the food people eat comes from just three plants – maize, wheat and rice – and nine-tenths of human nutritional needs are supplied by thirty food crops; yet there are said to be 75,000 species of edible plants. Locally used tropical plants with significant food potential include fruit-bearing trees of the Amazon, palms that produce edible oils, the New Guinea winged bean, the potato-like taro and, said to be the world's best-tasting fruit, the mangosteen. Unforeseen solutions to the world's food problems may lie ahead in this vast gene pool.

Natural diversity is used to revitalize domesticated crops. Modern monocrops, inherently vulnerable to pests and diseases, need regular cross-breeding with wild genetic strains or with the robust traditional varieties grown by peasant farmers. After a sample of Indian wild rice was interbred with commercial strains to develop resistance to a disease that had destroyed 100,000 hectares of rice in the 1970s, the new hybrid became the most widely grown in the world. Canada's wheat stock has been enriched by genes introduced from fourteen countries, while the US economy is said to be "more dependent on foreign sources of germ plasm than it is on foreign sources of oil".[5] Barley, cassava, cocoa, coffee, peanuts, sunflowers, tomatoes and wheat are among the other crops that have been strengthened against pests, diseases and weather damage by cross-breeding with wild relatives.

Animals supply much of the world's food, and not just for the rich. Wild game ("bush meat") has an important traditional dietary role in many African countries, and animal protein eaten by the rural poor in Latin America also comes from wildlife. Among domesticated livestock, cattle and other species are undergoing genetic deterioration because of factory farming and inbreeding to promote commercially desirable characteristics (such as large milk yields). As with commercial food crops, these domesticated stock will have to be interbred with hardy traditional strains if they are to survive. Once genetic diversity is lost, this will become impossible.

Medicinal plants
The natural world is an irreplaceable source of medical treatments, although few of the 20,000 plants identified as having healing properties have as yet been put to use by modern medicine. The $18-billion-a-year world pharmaceutical industry nevertheless relies largely on natural extracts, and a quarter of the commonest medicines are derived from rainforest plants. Antibiotics, aspirin, atropine, digitoxin and other heart drugs, hormones, morphine, quinine, tranquillizers and ulcer treatments, for example, are all plant- or animal-derived. Tropical plants have made important contributions to the treatment of child leukaemia, multiple sclerosis, Parkinson's disease and other muscle disorders, and their derivatives are used in eye and abdominal surgery. The armadillo has helped provide a leprosy treatment; the Florida manatee has assisted haemophilia research; and the African green monkey supplies polio vaccine.

The US National Cancer Institute says that 3,000 plants have anti-cancer properties. One of these, the mayapple used by generations of North American Indians has been successfully incorporated into a cancer drug, while others are undergoing clinical trials. The world's indigenous peoples use thousands of plant species for contraception, a number of which scientists are studying, and the seeds of an Australian rainforest tree are currently being tested as an AIDS drug.[6] The world's rural people rely on natural remedies, and many poor countries in any case cannot afford to import modern medicines. The World Health Organization has launched a programme in low-income countries to make better use of indigenous species and traditional cures.

As with food crops, wild genetic stock is needed to safeguard the effectiveness of modern medicines. The malaria cure quinine, for example, was originally derived from the Peruvian cinchona tree, but since the 1940s scientists have made synthetic substitutes. Now, however, the malarial parasites carried by mosquitoes have developed immunity to the new compounds; with malaria on the rise, doctors need natural quinine again. Luckily the cinchona tree is still around.[7]

Untapped potential
Plants and animals supply the raw materials for countless human activites, and their future potential could be huge. The Chacobe tribe of Bolivia use hundreds of tree species for building materials, fuel and other purposes. In Japan the desert weed jojoba is grown in plantations to produce a waxy substitute for whale oil. The Amazonian babassu palm tree is said to produce oil that can be used in the manufacture of soap, detergents and biodegradable plastics.

Finally, even where we can see no practical use for plants and animals, it is criminal negligence to wipe out millions of them. "Whales...deserve to be saved, not as potential meatballs, but as a source of encouragement to mankind," says the environmentalist Victor Scheffer.[8]

Disappearing worlds

Habitat destruction is the single most important factor in the world's current loss of plant and animal species. Habitats are shrinking because of the effects of rapid human population growth, poverty in the South and excessive consumption in the North. Besides the species they contain, habitats have value in themselves. The world's remaining wilderness areas are a living laboratory, the only places left where uninterrupted evolution can be studied and understood.

The rainforests
Richest in species and most vulnerable are the tropical

rainforests of Central and South America, Central Africa and South-east Asia. Tropical rainforests cover only about 6 per cent of the world's land but contain between one-half and nine-tenths of all species, many of which are endemic (found nowhere else). The majority of the world's insect, reptile and amphibian species are rainforest inhabitants.

A thousand hectares of rainforest are said to contain up to 1,500 species of flowering plant plus 750 tree, 400 bird, 150 butterfly, 125 mammal, 100 reptile and 50 amphibian species. Just one hectare of Peruvian rainforest was found to yield 41,000 insect species, and a single Peruvian tree can support as many kinds of ant as found in the UK. The Amazon Basin contains the world's richest collection of fish; in a single tributary, the Rio Negro, there are said to be several times more species than in all Europe's rivers.[9]

The rainforests were the original source of such taken-for-granted foods as bananas, citrus fruits, coffee, maize, peanuts, pineapple, rice, sugar, tea and the domestic hen, as well of industrial materials such as dyes, latex, lubricants, resins and rubber. Their great age (an estimated 75 million years of continuous evolution) and warm and moist conditions have produced the planet's largest "genetic library". Most rainforest species have short life cycles but reproduce all year round; with this fast turnover of generations, species differentiation occurs rapidly.

Genetic richness makes the rainforests vulnerable, however. As Catherine Caufield writes: "With so many different species, there can be relatively few individuals of each. So, compared with the plants and animals of temperate forests, most tropical species are rare." As an example Caufield cites a 24 hectare patch of rainforest on the Malay peninsula that contains 381 tree species, nearly half of which occur just once.[10] Some rainforest bird species inhabit only one island or mountain range; if that habitat is destroyed, the species will probably be lost.

The burning of the rainforests has been compared to setting fire to a library of priceless unread books. If deforestation is allowed to continue, and only those areas currently protected remain (less than 10 per cent of the original extent), one-fifth of the world's plant and animal species could perish along with the trees.[11]

The usual pattern of forest destruction – by commercial

logging, dam building, mineral extraction, ranching and slash-and-burn agriculture – is piecemeal. Forests become fragmented before they are eliminated, isolating vulnerable animals but allowing opportunistic scavenger species to thrive. Animals may not be able to find mates or may degenerate through inbreeding; plants, too, may fail to reproduce.

Wetlands and coral reefs

Two other species-rich and vulnerable habitats are the wetlands and the coral reefs, which together contain nine-tenths of all aquatic species. Wetlands – marshes, swamps, mangrove forests, flood plains and river estuaries – are the home of plants that purify water by decomposing organic waste matter; they absorb peak river flows and help prevent flooding. River estuaries and mangroves support fish nurseries and feed migrating birds. Mangroves also help prevent coastal erosion. Wetlands provide people with building and industrial materials, salt and sugar, firewood, peat and a place to cultivate rice and oil palms. Flood plains supply grazing lands for livestock, supporting more than a million people. Despite wetlands' greater long-term value when left alone rather than reclaimed for agriculture, industry or urbanization, half of these habitats have already been degraded or destroyed.[12]

Coral reefs are colonies of marine organisms living in warm waters on the layers of limestone secreted over thousands of years by their predecessors. Feeding by day on photosynthetic algae and at night on plankton, corals support a vast array of marine life, including a third of all fish species. The best-known coral reef, Australia's Great Barrier, may be as rich an eco-system as the tropical rainforests. Corals are fragile, however: vulnerable to limestone mining, to silting from soil erosion and dredging, to any pollution that cuts off light and oxygen and to damage by human activities such as tourism and oil and gas exploitation.

Islands

Islands are another species-rich habitat with a large proportion of rare endemic species. Many tropical islands were once covered in forest. Their species are menaced by environmental disruption and by the introduction of non-native competitors or predators against which they have had no chance to develop survival strategies. Three-quarters of all bird and mammal extinctions over the last two centuries have been of island species, the most famous case of which, the elimination of the flightless dodo, took place on Mauritius within 150 years of the arrival of Europeans.

Madagascar, the world's fourth largest island (Greenland, New Guinea and Borneo are bigger), is an example of the wholesale destruction of island habitats by human activity. After an estimated 100 million years of undisturbed evolution, it has taken people just 1,500 years to ruin three-quarters of the island's dense forests. Three unique kinds of flightless bird, two giant tortoise species and eleven varieties of lemur have been wiped out.

Grassland and wilderness

Among other habitats, half the world's grasslands have been degraded or destroyed by overgrazing, livestock trampling, burning, desertification and ploughing up. Original grass species are often replaced by hardier but less productive weeds. Most of the original grasses of the Sahel were lost in this way, as were 98 per cent of the USA's prairies. In the UK and other parts of Northern Europe, semi-natural woodlands, species-rich hedgerows and ancient meadows have also largely disappeared; where native broad-leaved trees are replaced by conifers, the result is dense shade, little undergrowth, few insects and hardly any birds or mammals.

Estimates of the total extent of habitat destruction are not reassuring. Sixty-eight per cent of South-east Asia's wilderness areas are said to have gone and 65 per cent of those of sub-Saharan Africa. Several West African countries have lost over 78 per cent of their original habitats, with Gambia suffering 89 per cent destruction. In Bangladesh all but 6 per cent of the original wild habitats have been eliminated.[13]

Antarctica

Antarctica, comprising one-tenth of the Earth's land surface, is the world's last great untouched wilderness. Argentina, Australia, Chile, France, New Zealand, Norway and the UK all have territorial claims to the continent, and thirty-five countries are involved in discussions about its future. This huge frozen land mass is the last unexploited region of the planet. Its harsh and fragile environment supports large colonies of a few major species – penguins, seabirds, seals and whales – in a food chain based on plankton and krill.

Antarctica has been an important location for atmospheric research, especially into ozone depletion. Even without much human activity, pollution is building up (scientific staff also kill sizeable numbers of seals every year to feed their huskies); mineral exploration and exploitation are now under international discussion. Coal, gold, oil and platinum reserves are thought to be held under the ice, although possibly only in minor deposits. Exploration would have to take place along the coasts where the ice melts in the summer and where the continent's wildlife breeds. Offshore oil rigs would have the problem of fending off massive floating icebergs. Accidents could have devastating consequences if oil were to spread under the ice or disrupt the marine food chain.

Vanishing species

Nearly four hundred bird and mammal species and subspecies are thought to have died out since the seventeenth century. Most estimates of the current rate of extinction agree that at least one plant or animal species disappears every few hours, one rainforest species each day. Some environmentalists consider that the rate is faster, with something like a hundred species lost daily, most of them small fish, bats and reptiles, insects and plants. The US National Science Foundation believes that the speed of loss may multiply a thousand times over the next few decades. The next half-century could witness the greatest mass extinction since the dinosaurs died out 65 million years ago.[14]

"In earlier mass extinctions...most of the plant diversity survived; now, for the first time, it is being mostly destroyed," says biologist Edward Wilson of Harvard University.[15] The disappearance of a plant species that bears fruit at a time few others do can mean the loss of fruit-eating animals that depend on it.

The total extinction of a species often follows a period of numerical decline. As numbers fall, genetic deterioration caused by inbreeding may set in, or adults may fail to mate or to produce enough offspring. Such population decreases, which can sometimes be reversed if recognized in time, are at present more common than extinctions. For example, 12 per cent of the Amazon's bird species and 15 per cent of Latin America's plant species are categorized as belonging to the "living dead"; some individuals survive, but the populations are probably no longer viable without human intervention.[16]

Wildlife trade

The $5-billion-a-year wildlife and wildlife product trade, a third of which is illegal, is the main reason for the rapid decline of many of the more attractive and "useful" species. This trade supplies such products as elephant ivory, rhino horn (in demand for dagger handles in North Yemen and for dubious medical purposes in the Far East) and the pelts of wild cats. South American alligators and anacondas and South Asian species such as the pangolin are used as a source of fabric for handbags and luxury footwear.

Widely collected live specimens include chimpanzees (for medical research) and a whole variety of plants and animals for private collectors, ranging from orchids (changing hands illegally for as much as $5,000 each), rare cacti and wild ginseng to parrots, exotic reptiles, butterflies and tropical fish. Many exotic creatures die within a year of being taken from their natural habitats. Prices rise to reflect increasing rarity; but as with trade in other natural resources, the rich consuming countries take most of the profits, while the low-income suppliers receive only a fraction of the market price.

Plants

Which species are most in danger? Taking plants first, a total of about 380,000 species have been discovered, of which between 10 and 15 per cent, many of them island varieties, are at risk. These include 60 per cent of the native plants on the Galapagos Islands, 40 per cent of Hawaii's native plants and three-quarters of the vegetation on the Canary Isles. In the North, 680 native North American plant species will probably disappear by the year 2000, while 17 per cent of those of Europe may soon be lost, including almost a third of West Germany's native species.[17]

The majority of the plants at risk are in the poor countries, where genetic diversity is greater, species more vulnerable and socio-economic pressures heavier. Forest clearance is the chief factor. When one 2,000 hectare patch of Ecuadorean forest was cleared, for example, ninety endemic species were reportedly lost for ever.[18] Tropical hardwood trees are particularly vulnerable because they have long life spans and grow slowly, while many are endemic to particular localities.

The modernization of world agriculture has resulted in the loss of thousands of varieties of traditional food crops. The process has been called a "botanical holocaust".[19] Cornering the international market in the supply of seeds to farmers, the multinational corporations have eliminated small plant breeders. In Western Europe agricultural uniformity is thought likely to erase three-quarters of the traditional vegetable varieties, if present trends continue.

Invertebrates
What of the animals? Vast numbers of insect and other invertebrate species have probably already been destroyed. After one year's logging of a single forest in Sarawak, over half the known termite species had disappeared, while 6,000 European insect species are said to face extinction because of habitat destruction and the use of pesticides.[20]

Fish, amphibians and reptiles
The vertebrates – fish, amphibians, reptiles, birds and mammals – are equally at risk. The greatest threat to fish is overfishing, which, along with river damming and the pollution of rivers and coastal waters, has drastically depleted stocks of many edible species. A number of fish, such as the sturgeon (the much-prized source of caviar), could disappear over the next few decades. In the Amazon River and its tributaries the threat comes, oddly enough, from deforestation, because many fish there have a diet of falling fruit. Pacific species are menaced by the 60-kilometre-long fine-meshed drift nets used by Japanese, South Korean and Taiwanese fishing operators, who have exhausted their own coastal waters. Banned by Australia, New Zealand and the USA, these wall-of-death nets are designed to catch salmon, squid and tuna but scoop up everything in their path.

Smaller amphibians and reptiles, such as the UK sand lizard and common frog, are among the industrialized countries' most endangered species. Elsewhere, larger animals in these classes have also been lost or are in danger. Four unique species of Galapagos tortoise are extinct, and the giant salamander of China and Japan is at risk. Turtles are among the many casualties of the drift nets used in the Pacific, while the loggerhead turtle and others are threatened by the disturbance of breeding beaches and by overexploitation for food and by shell collectors.

Birds

Out of almost 10,000 identified bird species, 1,000 are said to be approaching extinction. The fate of many depends on the survival of their habitat, the Amazon rainforest. Among island species, there were once twenty-two kinds of honeycreeper bird on Hawaii, but nine have died out. Several other large flightless birds besides the dodo used to inhabit the Indian Ocean islands; all have long since perished.

In the industrialized countries, large numbers of domestic species are endangered by loss of habitats. Such splendid large birds as the Californian condor have disappeared, along with what is said to have been the most numerous bird in the world, the North American passenger pigeon. Hunted to extinction during the nineteenth and early twentieth centuries, the last known survivor of this species died in a US zoo in 1914.

In New Zealand the introduction of 100 competitor species from Europe has wiped out seven kinds of native bird and may cause the extinction of another seventeen. Introduced starlings and sparrows are squeezing out the native eastern bluebird of North America, while the bringing of Asian mongooses to the Caribbean has eliminated native birds there, too.

Many birds are migrants, vulnerable at both ends of their journey as well as at stop-over places. Brent geese, which breed in the Arctic summer, are at risk because of the destruction of wetlands and grasslands further south where they overwinter, while the common crane is in danger of losing its breeding sites south of Scandinavia and its winter feeding grounds in Spain. Many European birds that overwinter in the Sahel have been in decline because of drought and deforestation there.

Every spring large numbers of migrating doves, egrets, falcons, songbirds and other species cross Southern Europe. As they fly overhead, millions of these birds are shot by local people, for whom the seasonal catch is an old custom. This traditional cull to protect crops and supplement the local diet has begun to make major inroads into bird populations, with hunters increasingly using sophisticated firearms.

Seabirds are among the victims of modern fishing practices

and marine pollution. Each year tens of thousands die in the Pacific, caught in drift nets, and over 2 million die from ingesting or becoming tangled in plastic dumped at sea.[21] Tens of thousands of seabirds and marine mammals were killed by the crude oil spill from the *Exxon Valdez* in Prince William Sound, Alaska, in 1989.

Pollution can strike at birds through the food chain, because toxins absorbed by plankton, fish, insects and small mammals become concentrated in predators' body tissue. Pesticides such as DDT, which remain biologically active for years, threaten the survival of several species, including the bald eagle, osprey and peregrine falcon. The toxins produce reproductive disorders and weaken the shells of the birds' eggs, so parents may crush the eggs in the nest.

Larger mammals

Any mammal that is large or a meat-eater or reproduces slowly is probably endangered today. The larger mammals, represented by relatively small numbers of individuals, are often the animals people want to hunt. In view of their low reproductive rates, the loss of just a few hundred or thousand large mammals can have a major impact on species survival. Carnivores, which depend on a longer food chain than herbivores, are imperilled when the numbers of their prey go into decline.

More than 700 well-known mammal species are said to be seriously threatened with extinction, including 60 species of wild cat (notably the tiger, jaguar, leopard, cougar and cheetah), 2 species of panda, 10 species of bear, 23 species of whale, the African and Asian elephant and the mountain gorilla.[22] Many of these creatures are killed for their meat and skins, for trophies and decorations or because people think of them as competing with humans for food or territory. In Africa in particular, population pressure on wilderness areas, chronic poverty and the ravages of civil war have caused massive declines in some mammal populations.

Elephants

Elephants are the largest land mammal and the slowest to reproduce. With their unique size and trunk, elephants exploit vegetation that other herbivores cannot use, open waterholes during the dry season, disperse the fruits and seeds of trees and keep grasslands open for game and carnivores. Unless the elephants survive, it has been said, all of Africa's mammals could be doomed.

The African elephant population has fallen from 1.3 million individuals to about 600,000 in the past ten years, with 70,000 beasts killed for their tusks annually, mostly by poachers. Without a halt to ivory poaching or an easing of human population pressure, it is feared that the species could disappear from East Africa within five years and from the southern part of the continent by the end of the century. Elephant numbers are declining in 31 of the 36 African countries where they survive in the wild, with extinction imminent in Senegal, Somalia, Uganda and Zambia. Herds have been successfully protected in Southern Africa, but these are likely to become the poachers' next target if East Africa's elephants are eliminated.

Most countries suffering from elephant poaching are too poor to protect the animals properly. (The poachers earn more than the wildlife rangers opposing them.) African ivory has traditionally gone to Hong Kong and Japan, to be worked into jewellery, carvings and piano keys for re-export or for the large Japanese home market. Of the $900 million a year generated by this trade until 1989, only 1 per cent returned to African countries.

Even if smaller African elephants escape the poachers, who prefer to kill the larger adults, the herds may be doomed. Elephants are unusually intelligent, and adults teach younger individuals over many years. Deprived of adult leadership and knowledge, the young may not survive.

Rhinos

All four rhinoceros species are endangered, their total numbers having fallen 84 per cent since 1971. In the past decade the African black rhino has declined by almost half to less than 9,000 individuals, and extinction of the northern white rhino (less than thirty left in the wild) seems inevitable. Asia has fewer than 2,500 of its rhinos left. Again, poaching is largely responsible; rhino horns are illegally sold for up to $30,000 apiece.[23]

On the brink

With their numbers reduced to a few hundred or even less, other mammals that will probably soon be extinct without swift intervention include the Amazonian woolly spider monkey and giant otter, the South-east Asian tiger and tapir, the Central African gorilla and the Central American jaguar. Only about 200 Siberian and less than 30 Manchurian tigers remain in the wild. Despite efforts by the Chinese government and the World Wide Fund for Nature on behalf of the giant panda, its survival remains in doubt; only about a thousand giant pandas are left in the bamboo forests of China's Sechuan province, endangered by encroachments on their habitat and by the periodic mass flowering and die-off of their staple diet.

Migration routes
Like migratory bird species, some mammals are at risk from the disruption of their migration routes. The caribou of Alaska and north-west Canada, an important resource for 10,000 Inuit people, may shortly cease to be North America's last great animal herd as oil and gas exploration proceeds in the region. One proposed new raised pipeline, said to represent less than a year's supply of oil for the USA, would bisect caribou migration routes and probably stop the herds completing their seasonal journeys, with unforeseeable consequences. The disruption of migration patterns is a factor in Africa, too. Fencing erected by export cattle ranchers in Botswana has blocked the seasonal migrations of wildebeest, hartebeest, gemsbock and giraffe, resulting in a great many animal deaths from thirst and starvation.

The big cats
Living at very low densities, the large carnivorous mammals, notably the bear and cat families, need a sizeable range with a large supply of prey. Fragmentation of habitat or overhunting can drastically reduce their chances of mating and reproducing successfully. According to zoologist Lee Durrell, the big cats were overhunted in the past mainly because they were seen as a threat to domestic livestock or a direct menace to human life. Yet this is usually the end result of another process: "It should come as no surprise that the big cats turn to goats, cattle, dogs or people if their usual prey has been shot out or their hunting ranges fragmented."[24]

Primates
Primates, the highest order of mammals, depend on the tropical forests for survival and are therefore high on the danger list. Species at risk include Zaire's pygmy chimpanzee, Cameroon's

chimpanzee, red colobus, mandrill and drill, Madagascar's little aye-aye, indri and sifaka, the orangutan of Indonesia and Malaysia, southern India's lion-tailed macaque, Borneo's proboscis monkey, China's snub-nosed monkey, Brazil's woolly spider monkey, lion tamarin, white uakari, southern bearded saki and pied tamarin, Colombia's cotton-headed tamarin and Peru's yellow-tailed woolly monkey.[25]

Modern farming

Are domesticated animals any better off? Modern livestock, especially cattle, are prone to degeneration as a result of inbreeding, genetic erosion or diseases caused by intensive farming. Traditional cattle breeds evolved around the world over centuries according to local conditions, but modern farming eliminates such useful genetic variations in order to maximize milk or meat production. The writer Vandana Shiva relates how the light skin colour of Indian cattle (for comfort in strong sunlight), long ears and tails (to keep insects away) and hump (to store muscular fat) have been lost through cross-breeding with cattle from temperate climates. The result is that animal ailments previously unknown in India, such as viral pneumonia and bovine rhinotractitis, are now common.[26]

Modern factory farming alone can cause genetic deterioration. Penned in narrow stalls or cages, fed unnatural diets and pumped full of drugs, animals cannot and do not behave naturally. Stress weakens their resistance to disease. According to the farmer and environmentalist John Seymour, modern livestock are prone to illnesses that were unknown fifty years ago.[27] The feeding of factory-farmed cattle on the remains of sheep and other animals has produced BSE (bovine spongiform encephalopathy), the "mad cow" disease, in the UK.

Mammals at sea

The marine mammals - whales, dolphins, porpoises, seals, sea cows and sea lions – are also in jeopardy. Whales have declined more than most.

The first commercial whalers, the Basques, were energetic hunters of the right whale ("right", because it yielded an abundance of oil and whalebone and stayed afloat when killed); it was commercially exhausted as early as the seventeenth century. European whalers next turned their attention to the North Atlantic bowhead and the humpback, almost wiping these out by the late 1700s. The sperm whale followed, hunted close to extinction by European and North American whalers over the next few decades. Later in the nineteenth century, now using steamships and explosive harpoons, the whalers turned south in pursuit of first the blue and then, when that had been virtually eliminated, the smaller fin and sei whales. Tens of thousands of fin and sei were caught every year until, by the early 1960s, few remained.

Recent surveys indicate whale numbers to be well below previous forecasts. There may be as few as 500 of an original 100,000 blue whales left and only 2,000 fin whales. About 4,000 sperm and 3 per cent of the original humpback population are believed to survive. Only one whale remains relatively numerous, the small minke – hunted by a few countries in defiance of the world ban on whaling, often under the guise of "scientific research". According to some, even the minke is halfway to extinction.[28]

Many sea mammals are endangered by loss of food due to overfishing, pollution of their inshore feeding waters and human intrusion on their breeding beaches. Others are at risk from the wall-of-death drift nets in the Pacific, which kill tens of thousands of dolphins, porpoises, seals and smaller whales each year. Many more marine mammals are killed by plastic debris.

Recent tests in various seas show the blubber of seals, sea lions, walruses, dolphins and killer whales to contain increasing amounts of polychlorinated biphenyls (PCBs, the industrial poisons now banned), pesticides and other toxins. Released into the atmosphere or dumped on land or at sea, such pollutants pass up the marine food chain and reach deadly levels in the tissue of top predators such as seals. Besides kidney and intestinal disorders, this is thought to cause reproductive failure, threatening to wipe out marine mammals. The grey seal population of the polluted Baltic Sea has decreased by 98 per cent; and the Canadian genetics professor Joseph Cummins, who has studied the effects of PCBs in the food chain, predicts that all marine mammals could be extinct within fifty years.[29]

In 1988 a contagious seal virus killed 17,000 of Europe's Baltic and North Sea common seals. Possibly related to canine distemper and the cattle disease rinderpest, and reportedly carried to Europe by Arctic harp seals, the virus has not (so far) struck again. Was the epidemic of purely natural origin or did pollution of the seas play a part in it? Environmentalists argue that the seals' resistance to the virus was probably weakened by the toxins in their bodies. In the words of Olof Linden of the University of Stockholm: "The virus may be natural, but it is working on an ecosystem in stress."[30]

A similar mystery epidemic caused about 3,000 dolphin deaths on the USA's Atlantic coast in 1987. Although it was explained by some in terms of "naturally occurring" poisonous algae, industrial pollution was a suspected cause. A lesser outbreak of deaths among dolphins occurred in 1990 in the Gulf of Mexico, with Greenpeace supporting its claim that the deaths were symptoms of "an ecosystem that is dying" by citing oil spills and toxic waste dumping.

Action

Habitats and species

"To save the tiger," says the WWF, "you must maintain the forest, and you must ensure there are spotted deer or other prey for it to eat. To preserve the deer, you must preserve vegetation, and that means you must preserve the soil; water contamination is an important factor too. So, in the name of the tiger, a total environmental conservation programme takes place."[31] The task of habitat and species protection is formidable. Success depends on our making the best use of the existing conservation machinery as well as on new approaches.

Parks and reserves
In 1872 the USA became the first country to set up a national park. Worldwide, more than 3,500 national parks or reserves, covering 400 million hectares (about the size of Western Europe), are now recognized by the International Union for the Conservation of Nature and Natural Resources (IUCN). Valuable as these protected areas are, they are probably not enough. The Brundtland Commission concluded that to protect a truly representative sample of the planet's ecosystems would require three times this area.[32]

Traditional-style nature reserves have been criticized for ignoring the needs of local people. In response, "parks for development" or "biosphere reserves" have been set up as part of the UNESCO Man and Biosphere programme. These protected habitats aim to combine protection of nature with assistance for local people to improve their livelihoods. Instead of a single, fenced-off area, biosphere reserves have two or more zones: a central wilderness from which people are almost completely excluded, and one or more multiple-use buffer zones where scientific research, limited wildlife tourism and controlled natural resource use take place. Local people are involved as wildlife rangers, tourist guides or scientific aides and share the financial benefits of conservation.

Like every conservation programme, Man and Biosphere is underfunded, but there are now more than 250 biosphere reserves worldwide in more than sixty countries. Some of the best are said to be in Mexico; as well as scientific study, in these Mexican reserves environmental education and practical research take place to help improve the quality of life for people.[33]

Even an expanding network of wildlife and biosphere reserves has its problems. Lukewarm government commitment to habitat conservation in high-income countries has allowed countless semi-protected sites to be destroyed, while low-income countries are often unable to finance wildlife protection. Also, in even the best-protected reserves, species survival cannot be guaranteed. A study of the USA's Rocky Mountain and Yosemite national parks found that up to a third of the native mammals have disappeared; these sizeable areas may still not be big enough to sustain viable populations.[34]

Wilderness corridors
Where large carnivores and other animals need to roam widely or migrate, one solution is to set up "wilderness corridors" linking reserves. Wildlife corridors for birds and mammals are part of a massive forest-restoration programme under way in Costa Rica that involves NGOs, the Costa Rican government and farmers.[35]

Success stories
Conventional wildlife conservation does have its success stories. These include the Indian tiger, whose numbers have doubled since Project Tiger was launched by the WWF in 1972, the North American bison, the Arctic bear, the Asian rhino and the Russian saiga. Birds of prey in the industrialized countries are making a gradual comeback with the help of

conservationists, as the benfits of the ban on DDT work their way through the food chain

Besides preserving what remains of habitats and species, a further important step is to restore and rehabilitate damaged ecosystems. Damaged or waste land is sometimes available for this sort of work, although economic injustice usually means that people need the land too. Vulnerable species can be helped by supplementary feeding programmes and the transfer of individuals from established locations to new sites. In the case of birds, the provision of artifical nesting sites and double clutching (removing new-laid eggs from the nest, prompting the mother to lay more, and transferring them to a non-breeding pair to incubate) are now well-established practices.

Zoos and gardens
Despite limitations of size and budget, many zoos and botanical gardens are skilled at reintroducing captive-bred species into the wild, work they see as additional to their function as environmental educators. London Zoo has helped restore the Arabian oryx, Pere David's deer and the golden lion tamarin in this way. Zoo managements increasingly believe they will have to maintain some species in captivity for many years until habitat recovery makes reintroduction into the wild possible. Mammal populations of about several hundred individuals may have to be kept around the world to ensure a viable gene pool. To maintain 200 species for twenty years along these lines could cost $25 billion.[36] Where will the money be found?

Farming for conservation
Where food crops and domesticated livestock are threatened by genetic erosion, the answer is the same as in several other chapters of book: we need to phase out monoculture and industrialized, profit-maximizing farming; reduce our meat and dairy consumption; and revitalize the small-farm sector, supporting it with government subsidies, land reform and small-scale technology. The multinationals that dominate the supply of modern seed varieties could be taxed to fund a subsidy for small farmers growing traditional varieties.

Strategy for survival
Current thinking about conservation is strongly influenced by the World Conservation Strategy (WCS), prepared by the IUCN and launched in 1980 jointly with the WWF, the

UN Environment Programme, the UN Food and Agriculture Organization and UNESCO. The Strategy has three priorities: to maintain life-support systems such as climate, the water cycle and soil renewal; to preserve genetic diversity; and to ensure the long-term survival of species and ecosystems.

The WCS was intended to help and encourage individual countries to produce national conservation strategies, balancing their economic goals with ecosystem protection. Between thirty and forty countries have so far responded. Some governments, such as that of the UK, argue that their existing conservation legislation is adequate – a conclusion disputed by environmentalists. Many species-rich Southern countries where conservation is especially urgent, such as Brazil and Zaire, have made little progress towards a national strategy, and poor countries usually lack the funds to fulfil any such commitments. Besides, little attention has been given to involving ordinary people in national plans. The IUCN is currently working on a second Strategy with the aim of overcoming such problems.[37]

Species census

Lack of information hampers conservation work. The IUCN's international computer network monitors the survival of endangered species listed in its "Red Data Books", but many threatened plants and animals are not listed at all. A census of the great many unknown rainforest species should be a priority. Research is also needed into habitat regeneration rates, into the relation between reserve size and species survival and into the sequence in which an ecosystem's species die out or may be reintroduced (although not, as has sometimes been proposed, by felling more rainforest). These studies should involve local people, who often have a deep understanding of their country's ecosystems and whose co-operation is essential for conservation to succeed.

The rainforests

Since 1985 international efforts to protect the rainforests have been dominated by the World Bank/United Nations Tropical Forestry Action Plan (TFAP), one of whose stated aims has also been the expansion of commercial logging on "sustainable" lines. In practice, TFAP has done little to prevent rainforest destruction, and even the most careful attempts to cut rainforest timber have degraded habitats and wiped out wildlife

256 The Earthscan Action Handbook

(see Chapter 6). A reassessment of "sustainable forestry" and restriction of the international hardwood trade are needed. The World Bank itself admits that "remaining wildlands can contribute more to economic development in their natural state than if converted to some other use".[38]

Wildlife trade convention

Control of the wildlife trade takes place through the Convention on International Trade in Endangered Species (CITES), dating from 1973 and now signed by more than ninety countries. Several hundred species threatened with extinction are listed in CITES Appendix 1, and trade in them is prohibited. Species that would be endangered by uncontrolled trade are listed in Appendix 2, which permits quota trading.

The CITES system has limitations. It does not cover internal trade within countries; any country can legally exempt itself from a prohibition it disagrees with; and there are enforcement problems because of the massive illegal trade. CITES requires countries exporting or importing endangered species to keep written records, but these logs are plagued by discrepancies and forged permits, while customs officers often cannot distinguish between legally and illegally traded species. Several countries – notably Argentina, Indonesia, Spain and Thailand – have been identified by the WWF as permitting the large-scale illegal smuggling of endangered species.

Improved record-keeping, better training for enforcers and stiffer fines for law-breakers, already in force in some countries, will help make CITES more effective. Participants will have to commit more money; and as with every form of environmental conservation, local people in the exporting countries will need to be given a financial incentive in the elimination of illegal wildlife trading.

Until very recently the CITES governing body favoured some trade in elephant ivory, arguing that the proceeds help finance conservation. The United Nations permits CITES to receive contributions from wildlife dealers and to profit from sales of captured illegal wildlife products. Accusations of corruption were made against CITES in 1989 by Kenya, Tanzania and other countries demanding a total ban on the ivory trade. Only outright prohibition would, they said, prevent illegal ivory from being traded with forged permits and thus bring an end to elephant poaching.

Several Southern African counties, led by Zimbabwe, whose elephant populations have so far been spared the onslaught of the poachers, opposed the ban. In 1989 the CITES signatories agreed as a compromise a two-year suspension of all international ivory trading. Three months later, however, the UK gave Hong Kong permission to reopen its ivory markets for six months and clear stockpiles (most of which probably come from poached sources); this controversial decision was said to "open the door to the destruction of the African elephant".

Alternatives to trade

Is there a viable alternative to the wildlife trade? Safari tourism in Kenya has shown that there is. Kenya's revenue from keeping its elephants alive is said to approach $22 million a year, more than Africa's annual pre-1989 income from ivory. Similarly, the value of a live lion for wildlife tourism is up to fifty times greater than that of one killed, carved up and sold.[39] Safari tourism must be sensitively handled, however, so as not to disturb animals and degrade habitats. It can also cause resentment and lead to poaching by local people if they are denied a share of the proceeds.

Zimbabwe has approached the problem differently, harvesting its elephant population and selling the meat and hides, as well as the ivory, for $4.5 million a year. All the money, the Zimbabweans say, is ploughed back into wildlife conservation. Zimbabwe's successful conservation programme has also benefited from the involvement of rural communities in game protection and management and in sharing the economic benefits of wildlife tourism and culling.

The conflicting needs of East and Southern Africa when it comes to protecting the elephant have yet to be resolved. Poaching will probably continue as long as the demand for ivory products exists and people in poor countries have few viable sources of income. In the words of one conservationist: "Until it becomes as socially unacceptable to use ivory as to have a gorilla-hand ashtray or a leopard-skin coat, the ivory trade will flourish, and the elephants will continue to perish."[40]

Reports during 1990 suggested that the worldwide demand for ivory had begun to fall. It was thought that this would produce a decline in elephant poaching.

Some conservation-conscious piano manufacturers now use

plastic rather than ivory to make the white keys, and public education campaigns and the use of substitute materials could help reduce the threat to many animal species. An international campaign against the fur trade has had some success, although the position of the Arctic Inuit who rely on seals as a source of income needs to be resolved.

Wildlife ranching
Wildlife ranching is another useful approach when a species is in danger of overexploitation. This is based on the idea of combining controlled commercial exploitation with long-term conservation. On crocodile farms in Asia, for example, the larger adults are killed for their skins while the younger ones are protected. Conservation farming of the Himalayan musk deer in China allows the musk to be removed without killing the animal, and the fleece of the once-endangered vicuna is similarly farmed in Peru.

Visitors to African wildlife ranches can now buy a meal of low-fat giraffe, zebra or camel steak. The income funds both conservation and, ideally, local people's economic development. By using indigenous animals rather than non-native cattle, wildlife ranching is said to be kinder to both animals and environment. However, this is a stop-gap measure, based as it is on the maldistribution of resources whereby rich visitors eat meat while Africans starve.

Whaling ban
International agreements have been signed to protect wetlands, waterfowl habitats, migrating species and, after years of public pressure, whales. Proving that governments do (eventually) respond to public demands for better conservation measures, the International Whaling Commission agreed a five-year whaling ban in 1985 (extended in 1990 for another year). Two exceptions were allowed: indigenous peoples such as the Greenlanders could continue whaling for local needs; and scientific research that would help the species survive was permitted.

Was it all too little too late? Whale populations have shown no signs of recovery; and the Japanese (with their traditional diet of cheap whale meat), Iceland, Norway, South Korea and the Soviet Union refused to honour the ban. Exploiting the research loophole, Japan's Joint Whaling Company changed its name to the "Cetacean Research Institute" and has continued to take hundreds of minkes from the sea each year, while until mid-1989 Iceland continued to sell Japan whale meat as a by-product of its so-called research.

Iceland and the USSR have now stopped whaling, however, and Norway promised to kill just five whales during 1990. Iceland's change of heart was probably brought about by the international boycott of its fish exports organized by Greenpeace. As for Japan, Greenpeace vessels have harried Japanese fishing ships, and the US government has banned the Japanese fishing fleet from US territorial waters.

A worldwide prohibition on drift-net fishing has been called for by several governments and by conservation NGOs. In response to pressure from US conservation groups, Heinz and other tuna canning companies announced in 1990 that they would stop selling tuna that had been caught in drift nets. Measures to tackle the other major threat to marine species – pollution – are described in Chapter 7.

"World park" for Antarctica

Antarctica is protected by a series of international agreements, but several countries, notably the UK and the USA, are eager to explore the continent's mineral resources. Australia, France and many environmental groups are calling for Antarctica to be declared a "world park" when the present Antarctic treaty expires in 1991. The veteran French marine biologist Jacques Cousteau has collected more than a million signatures in support of this campaign. Such a move would bring the Antarctic and its species permanently under UN protection, permitting only internationally managed scientific research; it could be an important success to achieve.

A new outlook

Few habitats or species will be secure without efforts to solve the key human problems of rapid population growth, poverty and overconsumption, all of which lead to the overexploitation of natural resources. It is no good the rich North telling the poor South to protect its mammals, birds, forests or wetlands as long as the South can see no way of feeding its people without stripping nature bare. If we in the rich countries want the Earth's natural diversity to be protected, we must be prepared to make some material sacrifices to pay for it. An international conservation banking programme, as proposed by the Brundtland Commission, or regional conservation funds may be the best channel for the large sums needed.[41]

Ultimately, we are faced with the choice of putting the good of the global environment before our desire for unnecesary comfort, convenience or amusement. As Lee Durrell says: "Few animals would be threatened today if they were taken only for immediate human needs." *Ecologist* editors Edward Goldsmith and Nicholas Hildyard agree that avoiding a mass extinction will require "a fundamental reappraisal of our whole way of life, with priority being given to ecological imperatives rather than the pursuit of economic gain".[42]

Getting Involved

Related subjects covered elsewhere in this book include: food crops and biological diversity – Chapter 1; the future of indigenous peoples – Chapter 5; rainforests and woodlands – Chapter 6; pollution of rivers, lakes and seas – Chapter 7. To find out more about the threat to habitats and species and how they might be saved, see "Recommended Reading" (pages 324–9).

Consumer and lifestyle choices

Natural diversity is endangered by many of our consumption habits. We have to be prepared to act differently if we are to save habitats and species from continual destruction. The crucial contribution that comfortably off people have to make (most of us in the industrialized countries) is to reduce our consumption of raw materials and energy. We cannot go "green" and save nature without, as a society, making material sacrifices – because the rapid consumption of resources is what puts pressure on the natural resource base and disrupts ecosystems.

Interrelated action

Many of the ways we need to change our habits are described in earlier chapters. By switching from your private car to other forms of transport (see the "Getting Involved" section in Chapter 8), for example, you relieve the pressure for new roads that causes habitat destruction; you reduce the demand for the raw materials and fossil fuel energy (whose extraction, transportation and use damage habitats) needed to produce a replacement; you ease the environmental disruption caused by oil drilling, refining and petrol distribution to produce vehicle fuel; you help to lessen the mechanical violence of our towns and cities; and depending on your vehicle, you may delay the acid-death of a tree or stream. These are small contributions; but made often over a wide range of human activities by enough people, they can have an effect.

Care for wildlife
Don't buy exotic species as pets, endangered imported plants or such wildlife products and souvenirs as shells, animal skins, furs or ivory. If you are visiting another country to enjoy the wildlife, write to their tourist office and their ambassador expressing your concern about nature conservation, especially if you know of particular habitats and species that have been lost or are under threat in that country. Points you could make include:

- Habitats and species are rapidly disappearing all over the world, including in the country you are visiting.
- The natural beauty of the countryside and the richness of wildlife are one of the main appeals of visiting another country.
- Unless more is done by governments to halt the destruction of our natural heritage, many people will not want to continue visiting different places, because every country will end up the same.

Consume carefully
Try to do without tropical hardwoods (see Chapter 6). Buy locally produced vegetarian food rather than agribusiness or imported cash crops or beef (all produced at the cost of destroying traditional landscapes and habitats). Eat organic, pesticide-free food, reducing the market for species-endangering pesticides (see Chapters 1 and 3); cultivate your own plants or crops organically for the same reason.

Greenpeace want shoppers to ask food stores to guarantee that their tuna have been caught by rod and line, thus causing no harm to dolphins.

Criticize and boycott
Criticize or boycott any company whose operations you know cause significant habitat or species destruction. (There are

probably a great many companies doing this a lot of the time.)
Tell other people what you are doing and why, and write to the
firm and the press explaining your actions and point of view.
Consumer pressure can be effective; when Exxon failed to act
quickly to clean up its disastrous oil spill off the Alaskan coast
in 1989, thousands of US customers cancelled their credit card
accounts. For more about consumer boycotts, see Chapter 2.

Teach respect
Respect the countryside wherever you go and teach children
in your care to do the same. Educational materials for young
people on the threats to habitats and species and on nature
conservation are available in the UK from:

- Conservation Trust for Environmental Education, George
  Palmer Site, Northumberland Avenue, Reading RG2 7PW.
- Watch Trust for Environmental Education, 22 The Green,
  Nettleham, Lincoln LN2 2NR.
- World Wide Fund for Nature Education, Panda House,
  Weyside Park, Godalming, Surrey GU7 1XR.
- Young People's Trust for the Environment and Nature
  Conservation, 95 Woodbridge Road, Guildford, Surrey
  GU1 4PY.

Wildlife gardens, trees, recycling
Set aside part of your garden as a wildlife area. Plant trees; the
UK has far less natural woodland than most other European
countries (see Chapter 6). Recycle as much waste as you
can, to avoid the land and water pollution caused by waste
disposal (see Chapter 7). Paper recycling will help slow the
conversion of moorland and other natural habitats in the
northern UK to low-wildlife-value conifer forests intended
to provide woodpulp. Use water and energy sparingly (see
Chapters 7 and 8).

Join a nature conservation group (see below) and make its
activities an essential part of your life.

Community and political action

Protect local habitats
Keep a watch on any places of natural interest near where you
live and work. If you think the local natural environment is

threatened by planning applications, new building or changes of use, contact (in the UK) the Royal Society for Nature Conservation or Friends of the Earth (addresses below) and ask them what you can do. Many conservation groups appear at planning applications in order to protect wildlife sites, and this costs money; your financial support will help. For more about defending the UK's natural heritage from potentially destructive planning applications, see *Friends of the Earth Handbook* edited by Jonathon Porritt (London: Macdonald Optima, 1987).

Conservation volunteers
Give your support to local small-scale projects such as neighbourhood wildlife gardens, city farms and ecology parks. See if you can start one up yourself.

For people of all ages who enjoy practical conservation work, the ideal UK organization to be involved with is the British Trust for Conservation Volunteers (BTCV; address below), which trains thousands of people of all ages each year to work on environmental projects around the country. Membership is open to individuals and families; there are hundreds of active local groups; and schools can become affiliated. Activities include tree planting and woodland management, protecting wildlife habitats, clearing ponds and canals, restoring footpaths, drystone walls and rural buildings. BTCV organizes conservation holidays in the UK and elsewhere in Europe in association with groups in other countries.

Lobby the government
Wildlife sites are rapidly being destroyed everywhere. In the UK more than 200 Sites of Special Scientific Interest were damaged during 1989 by farming, peat extraction, drainage and planned development.[43] Write to local councillors, your MP and the Secretary of State for the Environment (Department of the Environment, 2 Marsham Street, London SW1P 3EB), expressing your concern about the rate of damage to officially protected sites and asking for more government resources to be given to nature conservation. A suggestion you could also make, which is gaining ground among environmentalists, is that the UK needs a strong and politically independent environmental protection agency or executive like those in the Netherlands, Sweden, the USA and West Germany.[44]

Support campaigns
Join the political movement for global economic and social justice and for the decentralization of power to local communities (see Part One of this book). How will this help? As long as so many of the world's people are impoverished, denied essential rights and freedoms and without control over their environment, human problems will always lead to the abuse and destruction of habitats and species. Nature cannot be saved unless we root out human injustice and people gain control over their lives.

Take part in one or more of the many international campaigns to save the rainforests, where most threatened species live, and to reforest other lands (see Chapter 6).

If you are concerned about the threat to Antarctica from future mining and oil exploration, support the calls for the establishment of an Antarctica World Park. The World Wide Fund for Nature suggests you write to your MP along the following lines; you could also address similar letters to your MEP and to the Foreign Secretary (Foreign and Commonwealth Office, Downing Street, London SW1A 2AL), as well as raising the subject in community newsletters and the press and on radio phone-ins:

- Antarctica is the world's last great wilderness left on Earth and the only international zone free of military activity.
- The Antarctic icecap plays a major role in regulating the global climate.
- Antarctica is home to a vast number of seabirds, penguins, seals and whales, and its ecosystems might not survive being disturbed by industrialization.
- The best way to preserve Antarctica would be to have it declared a World Park.
- There should be no mining or oil exploration there.
- Pollution is already building up just from scientific activity in Antarctica, and the establishment of a World Park is an urgent priority.

Organizations

Organizations campaigning to protect habitats and species nationally and internationally include:

UK and Irish Republic

British Trust for Conservation Volunteers, 36 St Mary's Street, Wallingford, Oxon. OX10 OEU (0491-39766).

Common Ground, 45 Shelton Street, London WC2H 9HJ (071-379 3109).

Compassion in World Farming, 20 Lavant Street, Petersfield, Hants. GU32 3EW (0730-64208).

Earthwatch, Harbour View, Bantry, County Cork, Irish Republic.

Friends of the Earth, 26–28 Underwood Street, London N1 7JQ (071-490 1555).

Friends of the Earth Scotland, Bonnington Mill, 70–72 Newhaven Road, Edinburgh EH6 5QG (031-554 9977).

Greenpeace, 30–31 Islington Green, London N1 8XE (071-354 5100).

Marine Conservation Society, 9 Gloucester Road, Ross-on-Wye HR9 5BU (0989 66017).

Nature Conservancy Council, Northminster House, Northminster Road, Peterborough, Cambs. PE1 1UA (0733-40345).

Plantlife, c/o Conservation Foundation, 1 Kensington Gore, London SW7 2AR (071-823 8842).

Royal Society for Nature Conservation, 22 The Green, Nettleham, Lincoln LN2 2NR (0522-752326).

Royal Society for the Protection of Birds, The Lodge, Sandy, Bedfordshire SG19 2DL (0767-680551).

Whale and Dolphin Conservation Society, 20 West Lea Road, Bath, Avon BA1 3RL (0225-334511).

Woodland Trust, Autumn Park, Grantham, Lincs. NG31 6LL (0476-74297).

World Society for the Protection of Animals, 106 Jermyn Street, London SW1Y 6EE (071-839 3026).

World Wide Fund for Nature, Panda House, Weyside Park, Godalming, Surrey GU7 1XR (0483-426444).

USA and Canada

Canadians for Conservation of Tropical Nature, Faculty of Environmental Studies, York University, 4700 Keele Street, Toronto, Ontario M3J 1P6, Canada.

Environmental Defense Fund, 257 Park Avenue South, New York, NY 10010, and 1616 P Street NW, Washington, DC 20036, USA.

Friends of the Earth, 218 D Street SE, Washington, DC 20003, USA.

Greenpeace, 1436 U Street NW, Washington, DC 20009, USA.

Greenpeace, 578 Bloor Street W, Toronto, Ontario M6G 1K1, Canada.

National Resource Defense Council, 122 East 42nd Street, New York, NY 10168, USA.

Rainforest Action Network, 300 Broadway, San Francisco, Calif. 94133, USA.

Sierra Club, 730 Polk Street, San Francisco, Calif. 94109, USA.

Society for the Promotion of Environment Conservation, 2150 Maple Street, Vancouver, British Columbia V6J 3T3, Canada.

Wilderness Society, 1400 Eye Street NW, Washington, DC 20005, USA.

World Wide Fund for Nature, Suite 201, 60 St Clair Avenue East, Toronto, Ontario M4T 1N5, Canada.

World Wide Fund for Nature, 1250 24th Street NW, Washington, DC 20037, USA.

Australia and New Zealand

Australian Conservation Foundation, 672B Glenferrie Road, Hawthorne, Melbourne, Victoria 3122, Australia.

Friends of the Earth, PO Box 530E, Melbourne, Victoria 3001, and GPO Box 1875, Canberra, New South Wales, Australia.

Friends of the Earth, PO Box 39-065, Auckland West, New Zealand.

Greenpeace, Private Bag No. 6, 134 Broadway, Sydney, New South Wales 2007, Australia.

Greenpeace, Private Bag, Wellesley Street PO, Auckland 1, New Zealand.

Native Trees Coalition, PO Box 756, Nelson, New Zealand.

Pacific Concerns Resource Centre, PO Box 9295, Newmarket, Auckland, New Zealand.

Rainforest Information Centre, PO Box 368, Lismore, New South Wales 2480, Australia.

Tasmanian Conservation Trust, 102 Bathurst Street, Hobart, Tasmania, Australia.

Total Environment Centre, 18 Argyle Street, Sydney, New South Wales 2000, Australia.

Wilderness Society, 130 Davey Street, Hobart, Tasmania 7000, Australia.

Wilderness Society, 362 PH Street. Sydney 2000, Australia.

World Wide Fund for Nature, PO Box 6237, Wellington, New Zealand.

World Wide Fund for Nature, Level 17, St Martin's Tower, 31 Market Street, GPO Box 528, Sydney, New South Wales, Australia.

Africa and Asia (Commonwealth)

Asian Pacific Environmental Network, 43 Salween Road, 10050 Penang, Malaysia.

Centre for Science and Environment, 807 Vishal Bhavan, 95 Nehru Place, New Delhi 110019, India.

Friends of the Earth, PO Box 3794, Ghana.

Friends of the Earth/Sahabat Alam Malaysia, 43 Salween Road, 10050 Penang, Malaysia.

Friends of the Earth, PO Box 4028, Boroko, Papua New Guinea.

Friends of the Earth, PM Bag 950, 33 Robert Town, Freetown, Sierra Leone.

Institute for Environment and Development Studies/Friends of the Earth Bangladesh, PO Box 4222, Ramna Dhaka 1000, Bangladesh.

Planetary Citizens' Council for Peace, Development and the Environment, Robinson Road, PO Box 2753, Singapore 9047.

Tanzania Envrionmental Society, PO Box 1309, Dar es Salaam, Tanzania.

10. A World without War?

"Nations spend obscenely large amounts of public funds on instruments of death and destruction. We know that a very minute fraction of that budget of death would ensure that God's children everywhere would have a clean supply of water, would have enough to eat, would have a reasonable chance of survival...The world will know no peace until there is global justice."

Archbishop Desmond Tutu[1]

The Problem

Are human beings naturally aggressive and warlike? Perhaps not. Prehistoric tribes had ample space, small populations and little need to fight for food or land. Armed combat was sometimes just a ritual of manhood, involving no bloodshed. It is said that the Arctic Inuit have never gone to war, and the African Bushmen told Laurens Van der Post that they gave up fighting among themselves for ever after one man was killed.[2]

Whereas animals behave aggressively when their food or territory is threatened, humans have social and political ways of dealing with such problems. Most wars, the psychologist and philosopher Erich Fromm believes, have been fought as a result of deliberate decisions about land, wealth, slaves, raw materials and markets, not out of blind instinct. "The thesis that war is caused by innate human destructiveness is plainly absurd to anyone who has even the slightest knowledge of history," Fromm argues.[3] If he and other thinkers like him are correct, war may not be essential to the human condition. There must therefore be a chance that we can prevent it.

Weapons and wars

"We are living in a war zone called Earth."[4] Modern technology has given the world weapons of enormous destructive power. The 6,000 kilotonnes of one US MX missile equal all the explosive energy released during the Second World War. One Trident submarine can destroy 240 cities. The world's 50,000 stockpiled nuclear weapons could do as much damage as a million Hiroshima-type bombs.[5]

The nuclear threat
The use of even a fraction of these weapons would destroy civilization, causing millions of instantaneous deaths and slower fatalities through radiation sickness, famine and disease. Scientists believe that a major nuclear explosion would cause a "nuclear winter" by throwing up enormous quantities of debris and smoke into the atmosphere to block out the sun for months. Temperatures would fall by perhaps 15°C, wiping out harvests. Environmental catastrophe and radiation-induced sterility would probably kill off the human race.

Who has the bomb?
Besides the official nuclear weapons countries – the USA, the USSR, the UK, France and China – many other countries have the technology to operate nuclear power stations and make weapons-grade plutonium, as well as possessing missiles capable of carrying nuclear warheads. Since nuclear energy is expensive and unsafe, governments are perhaps led to develop it as much for the capacity to produce weapons as to generate energy. Israel, South Africa, India, Pakistan, Iraq, Argentina and Brazil could probably build a nuclear weapon (Israel and South Africa are believed to have done so already), and Libya wants one. Just 10 kilos of plutonium are needed for a nuclear device, and the possibility of a terrorist plutonium theft has been considered by the US Congress.

Chemical and other weapons
Besides its nuclear arsenals, the human race has many other weapons of appalling destructive power. Stockpiles of chemical weapons are widespread, despite an international ban dating from 1925. Among the countries known or thought to have such weapons are the USA and USSR, France, Syria, Libya,

Egypt, Israel, Iraq, South Africa, Romania, China, North Korea and Pakistan. The Arab countries reportedly consider their chemical weapons to be the "poor man's nuclear bomb". Even conventional weapons are now so destructive that there is little difference between, say, fragmentation bombs and the lowest-yield tactical nuclear weapons, a fact that could increase the possibility of escalation from conventional to nuclear war.

Worldwide war

We are sometimes told that nuclear weapons have kept the peace since 1945. True, no international wars have been formally declared; but there have been scores of armed conflicts within or between countries, resulting in close to 40 million deaths, mostly in the South and almost equalling the total loss of life caused by the Second World War. One million people were killed during the 1980–8 Gulf War alone.

Many of these conflicts have been partly or wholly civil wars, and the majority of casualties have been civilians. In the First World War 95 per cent of deaths were of military personnel; the first heavy bombing of cities and deliberate attacks on civilian populations occurred in the Second World War. By the 1960s and 1970s, when the USA fought in Vietnam, 80 per cent of deaths were civilian. More recently still, 85 per cent of those killed during the conflicts of the 1980s are said to have been civilians. Across the world, non-military populations are now prime targets in warfare.[6]

All the main nuclear powers have been directly involved in war: the USA and the UK in Korea (1950–3), France in Algeria (1954–62), France and the UK in Suez (1956), China with India (1961–2), the USA in Vietnam (1965–73), the USSR in Afghanistan (1979–89) and the UK with Argentina (1982). Involvement also occurs indirectly, when wars take place between the superpowers' clients; Israel, UNITA, the Eritreans and El Salvador are or have been funded and supplied by the USA, while their opponents – Syria, Angola, Ethiopia and the Salvadoran guerrillas – have had Soviet (or Cuban) backing.

Today's battlefields

Where are today's wars being fought? As the 1990s began, armed conflicts involving significant numbers of people were taking place in Afghanistan, Angola, Borneo, Colombia, East

Timor, El Salvador, Ethiopia, Guatemala, the Israeli-occupied territories, Kashmir, Lebanon, Liberia, Mozambique, Northern Ireland, Peru, the Philippines, the Punjab, Somalia, South Africa, Sudan and the Western Sahara. Most were civil wars, but some involved civilian struggles against occupying forces. At the heart of both kinds of conflict is a contest for political or economic power, although irrational fears and competition for scarce resources may also be involved.

Probably the worst armed conflict of the 1980s, the Gulf War was sparked off by a long-standing dispute over control of the Shatt el Arab waterway between Iran and Iraq, but the war was rooted in regional power rivalries. Both countries were ruled by tyrannical leaders whose political control involved the oppression of their own populations (war against an external enemy has often been used by repressive regimes to avoid domestic opposition). Many Arab states also feared the spread of Iran's militant religious fundamentalism, while Iraq may have wished to impress another rival, Syria, with a show of strength. The war was further complicated by the North's anxieties about the control of oil supplies.

Superpowers and cold war

The USA and the Soviet Union account for nearly a quarter of the world's armed forces, nearly two-thirds of its military spending (the US defence budget is currently about $300 billion a year) and 97 per cent of its nuclear arsenal. Each has armed forces six times larger than it had before the Second World War, as well as far more overseas bases. The superpowers' combined nuclear stockpiles have an explosive power of 15 billion tonnes of TNT.[7]

The cold war

The cold war between the USA and USSR arose from intense mutual distrust. Both countries, because of their size and power, showed themselves capable of inflicting terrible wrongs against their own citizens and against smaller, weaker countries – the Soviets mainly in Eastern Europe, the North Americans in the Caribbean, Latin America, South-east Asia and the Pacific. The mistrust was therefore justified on both sides.

In each superpower there was a corrupt elite that used this suspicion and rivalry as a pretext for further concentrations of power in its own hands – at the expense of ordinary people and weaker countries. While the Soviets applied the political stranglehold of Communism, the North Americans used the mighty dollar to knock their hemisphere into shape. In 1961 President Eisenhower, in his last presidential speech, warned against the growing influence of what he called the military-industrial complex, which he saw as moving beyond the democratic control of the US people.[8]

During the postwar years an atmosphere of menace and hysteria was fostered. The opposing sides spoke of "Communist subversion" and "US imperialism", "evil empires" and "class enemies". Both the USA and the Soviet Union assumed the right to provoke or intervene in armed conflict to serve their own interests.

The USA had used force in Latin America and South-east Asia since the start of the century, but the cold war provided the justification for US military action and covert operations after 1945. These were undertaken, for example, in Guatemala (1954), Brazil (1964), the Dominican Republic (1965), Vietnam (1965–73), Cambodia (1970), Chile (1973), Grenada (1983) and Nicaragua (1983–9). For its part, the USSR sent its forces into East Germany (1953), Hungary (1956), Czechoslovakia (1968) and Afghanistan (1979), and the threat of Soviet force lurked behind the imposition of martial law in Poland (1981). The USSR also kept such repressive regimes as the governments of Ethiopia and Syria heavily armed; between 1976 and 1983 it is said to have supplied ten times more weapons to sub-Saharan Africa than than the USA did.[9]

The cold war was a hot one for its victims. The US-backed "contra" war against the Nicaraguan government, for example, cost 31,000 lives.

The idea that US hawks have been as guilty as their Soviet counterparts of manipulating public opinion in order to justify international aggression is not just the view of radicals. The eminent economist and former US ambassador to India, J. K. Galbraith, has written: "The Soviet Union is indispensable to the American military power. Fear of the Soviet Union and tension in our relations...serve our military power...Tension is actually cultivated to support the military power."[10]

What was the military power wanted for? The Soviet Union's political deliberations have been shrouded in secrecy, but the reasoning behind the USA's global strategy is recorded in print. A 1948 State Department document reads: "We have fifty percent of the world's wealth, but only 6.3 percent of its population...In this position we cannot fail to be the object of envy and resentment. Our real task is to devise a pattern of relationships which will permit us to maintain this position of disparity without...detriments to our international security."[11]

The arms race

The arms race has been led largely by the USA and NATO, with the USSR and Warsaw Pact striving to keep pace. The USA opened the nuclear weapons age by dropping two atom bombs on Japan in 1945, at a time when massive conventional bombing had reportedly done much, and perhaps enough, to persuade the Japanese to sue for peace. Concluding that the US military wanted to prove its power to the USSR, some critics also believe that two explosions were decided upon to compare the effects of a uranium bomb (Hiroshima) with those of a plutonium device (Nagasaki).[12]

The West has invariably had more nuclear warheads than the Eastern bloc and has taken the lead in most major weapons developments, such as heavy intercontinental bombers, ICBMs (intercontinental ballistic missiles), submarine-launched cruise missiles, MIRVs (multiple independently targetable re-entry vehicles) and Star Wars-type research.

On the other hand, the Warsaw Pact presence has always been heavier on the ground. There were 2,317,000 Warsaw Pact troops and 58,500 battle tanks deployed in Europe (the world's most heavily armed zone) at the start of 1989, as against NATO's 2,243,000 servicemen and 21,900 tanks.[13] The Pact has also maintained an air advantage over NATO, although Western naval strength has been superior.

Overall, the Eastern bloc's numerical land superiority has been slim and well below a level needed to ensure victory. The West has never lost its economic and technological lead, while the Soviets have been hard pressed to maintain their empire. Thus even before the USSR began troop withdrawals in 1989, claims of Soviet intentions to invade Western Europe rang hollow, as did recurring statements about NATO's so-called loss of superiority. As Jonathon Porritt put it, several years before *perestroika* and *glasnost*: "Surrounded by enemies, outspent, outnumbered, outgunned, technologically and economically inferior, there is...no evidence either that the [Soviet Union] wants war or that it plans to invade."[14]

Despite the unlikelihood of a successful Soviet offensive in Europe, NATO devised the strategy of "flexible response": short-range nuclear weapons would be used if NATO's conventional forces failed to hold back a Warsaw Pact advance. A "limited" or "controlled" nuclear war would be waged. Nobody knows enough about the effects of using nuclear weapons or how a nuclear exchange could be limited, however. An accidental missile strike against a nuclear power station could cause a disaster well beyond human control. "Flexible response" was modified but not abandoned when NATO declared nuclear arms to be "weapons of last resort" at its July 1990 London summit.

Star Wars
In the early 1980s, already in command of the strongest armed forces in the world's history, US President Reagan wanted more. The President told the US people about a "window of vulnerability" to a Soviet nuclear strike against home-based US missiles. Public alarm gave his advisers the leverage they needed to justify a further massive arms build-up and the start of the Strategic Defense Initiative. SDI was offered to the US public as an all-protecting nuclear umbrella, safeguarding families and homes. Yet the presentation was misleading, and the logic was flawed. The atomic physicist Kosta Tsipis has called the project "militarily and technologically absurd...a political and psychological ploy...voodoo science".[15]

On grounds of cost (projected to top $1 trillion) and technological feasibility, SDI's supposed all-embracing defence has always looked impossible. If the system were deployed, anti-missile lasers would have to be mounted in space on nuclear-powered battle stations. No such system could be realistically tested for reliability, kept ready to fire or permanently safeguarded from attack or sabotage. It would offer no protection against nuclear weapons components being smuggled into the USA and reassembled to make a bomb (said to be one of the surest ways of delivering a nuclear attack). Nor would it protect against contour-hugging cruise missiles or low-level nuclear bomber attack.

In the late 1980s the Star Wars research director, a lieutenant-general, said defensively: "Nowhere have we stated that the goal of the SDI is...a 'leakproof' defense."[16] The official purpose had shrunk to that of protecting US missile silos rather than cities and people. (Even so, the deployment of space laser weapons could increase an aggressive US administration's willingness to use nuclear blackmail or to launch a pre-emptive first strike.) The underlying motive behind SDI was probably, at least in part, to inject public money into the US arms and technology industries through research and development contracts. As the *Wall Street Journal* put it during the project's brief heyday, SDI was "the business opportunity of a generation...that pot of gold".[17]

The future

The post-cold-war world has arrived. The Soviet Union has abandoned the doctrine of total war capability in favour of a policy of "reasonable sufficiency" in defence and has unilaterally withdrawn troops and tanks from Central Europe and called for a nuclear-free Germany and a "common European home". (Although the USSR is said to be still building warships and modernizing its forces in other ways.)

In response, President Bush's 1990 defence budget showed an overall reduction in military spending, most of the cuts made in conventional forces and military bases, and further cuts are forecast for 1991. However, the USA still wants to modernize and expand its armoury. Plans include new submarine-launched missiles systems (Trident), the costly B-2 Stealth bomber (although fewer will now be produced), the new Tactical Air-to-Surface Missile (TASM) and a continuation of SDI.

NATO's 1990 London Declaration recognized the new realities to some extent. It proposed a joint East–West peace declaration and further weapons reductions. Yet NATO strategists still insist that there is enough potential threat in Europe to require a strong Western military alliance equipped with nuclear weapons.

The real cost of military spending

Military spending has grown fast since 1945, outstripping both inflation and increases in industrial output. The countries of the world spent $16 trillion on "defence" in the twenty-five years prior to 1988, a sum greater than the income of the poorer half of humanity. Estimates put current arms spending at about a trillion dollars a year, $1.6 million a minute.

NATO and the Warsaw Pact have in the past accounted for three-quarters of this sum, with the industrialized North spending four times more than the developing South. In recent decades however, arms spending has increased three times faster in the South than in the North. The highest per capita spenders are now in the Middle East; Saudi Arabia, for example, spends over $2,000 a year on arms for each of its citizens. Canada and Sweden spend less than $500.[18]

During the world recession and debt crisis of the 1970s and 1980s, military budgets held steady, while social expenditures fell. Three out of five countries, many of them the poorest ones, devote more money to defence than to health and social welfare combined. In the late 1980s Ethiopia spent six times more on arms than on health care, while Iraq was said to spend seven times more on the military than on education and health combined, Iran almost four times more. By contrast, Mexico spends ten times *less* on arms than on health and education; a 1985 survey found that while militaristic Argentina had high infant mortality and poor quality-of-life indicators, Mexico's population, with much lower per capita incomes, fared better.[19]

Opportunity costs
Sacrifices and trade-offs are made when money is spent on one thing rather than another. What could be done by diverting some of today's military expenditure? Here are a few examples:[20]

Hunger: the elimination of famine in Africa would cost about five weeks' world military spending ($100 billion); a transfer of 0.5 per cent of the global arms budget would buy all the agricultural equipment the South is said to need to achieve food self-sufficiency.

Health: the World Health Organization estimates that it would cost eighteen days of world military spending each year for ten years to provide safe water for the 2 billion people who lack it; one Trident submarine would pay for a five-year worldwide child immunization programme, saving a million lives annually.

Education: the cost of training one soldier would educate about a hundred schoolchildren; the price of a single battle tank would finance 1,000 classrooms in the South for 30,000 children; a nuclear submarine would pay for a year's education for 160 million schoolchildren in twenty-three low-income countries.

Environment: three days of world military spending would finance five years' global rainforest conservation; one month's worth would pay for most of the twenty-year UN action plan to halt desertification in the South; the SDI budget for 1987 would have paid for solar power for a city of 200,000 people or for twenty years of energy conservation research; a year's European Community military spending would finance a ten-year clean-up of the EC's hazardous waste sites.

While opponents of disarmament claim that military spending helps the economy, the opposite is usually the case. In the Eastern bloc, the cost of a high level of militarization has included economic stagnation and a severe shortage of useful goods. In the Western democracies, public money, raised through taxation or international borrowing, is eaten up in expensive technology for its own sake, budget overruns, mismanagement, excessive secrecy and corruption. There is a well-known story, possibly apocryphal, of the US air force being billed hundreds of dollars apiece for ashtrays, toilet seats and coffee pots. More reliable was the announcement in early 1990 that the unit price of the US air force's new air-to-air missile had shot up by almost 50 per cent in a single year.[21]

Inflation and jobs

Military expenditure is completely inflationary. It injects cash into the economy without producing goods and services for the money to be spent on. This is pure consumption, doing nothing to increase a country's ability to meet its people's needs.

Arms spending is also a poor way of creating jobs. As military technology grows more sophisticated, production becomes capital- rather than labour-intensive. Studies by the US Bureau of Labor Statistics show that far more jobs are created, dollar for dollar, by federal spending on construction, education, health, transport, civilian industry or government services than by military expenditure. In the UK, while arms exports tripled between 1981 and 1986, jobs dependent on these sales fell by a third.[22]

The myth of the spin-off

Another myth is that military research and development produce valuable spin-offs for civilian industry. Just compare the industrial performance of high military spenders with low spenders: defence budgets absorb 50 per cent of government R&D funds in the USA, USSR and UK but only 10 per cent in West Germany and just 2 per cent in Japan. The result? Japanese and West German civilian industries and products are world beaters. "The Japanese apply their research directly to the purposes for which they seek relevant solutions...Accordingly the United States bristles with Japanese goods."[23]

Social costs

Then there is the harm done to the position of disadvantaged social groups, such as women, ethnic minorities, the elderly and people on low incomes. When resources are switched from civilian industry and services to the military, as they were in the NATO countries during the 1980s, women's jobs and social welfare spending are cut back. In the USA cuts were made in food stamps, health care, public transport and public education. It is generally women, not men, who pick up the tab when the welfare state gets mean.

Knock-on effects

The effects of President Reagan's $1.6 trillion arms programme launched in 1982 were felt far beyond the USA's shores. The sum was estimated as equivalent to a year's combined GNPs of Latin America, Australia, South-east Asia and India, plus a year's Middle East oil.[24] Most of the money had to come from abroad to keep US taxes low; people in other countries had to foot the bill.

To attract the necessary foreign lending, and to combat the inflation sparked off by bigger military expenditure, the US Federal Reserve raised its interest rates high. As other US banks followed suit, the higher cost of borrowing caused bankruptcies among small US business, such as family farmers. US manufacturers suffered as the value of the dollar climbed in response to the influx of foreign money, overpricing US goods and reducing their competitiveness; unemployment followed. With the UK and other Western countries adopting the same policies, bank lending rates rose worldwide. Poor countries were forced deeper into debt. By 1990 the US deficit stood at about $2 trillion.[25]

The price of power
As for the Soviet Union and Eastern bloc, for years they had weapons to spare for Southern governments and revolutionary movements, but they could not provide their own people with food, useful work, a healthy environment or civil liberties. President Gorbachev and other new Eastern European leaders, however, recognize that large military budgets lie like a dead weight on their countries' economies.

In the UK, every postwar government has failed to notice the connection between the country's unusually high military spending and its poor economic performance. The UK's obstinate attachment to "great power" status has probably contributed more than any other cause to its economic and industrial troubles since 1945. Vast amounts of public money are pumped into military-oriented research at colleges and universities in the UK; is this the kind of work our higher education system should be geared to?

Wasting resources
Military spending in the South accounts for perhaps a third of the poor countries' debt burden and has steadily absorbed more and more of their disposable income. With so many economic and social problems needing solution, any diversion of resources to the armed forces allows domestic difficulties to build up, leading to civil unrest and government repression. The Brazilian metalworkers' union says that tax exemptions granted to arms manufacturers "mean that the government is effectively handing over to these companies money that could be spent on health, education, public transport".[26]

Besides the economic cost, excessive defence spending wastes human and other resources and causes environmental damage. The military is said to be the world's single largest employer, with 25 million soldiers under arms and another 75 million people in support roles. Weapons research is among the best paid occupations, and its uptake of half a million skilled scientists and technicians deprives the world of some of its most able problem-solvers. Another effect in the South is to drain resources away from the food-producing countryside. Cash crops are sold abroad to raise foreign currency to buy weapons, but little money is reinvested in rural areas. According to the United Nations, many low-income countries spend five times more foreign currency on weapons than on farm equipment. Land, food, mineral resources, housing and transportation facilities are among the other public goods lost to the community when military demands are made on them.

Environmental damage

As for environmental damage, consider for example the price paid by rural communities in parts of the UK where low-flying military aircraft make regular practice runs. Engine emissions from these aircraft pollute farmland, waterways, woodland and the air. People suffer noise and stress, and farmers lose livestock. Crashes and near-misses often occur, sixty-five people having been killed in the last six years. According to the Campaign for Nuclear Disarmament, these low flights are not practice *defensive* runs (which would require high-altitude flying) but practice long-range (and possibly nuclear) *offensive* bombing missions.[27]

The military obsession

Do enormous arms budgets genuinely increase people's security? Surely not. The USA was threatened with just four Soviet ICBMs in 1960, but twenty years later there were 8,000 of them. All around the world high military spending increases political tension, giving rise to regional arms races such as those between India and Pakistan, and Israel and Syria. Increasingly confident armed forces seek political power – a path that leads to repression and sometimes to civil war. Besides, as arms systems proliferate, the risk of accidental war or deliberate sabotage increases: official US sources acknowledge that faulty systems and human error caused 147 false nuclear alerts between 1979 and 1980.[28]

When countries concentrate on planning for war, they cannot make worthwhile progress in terms of social and political reform at home or the search for peace abroad. As the historian and peace campaigner E. P. Thompson has put it: "The drive to make the threat to your enemy ever more credible excludes the search for other ways of resolving conflicts...We are preparing ourselves to be the kind of societies which go to war."[29]

The arms trade

The international arms trade is worth about $250 million a year. Not surprisingly, most of this money travels from the South to the industrialized North, with the goods going in the opposite direction. Low-income countries buy far more weaponry than they can afford. Why?

The background
In the 1950s and 1960s, when Europe's former colonies gained political independence, the world seemed (and was) dangerous. Superpower rivalry dominated world affairs, and the Western allies and Eastern bloc were engaged in a hectic arms race. Not surprisingly, the newly independent countries followed suit. Many former colonies were in any case not natural political or cultural units but had been created haphazardly when the Europeans carved up the world between them, with little respect for ethnic or lingustic divisions (especially in Africa). The new governments were often hard pressed to keep their populations in order, and some Southern politicians opted for strong armed forces in an attempt to forge a sense of national identity and pride.

For all these reasons, low-income countries bought more and more arms. Southern leaders became dependent on the military, or themselves rose through the armed forces. High-ranking officers pressed claims for a greater say in national affairs and for more sophisticated weapons. By the 1980s "practically every African country had...at least one type of advanced weapon".[30]

Competitive market
What about the arms suppliers? The two superpowers, France, the UK and China are the big-time weapons exporters. Other European countries such as Czechoslovakia, Sweden and West Germany have gradually stepped up their sales efforts; and a number of Southern arms exporters including Brazil, Egypt, Israel, North and South Korea and Singapore have appeared on the scene.

Competition between exporting countries is intense, and the profit motive tends to overrule moral considerations. In 1980, for example, the UK reversed a previous government decision and resumed military sales to the Chilean dictatorship.

More than twenty other well-known human rights violators are regular UK arms customers, such as Indonesia, Malaysia and Saudi Arabia. Much of the hardware sold is riot-control gear and other equipment useless for external defence but handy when dealing with civil unrest.

To secure deals in what is a buyers' market, exporters may be obliged to grant easy conditions, special discounts and long-term low-interest credit; these are, in effect, subsidies paid for by taxpayers in the selling country. Thus, although overseas weapons sales are said to be good for the exporting country's economy, the reverse is closer to the truth. The true reason why manufacturing countries want to sell weapons abroad is that this is the only way they can recoup some of the astronomical costs of weapons research, development and production.

Prolonging war

The arms trade may not in itself cause wars, but it certainly makes them worse. The Iran–Iraq conflict of 1980–8, for example, was prolonged well beyond the point when the armouries of the combatants would otherwise have been exhausted because so many countries kept them supplied with weapons. At least twenty- six countries are alleged to have sold arms to both sides.[31] There have been ironic consequences of the trade, too, such as the sinking of HMS *Sheffield* during the Falklands/Malvinas conflict by an Argentinian Exocet missile (supplied by France) complete with UK-manufactured components. The Argentinian fleet included two warships refitted only weeks before in Portsmouth.

Secret deals

The weapons trade is highly secretive. Deals may remain undisclosed until governments have sealed them, or they may never be made public. This lack of accountability has allowed the illegal trade to flourish, sometimes with an added drugs connection. Private dealers are paid high commissions to circumvent embargoes such as the international ban on military sales to South Africa and to secure percentages for corrupt bureaucrats. The 1987 Iran–"contra" scandal implicated US government officials in illegal military sales to Iran and then in unlawfully siphoning the proceeds to the right-wing Nicaraguan rebels. Weapons purchases in Lebanon and Afghanistan have involved the proceeds of cannabis and heroin smuggling.

Arms trade secrecy breeds suspicion and destabilizes international relations. Alarmed by their neighbours' military strength and readiness for war (often exaggerated), governments that cannot afford to do so overarm and in turn give others cause to fear.

Action

War and the arms race

The role of the UN
Attempts have been made before and since 1945 to reduce the risk of war. Some of these efforts, for example the setting up of the League of Nations in 1919, were largely unsuccessful; others have produced positive results. The League's successor, the United Nations, has many achievements to its credit in such fields as health and disaster relief and as a peacekeeper in local conflicts. Yet the UN has been virtually powerless in the face of the world's military build-up, the proliferation of local wars and the threat of nuclear catastrophe.

Much of the blame rests with the permanent members of the UN Security Council – the USA, the USSR, the UK, France and China. The "big five", with their rivalries and ideologies, have distracted the UN from its true purpose and have clung to their privileged position in the organization (including veto rights) in the face of mounting opposition. Chiefly as a result, the UN has been unable to prevent acts of international aggression. In the opinion of the respected UN diplomat Brian Urquhart, "The deep and perennial disagreements of the permanent members hobbled the Security Council from the outset."[32]

The UN has also had financial problems. Accusations of wasteful spending have been made, and several countries have withheld financial contributions. The USA and the UK withdrew from UNESCO in the 1980s, accusing it of financial mismanagement and political bias. Low-income countries, meanwhile, are impatient with the UN's failure to make progress on issues of North–South economic justice and towards a new international economic order.

International treaties

Attempts to slow down the arms race through international treaties have had equally mixed results. The Partial Test Ban Treaty of 1963, for example, was endorsed by the Soviet Union, the USA and more than a hundred other countries. This agreement banned nuclear weapons testing in the atmosphere, underwater and in space, in response to worldwide anxiety about radioactive contamination. China and France nevertheless disregarded the ban, and underground tests continued. Two US writers on disarmament have suggested that the 1963 treaty "had about the same effect on the arms race as the ban on tv cigarette advertising and the surgeon general's warning had on the vitality of the tobacco industry".[33]

Other major international weapons agreements still in force include: the 1970 Non-Proliferation Treaty, which may have slowed but has failed to halt the global proliferation of nuclear capability; the 1972 Anti-Ballistic Missile Treaty, which prohibits the deployment of any Star Wars-type defence system; and SALT I, the 1972 Strategic Arms Limitation Treaty, which limits the number of ICBMs the USA and the USSR can possess.

The Intermediate Nuclear Forces Treaty, signed in December 1987 between Presidents Reagan and Gorbachev, was hailed as a breakthough. The treaty set in motion the removal of medium-range ballistic missiles and ground-launched cruise missiles from Europe; and it was the first ever agreement to dismantle missiles currently deployed and to allow verification by Soviet and US inspectors of each other's bases.

Some have argued, however, that such agreements have limited value. "Hardly had the ink dried on promises to remove 4 per cent of the world's nuclear arsenals," point out Green Party writers Sandy Irvine and Alec Ponton, "than NATO was planning new generations of nuclear-capable aircraft and sea-launched cruise missiles, which the Warsaw Pact powers will try to copy and overtake." Discussing the many years of arms control talks and agreements, historian Paul Kennedy concludes that "if anything, the banning or limitation of one weapon system merely led to a transfer of resources to another area".[34]

Critics of NATO's planned new TASM missile, which only the USA and the UK appear to want, agree. "As far as the Soviets are concerned, the effect of the TASM and of SLCMs [sea-launched cruise missiles, due to be deployed on NATO ships in European waters, within reach of Soviet targets, in the 1990s] is to nullify the intention of the INF Treaty," says retired US Admiral Eugene Carroll.[35]

Strengthening the UN

What of the future? The United Nations, despite its limitations, is our best hope for international conflict resolution. More support for the UN and its agencies is crucial if we are to build a more just and peaceful world. This means increased funding by governments, perhaps augmented with a tax on international trade, and a greater willingness to abide by UN decisions. No country, large or small, should be able to ignore rulings by the International Court of Justice in The Hague – as the USA did in 1986 when it refused to stop trying to destabilize the Nicaraguan government.

The role of the UN peacekeeping force should be strengthened, with the ultimate aim of setting up a permanent international force to guarantee countries' security and allow them to devote more resources to peaceful development. A corps of trained UN mediators could be established to help resolve tensions within and between countries. The dispatch of a small international UN peacekeeping and observer force to Nicaragua for its 1990 elections (the first ever deployment in the Western hemisphere) was a step in the right direction.

The UN's structure needs democratizing. It has been suggested that either the main decision-making body or a second chamber should consist of elected, not appointed, representatives from each country. Some have proposed a second chamber of representatives from NGOs. Greater democracy should also probably involve an end to permanent Security Council membership and to the veto powers of the big five.[36]

Peace dividend?

Beyond the UN, improvements in East–West relations have continued with Soviet troop cuts and political reform in Eastern Europe and NATO's 1990 "declaration of peace" towards the Warsaw Pact. Soviet defence spending is projected to fall steadily during the next few years, as it must if economic reform is to succeed. Further reductions in both sides' conventional forces are on the agenda at the Conventional Forces in Europe (CFE) talks in Vienna and a Strategic Arms Reduction Treaty (START) may well be signed by the superpowers at the end of 1990, leading to substantial cuts in long-range nuclear missiles.

In the USA former defence secretary and World Bank president Robert McNamara now believes the country could halve its defence budget over the next six to eight years. The US Congress and, to a lesser extent, President Bush both appear to want a scaling-down of defence spending, partly in recognition of the many domestic problems that accumulated during the Reagan military build-up. Despite the post-cold-war climate, however, some Pentagon policy-makers may try to fight a rear-guard action; in 1990 they were reported as seeking a 22 per cent increase in SDI funding.[37]

As for the UK, by reducing defence spending by up to a third (including the withdrawal of forces now stationed in West Germany), it would bring its military budget down to the level of its Western European neighbours, countries that are adequately defended at far less cost. This measure would release much of the money needed in the UK for investment in industrial and social infrastructure. In the event, in 1990 the UK announced sizeable manpower and hardware reductions for its armed services; but there will be only a small "peace dividend" as most of these savings are absorbed by rising costs.

Western leaders have refused to raise hopes of a "peace dividend", yet this is what the world needs. Friends of the Earth and the Safer World Foundation in the UK have proposed a Fifty Per Cent Initiative whereby NATO governments would halve military spending by the end of the century and use the money saved to deal with major environmental and economic problems.

NATO and the Warsaw Pact

For so long the pacesetters in the arms race, the USA and NATO have at least begun moving in the opposite direction, on what President Bush has called "a new path for peace". Proposals to reduce the number and type of nuclear weapons in Europe, and the declaration of nuclear arms to be "weapons of last resort", are welcome. But NATO should surely still also announce a policy of "no first use" of nuclear weapons, as the USSR and China have done.

The idea that US forces must remain in Europe, and that nuclear deterrence is needed, is now more than ever question-able. Richard Perle, once a hawkish assistant US defence secretary, admits that it is "no longer possible to imagine a cohesive Warsaw Pact, led by Soviet troops, forcing its way through the centre of Europe" to invade the West. The International Institute of Strategic Studies agrees: Soviet troop withdrawals "virtually eliminate" the danger of a surprise Warsaw Pact land attack. (In any case, NATO claims to have satellite surveillance that would give a month's warning of any such offensive.) Even the chair of the US House Armed Services Committee accepts that "We can defend conventional forces in Europe without nuclear weapons."[38]

As for US "protection" – Western Europe is one of the world's few rich and powerful groups of countries. From whom or what are US missiles, ships, bombers and ground troops meant to defend it?

Nuclear test ban
A comprehensive nuclear test ban is as desirable now as it was in the early 1980s when millions of anti-nuclear campaigners called for a weapons freeze. Seismic technology can identify even small nuclear explosions, so verification would be possible. Once all such tests had ceased, there would be little point in new weapons development.

Subsequent steps could include: phased reductions in existing nuclear arsenals in East and West; the establishing of more nuclear-free zones (such as a European one, centred on a demilitarized Germany, as suggested by President Gorbachev); and a phasing out of plutonium production, bringing the manufacture of weapons-grade material to a halt. The USSR has announced its intention to end plutonium production by the end of the century.

Dissolve the alliances
The long-term aim should be to dissolve NATO, the Warsaw Pact and every other regional military alliance. Czechoslovakia and Hungary have negotiated the withdrawal of Soviet troops from their soil, and Poland is likely to follow. Belgium and the Netherlands want to remove their armies from West Germany. It will be a backward step if a future united Germany becomes integrated into NATO's military strategy, as Western conservatives intend it should be. Czech President Vaclav Havel has called for NATO and the Warsaw Pact (if the latter survives) to be transformed into "instruments of disarmament",

alongside the construction of a new Europe-wide system of political co-operation. Such a system could be based on the 35-country Conference on Security and Co-operation in Europe that drew up the 1975 Helsinki Declaration on human rights and has since turned its attention to questions of political and military security. Both NATO and the Warsaw Pact say they intend to adopt a more political role.

Chemical weapons

International agreement is needed on chemical weapons. The "Australia Group" of governments is working towards a Chemical Weapons Convention that will allow "challenge inspections" of countries suspected of developing or holding chemical warfare agents.[39] The USA has announced plans to destroy all its stockpiles by 1997; and in mid-1990 it began the long and hazardous process of moving huge quantities of nerve gas from storage in West Germany to Johnston Atoll in the Pacific. There it will try to incinerate them.

Disarmament and development

By diverting as little as 5 per cent of their military budgets, the rich countries could double their overseas aid to the South. Such action would encourage other countries to reduce their armament levels, and this would strengthen their economies, meet more of the needs of their people and diminish the risk of war. Costa Rica, for example, has no army at all, is an unusually free and fair society by Central American standards and has been at the forefront of peacemaking efforts in the region. "National, regional and global security could be enhanced through expenditures quite small in relation to the level of military spending," argues the Brundtland Commission. "Common security", as the Palme Commission called it, means devoting resources to improving human well-being, whereas remaining armed to the teeth has the reverse effect.[40]

The UN has sponsored work on the links between disarmament and development. A tax on international arms sales is one of several proposals put forward for the transfer of resources from military activities to development. And despite some opposition from Western governments, a forthcoming UN conference will consider the idea of a "disarmament and development fund". In 1989 World Bank president Barber Conable called for a diversion of funds from arms to spending on health, education and welfare; while the IMF is said to have persuaded Jordan not to buy $800 million of UK Tornado aircraft.[41]

Controlling sales
Arms exports to violent regimes must be halted, a policy so far fully implemented only by a few countries such as Canada, the Netherlands and West Germany. To reduce corruption and political tension, weapons transfers should no longer be secret. The UN has discussed setting up an open register of international arms transfers; or there could be a licensing system for arms sales, with the aim of steadily reducing the volume of trade.

Arms conversion
Debates about disarmament often focus on the conversion of weapons industries to civilian production. While opponents of disarmament argue that military industries are important providers of jobs and profits, the evidence indicates otherwise. In the early 1970s Lucas Aerospace, then the UK's largest private military contractor, suffered thousands of job losses. Lucas's trade unions then presented an alternative corporate plan to the management, suggesting the company switch production from military to civilian goods. Adopting many of these ideas, the management avoided further large-scale job losses.

Military contractors in other countries have converted to making heat pumps, road/rail vehicles and medical equipment, and further areas of potential include solar energy products, pollution control technology and weapons destruction and disposal systems. Only 6 of a total of 127 US occupational groups studied in 1967 were thought to need retraining for the change-over from military to civilian production.[42]

Few civilian industries are as wasteful and inflationary as weapons manufacturing. Most are more labour-intensive and less dominated by large corporations. Arms conversion can therefore cut waste, reduce inflationary pressure, create jobs, give better opportunities to small companies and help spread wealth through the community. The production of socially useful goods should also improve living standards. Major European military manufacturers said to be looking into conversion include Thompson CSF in France, Philips in the Netherlands and MBB in West Germany. In the UK, Lloyds Bank has expressed interest, and research has been undertaken by the Transport and General Workers' Union and some local authorities.[43]

The main obstacle to conversion is an unwillingness to change. Arms manufacturers want to hold on to their economic power, while government propagandizing encourages people to see weapons industries as essential to the national interest. Managements and trade unions could prepare for conversion together by drawing up feasibility studies and running pilot projects; government funding could be provided to assist this research.

Driven by its economic problems, Eastern Europe may be ahead of the West in turning tanks into tractors. The USSR is said to have cut tank and fighter aircraft production, halted work on a nuclear-powered cruiser and begun to "reprofile" defence enterprises to help the civilian economy. Bulgaria has announced plans to convert most of its military production to civilian purposes within five years.

As for the poorest countries, the UN Environment Programme is reportedly prepared to help them switch resources from arms to environmental protection.

Besides the arms industry, armed forces themselves could be converted. Military training, skills and resources may prove crucial in the global environmental battles ahead; the international community may need a rapid-deployment disaster force, for example.

The peace movement

Despite being sometimes ridiculed or harassed by governments, peace campaigners in many countries have helped remind the world that there are alternatives to endless militarism. Public pressure was the main factor in the USA's decision to withdraw from Vietnam in 1975, and since then US foreign policy has been more restrained. Public opinion also led to Israel's military withdrawal from Lebanon in 1982. In 1984 New Zealand's peace movement helped persuade Prime Minister Lange to declare a nuclear-free zone and ban visits by nuclear-armed ships. Greenpeace's anti-nuclear protests in the Pacific so alarmed the French secret service that its agents blew up the *Rainbow Warrior* in 1985. After years of struggle, peace groups and human rights campaigners have been in the forefront of the political changes sweeping Eastern Europe. Solidarity, now in power in Poland, has long called for the abolition of nuclear weapons.

"Since war begins in the minds of men, it is in the minds of men that the defence of peace must be constructed,"

UNESCO's constitution begins. More cultural and scientific exchanges and greater efforts to enhance respect and understanding between countries – for example, through international environmental co-operation – are crucial if peace is to be won. Peace is being adopted as a subject of study in a growing number of countries, for both children and adults; such studies focus on the interdependence of people, countries and the planet, and on an understanding of human psychology and behaviour, conflicts and conflict resolution.

Peace campaigners in many lands have argued for non-violent defence strategies (sometimes called social defence). Drawing on Gandhian principles of civil disobedience, such a defence would immobilize and undermine any occupying power through strikes, disruption of transport and services, public demonstrations and so on. Similar tactics contributed to the success of the US civil rights movement.

This kind of approach to defence has been ridiculed. Rumours that something similar lay behind the UK Labour Party's unilateralist defence policy are said to have damaged the party's performance in the 1987 general election. But is non-violent defence really such a non-starter? Soviet President Gorbachev, admired by Western leaders for his realism, has spoken of "the process of lowering, and then eliminating, military confrontation *and making the transition to non-offensive defence*".[44]

Getting Involved

Related subjects covered elsewhere in this book include: extremes of wealth and poverty – Chapter 2; male violence – Chapter 4; human rights and regional conflict – Chapter 5; nuclear power – Chapter 8. For more information on war, the arms race and the potential for disarmament, see "Recommended Reading" (pages 324–9).

Consumer and lifestyle choices

Most of the individual action suggested in earlier chapters should help create a more just and self-reliant society, one less threatening to other countries and oriented towards peace rather than towards war. This will not necessarily create a world free from conflict, because there will always be disagreements and disputes; but it should mean a world less prone to violence. The more a country such as the UK gains a reputation for economic and social justice, the better it can act as a peacemaker worldwide.

Make do with less

By being satisfied with less materially, avoiding unethically produced goods and working in a peace-enhancing occupation (see the "Getting Involved" sections in Chapters 1, 2 and 5), you can help reduce the risk of war arising from brutal exploitation and extreme inequalities of power and wealth. Affirmative action in favour of women (Chapter 4) will weaken male domination, an essential aspect of the aggressive state, and enhance the role of peaceful conflict resolution. By reducing your consumption of hardwood timber, water and fossil-fuel energy (Chapters 6, 7 and 8), you can help ease the inequalities of resource use that lead to the South's often bitter resentment of the North.

Avoid competition

Other choices we can make will probably come naturally to most people reading this book. One is to avoid competitive behaviour at work and in the community; the competitive spirit got men to the moon, yet it left the country that achieved this, the USA, as crime- and debt-ridden and as prone to violence as ever. "A competitive mode of action", it has been said, "can never achieve an equitable and just society, since it requires a constant supply of failures."[45] Trying to do worthwhile things well, of course, is another matter entirely.

Oppose violence

Speak out against hidden violence in everyday life, such as the domination of one person or one section of the community by another. Oppose unjustifiable state, bureaucratic or commercial secrecy by joining a campaign for more open government, such as Charter 88 in the UK (see Chapter 5).

Avoid the glorification of violence and war in videos, films, other entertainment media and children's toys and games. Collections of co-operative, non-competitive games have been published, such as *Games for Social and Life Skills* by Tim

Bond (London: Century Hutchinson, 1986), which is suitable for teenagers and adults; the Peace Pledge Union (see below) publishes collections of younger children's co-operative games.

Workplace, community and political action

International links
Canvass for your town or borough to set up a "twinning" scheme with a town in Eastern Europe or a low-income country in the South. Take part in other international exchanges to help improve global understanding.

Industrial conversion
At your workplace, in your trade union or occupational association or in your community or political group, discuss industrial conversion from military to civilian production. Write a short article about arms conversion for your community or occupational newsletter or journal. If you work in the weapons industry, or if there are such industries in your area, try to persuade local councillors, your MP and MEP and the Secretary of State for Trade and Industry (Department of Trade and Industry, 1–19 Victoria Street, London W1) about the need for and usefulness of arms conversion studies and pilot projects; write about such studies and projects to the press and raise the subject on radio phone-ins. Here are some points you could make:

- The UK, NATO and the Warsaw Pact have for decades had far more weaponry than any of them need for legitimate defence, and there is now less cause than ever to fear the outbreak of war between East and West.
- Studies show that more jobs are created when governments invest in civilian industry and social services than when they put money into weapons production.
- The world's most efficient industrial economies – Japan and West Germany – are efficient largely because they are low military spenders.
- Arms spending is inflationary, pumping money into the economy without producing anything for people to spend the money on.
- In the face of so many urgent environmental and social problems, it is short-sighted and morally wrong to waste the

vast sums that we do (and will continue to do, despite recent cuts) on weapons and the armed forces.

In the UK, the Centre for Product Development Services (Cooper Buildings, Sheffield Science Park, Arundel Street, Sheffield S1 2NS) has been set up to link local authorities, co-operative development agencies, technology transfer centres and other organizations with an interest in arms conversion. Try to interest your workplace or local authority in contacting the CPDS to find out more about conversion possibilities.

Lobby for peace

Write to your local councillors, MP and MEP, to the Foreign Secretary (Foreign and Commonwealth Office, Downing Street, London SW1A 2AL) and to the press, or phone into your local radio station, about some of these measures that would strengthen peace and reduce the occurrence and risk of war:

- the withdrawal of US nuclear forces from the UK; Denmark, Norway and Spain, which are also NATO countries, will not allow US nuclear forces on their territory;
- an international treaty banning armed interventions in foreign countries;
- a comprehensive nuclear weapons test ban;
- further arms spending cuts in the UK and NATO;
- an end to arms sales to violent governments and human rights abusers;
- strengthening and reform of the United Nations, with larger budget contributions from the richer countries;
- an enlarged role for the UN peacekeeping force;
- a UN disarmament and development fund.

Peace studies

Find out more about peace studies and help campaign for more such courses in schools, colleges and workplaces; try to generate interest among like-minded colleagues. A good source of educational materials in the UK is the Peace Education Project run by the Peace Pledge Union (address below), which also arranges workshops for teachers, runs the Children and War Project (campaigning against the influences on the young that make war acceptable) and publishes practical books suggesting co-operative games for all ages. Peace education materials are also available from CND (address below).

Organizations

Organizations involved in the struggle for an end to injustice and a more peaceful world include:

UK and Irish Republic
Amnesty International, 99–119 Rosebery Avenue, London EC1R 4RE (071-278 6000), and (international secretariat) 1 Easton Street, London WC1X 8DJ (071-833 1771).
Campaign against Arms Trade, 11 Goodwin Street, London N4 3HQ (071-281 0297).
Campaign for Nuclear Disarmament, 162 Holloway Road, London N7 8DQ (071-700 2393).
Conscience/Peace Tax Campaign, 1A Hollybush Place, London E2 9QX (071-739 5088).
European Nuclear Disarmament, 11 Goodwin Street, London N4 3HQ (071-272 9092).
Greenpeace, 30–31 Islington Green, London N1 8XE (071-354 5100) .
Irish Peace Council/Irish CND, 29 Lower Baggot Street, Dublin 2, Irish Republic.
Medical Campaign against Nuclear Weapons, 601 Holloway Road, London N19 (071-272 2020).
One World Centre, 4 Lower Crescent, Belfast BT7 1NR (0232-241879).
Peace Pledge Union, 6 Endsleigh Street, London WC1 (071-387 5501).
Quaker Peace and Service, Friends House, Euston Road, London NW1 2BJ (071-387 3601).
Safer World Foundation, 82 Colston Street, Bristol BS1 5BB (0272-276435).
Scottish Campaign for Nuclear Disarmament, 3rd Floor Left, 420 Sauchiehall Street, Glasgow G2, Scotland (041-331 2878).
Scottish Campaign to Resist the Atomic Menace, 11 Forth Street, Edinburgh EH1 3LE, Scotland (031-557 4283).
Socialist Environment and Resources Association, 26–28 Underwood Street, London N1 7JQ (071-490 0240).

United Nations Association, 3 Whitehall Court, London
SW1A 2EL (071-930 2931).
United Nations Association, 22 Darley Terrace, Dublin 8,
Irish Republic.
United Nations Association of Northern Ireland, 1 Glesnharragh
Gardens, Belfast BT6 9PE.
Women's International League for Peace and Freedom, 29
Great James Street, London WC1N 3ES (071-242 1521).

USA and Canada
ACT for Disarmament, 456 Spadina Avenue, Toronto, Ontario
M5T 2G8, Canada.
Americas Watch, 739 Eighth Street SE, Washington, DC
20003, USA.
Amnesty International, 322 Eighth Avenue, New York, NY
10001, USA.
Amnesty International, Suite 900, 130 Slater Street, Ottawa,
Ontario K1P 6E2, Canada.
Campaign for Peace with Justice in Central America, 1747
Connecticut Avenue NW, Washington, DC 20009, USA.
Canadian Coalition for Nuclear Responsibility, PO Box 236,
Snowden, Montreal, Quebec H3X 3T4, Canada.
Center for Economic Conversion, 222C View Street, Mountain
View, Calif. 94041, USA.
Coalition for a New Foreign and Military Policy, 712 G Street
NE, Washington, DC 20003, USA.
End the Arms Race, 1708 West 16th Avenue, Vancouver,
British Columbia V6J 2M1, Canada.
International Center for Peace in the Middle East, PO Box
2051, Dag Hammerskjold Center, New York, NY 10001,
USA.
International Physicicans for the Prevention of Nuclear War,
126 Rogers Street, Cambridge, Mass. 02142, USA.
Project Ploughshares, Conrad Grebel College, Waterloo,
Ontario N2L 3G6, Canada.
United Nations Association in Canada, 63 Sparks Street 808,
Ottawa, Ontario KP1 5A6, Canada.
United Nations Association of the USA, 485 Fifth Avenue,
New York, NY 10017, USA.
Women against Military Madness, 3255 Hennepin Avenue S.,
Minneapolis, Minn. 55408, USA.

Women's International League for Peace and Freedom, 1102
   Ironwork Passage, Vancouver, British Colombia V6H 3P1,
   and PO Box 4781E, Ottawa, Ontario K1S 5H9, Canada.
Women's International League for Peace and Freedom, 1213
   Race Street, Philadelphia, Pa 1907, USA.
Women's Pentagon Action, 339 Lafayette Street, New York,
   NY 10012, USA.

Australia and New Zealand
Amnesty International, Private Bag No. 23, Broadway, New
   South Wales 2007, Australia.
Amnesty International, PO Box 6647, Wellington 1, New
   Zealand.
Australian Coalition for Disarmament and Peace, PO Box
   A243, Sydney South, New South Wales 2000, Australia.
Australian Peace Committee, Box 32, Trades Hall, Goulburn
   Street, Sydney, New South Wales 2000, Australia.
Campaign for International Co-operation and Disarmament,
   GPO Box 114A, Melbourne, Victoria 3001, Australia.
Campaign for Nuclear Disarmament, Box 8558, Auckland 1,
   and PO Box 6618, Te Aro, Wellington, New Zealand.
Nuclear-Free and Independent Pacific Movement, Pacific Con-
   cerns Resource Centre, PO Box 9295, Newmarket, Auckland,
   New Zealand.
Pacific Campaign to Disarm the Seas, PO Box 338, Fitzroy,
   Victoria 3065, Australia.
Pacific Peoples' Anti-Nuclear Action Committee, PO Box
   61086, Otara, Auckland, New Zealand.
Scientists against Nuclear Arms, PO Box 6289, Wellesley, New
   Zealand.
United Nations Association of Australia, 328 Flinders Street,
   Melbourne, Victoria 3000, Australia.
United Nations Association of New Zealand, PO Box 11-750,
   Wellington, New Zealand.
Women's International League for Peace and Freedom, GPO
   Box 2598, Sydney, New South Wales 2001, Australia.
Women's International League for Peace and Freedom, 56A
   Wai-iti Crescent, Lower Hutt, New Zealand.

Africa, Asia and Caribbean (Commonwealth)
Amnesty International, PO Box 872, Bridgetown, Barbados.
Amnesty International, PO Box 1173, Koforidua, Ghana.

Amnesty International, Palm Court Building, 35 Main Street, Georgetown, Guyana.

Amnesty International, PO Bag 231, Woodbrook PO, Port of Spain, Trinidad.

Amnesty International, c/o Dateline Delhi, 21 North End Complex, Panchkuin Road, New Delhi 110001, India.

Amnesty International, PO Box 59, Agodi Post Office, Ibadan, Oyo State, Nigeria.

Amnesty International, PO Box 4904, Dar es Salaam, Tanzania.

Gandhi Peace Foundation, 221–223 Deen Dayal, Upadhyaya Marg, New Delhi 110002, India.

Indian Campaign for Nuclear Disarmament, c/o Gandhi Memorial Committee, 59B Chowringhee Road, Calcutta, West Bengal 700020, India.

Planetary Citizens' Council for Peace, Development and the Environment, Robinson Road, PO Box 2753, Singapore 9047.

United Nations Association, c/o Kwame Nkrumah Conference Centre, PO Box 2329, Accra, Ghana.

United Nations Association, PO Box 58372, Nairobi, Kenya.

United Nations Association, PO Box 224, Kingston 7, Jamaica.

United Nations Association, c/o Nigerian Institute of International Affairs, PO Box 54423, Falamo, Ikoyi, Lagos, Nigeria.

United Nations Association of Singapore, PO Box 351, Tanglin Post Office, Singapore 9124.

United Nations Association, c/o Director of International Organizations, Ministry of Foreign Affairs, PO Box RW 50069, Lusaka, Zambia.

Women's International League for Peace and Freedom, c/o Joyce Lartey, PO Box 1949, Mamprobi, Accra, Ghana.

Women's International League for Peace and Freedom, Box 45922, Nairobi, Kenya.

Glossary

acid rain: more correctly, *acid precipitation*; acidic cloud, mist, rain, sleet or snow, resulting from the combination of moisture in the air with sulphur dioxide and nitrogen oxide emissions from fossil fuel burning.

agribusiness: industrialized form of farming based on large farms, heavy machinery and chemicals.

agrochemicals: chemical fertilizers and pesticides used in modern agriculture.

albedo: reflectivity of lighter-coloured areas of the Earth's surface.

alkalinization: soil deterioration caused when excessive irrigation water heavily laden with volcanic sodium or sodium bicarbonate salts evaporates.

Amerindians: indigenous people of the Americas.

appropriate development: forms of economic and social development in low-income countries that enhance the well-being of poor and powerless people and cause no environmental damage.

aquifer: underground layer of rock such as chalk or sandstone that holds water or allows it to pass through.

arms conversion: conversion of weapons industries to civilian production.

biodegradable: capable of being decomposed by living matter, such as bacteria.

biodiversity: rich variety of life forms.

biogas: fuel gas derived directly from living matter, such as methane (from decomposing organic waste) or ethanol (from sugarcane).

biomass: strictly, the chemical energy contained in growing plants; *biomass* fuels are those derived from plant matter, such as firewood, crop residues and *biogas*.

biosphere reserve: conservation reserve of two or more zones in which some forms of human activity, especially careful natural resource use by local people, scientific research and controlled wildlife tourism, take place.

bottom-up: approach to development in low-income countries where resources are directed to helping the poorest and most vulnerable people improve their lives.

bund: small, low stone or earth dike that slows rainfall runoff and helps prevent soil erosion.

carcinogen: cancer-causing substance.

cash crop: farm produce grown entirely for the cash or export market, not for local use.

co-disposal: dumping of domestic solid waste together with toxic industrial substances; prohibited in many industrialized countries but legal in the UK.

combined heat and power (CHP): harnessing of the waste heat produced during electricity generation, for example to heat offices and homes.

commodity: traded *cash crop* or industrial raw material (such as rubber or metals); usually refers to international markets.

conifer: cone- and needle-bearing, not leaf-bearing, tree.

crown dieback: symptom of acid pollution damage to conifer trees, where foliage turns yellow from top down and falls off.

DDT: dichloro-diphenol-trichloroethane; one of the earliest and most toxic chemical pesticides, used widely in fight against malarial mosquitoes; now banned in industrialized countries but still in use elsewhere.

debt/conservation swap: financial arrangement whereby a bank or non-governmental organization cancels or pays off a portion of a country's foreign-currency debt in return for that country's investment of its own currency in environmental conservation work.

debt/development swap: similar to a *debt/conservation swap*, except that local currency is diverted to human needs such as education and health rather than to nature conservation.

desertification: the advance of deserts into formerly fertile areas of land or the appearance of patches of desert in them.

dioxins: highly toxic group of synthetic compounds, by-products of pesticide manufacture, the chlorine bleaching of paper and other industrial processes.

drought–flood cycle: harmful cycle of alternating droughts and floods resulting in the dry tropics from deforestation and soil erosion.

drylands: areas of low and unpredictable rainfall comprising about a third of the Earth's land surface.

ecosystem: community of interdependent plants and animals in their habitat.

endemic: found only in one place.

eutrophication: overgrowth of algal plants in waterways as a result of excessive nutrients, such as fertilizers, in the water.

exponential growth: mathematical growth based on an ever-increasing variable; more and more rapid.

food chain: series of plants and animals each of which serves as food for the next in the chain.

forest death: translation of German term *Waldsterben*, referring to severe forest damage by *acid rain*.

fossil fuel: coal, gas or oil; derived from the ancient decay of living matter.

ghost acres: farmland areas of low-income countries that supply densely populated high-income countries with food and other produce.

grains: cereal crops.

greenhouse effect: effect of atmospheric gases that allow solar radiation to penetrate to the Earth and then prevent the heat from escaping back into space.

green revolution: name given to agricultural techniques developed since the 1940s that used large quantities of chemical fertilizer and irrigation water and specially bred strains of rice and wheat to achieve very large, but probably unsustainable, increase in cereal output.

gross national product (GNP): value of goods and services produced in an economy during a period of time; not an accurate measure of well-being because it includes costs of damage repair, such as dealing with environmental pollution, human illness and social problems; even war is good for GNP.

groundwater: underground water held in *aquifers*.

half-life: time taken by radioactive materials to lose half their radioactivity.

hardwoods: non-*coniferous* trees of hard, compact wood.

heavy metals: high-density elements, such as aluminium, lead and mercury, that can be converted from one compound to another but not destroyed.

hectare: metric unit of measurement of land area = 1/100 square kilometre or approx. 2.5 acres.

herbicide: pesticide for killing weeds.

high-yield varieties (HYVs): strains of rice or wheat bred by *green revolution* scientists to grow fast and produce large seed heads in response to lavish quantities of fertilizer and irrigation water.

humus: decomposed remains of plant and animal matter in soil.

hydrocarbon: compound of hydrogen and carbon in solid, liquid or gaseous form, for example coal-gas and petrol.

indigenous: belonging naturally to a region.

informal economy: unofficial, non-registered, non-taxpaying economic activity.

integrated pest management (IPM): farming technique based on natural means of pest control, such as predators, and the minimum use of chemicals.

intermediate technology: cheap and simple technology that can be widely used to improve the livelihoods of low-income people.

landfill: the disposal of large quantities of solid waste on land.

legume: pea- or bean-like plant or tree, bearing seeds in pods.

low energy path: conservation-based approach to meeting fuel-energy needs.

maldevelopment: economic development whose benefits are outweighed by environmental, social or other damage caused.

micro-hydro: small-scale hydroelectricity generation.

migration corridor: strip of forest or other natural habitat conserved or restored to allow species to migrate from one area to another.

monoculture: single crops cultivated on their own over large areas; an essential feature of *agribusiness*.

multinational corporation: large business enterprise with interests in several countries and usually in several industries.

new international economic order (NIEO): reformed system of world trade proposed by low-income countries to ensure a fairer and more sustainable distribution of resources, income and wealth.

newly industrializing countries (NICs): small group of countries such as Brazil, South Korea and Thailand that have achieved partial industrialization and export success in such sectors as textiles and electronics.

niche: well-suited position occupied by an organism in an environment.

nitrate: naturally occurring nitrogen compound heavily present in animal manure and artificial fertilizers.

non-governmental organization (NGO): independent non-commercial agency or action group involved in development or environmental protection.

North: usually refers to the market-economy industrialized countries of Western Europe, North America, Japan, Australia and New Zealand; sometimes taken to include Eastern Europe.

nuclear winter: scientists' prediction of global conditions after a nuclear war has lifted huge clouds of dust and debris into the atmosphere, blocking out the sunlight for an extended period.

ozone: form of oxygen containing three rather than two atoms; occurs naturally as part of the *stratosphere* but also an ingredient of low-level atmospheric pollution resulting from chemical reactions among other pollution gases.

PCBs: polychlorinated biphenyls; highly indestructible and toxic synthetic chemical compounds formerly used in a wide range of electrical applications; use now prohibited except in sealed equipment.

peace dividend: money that could become available as a result of major cuts in the armed forces of NATO and Warsaw Pact countries, especially the USA.

pesticide treadmill: repeated need for stronger pesticides because of pest species' development of genetic immunity.

phosphate: phosphorus compound widely used as artificial fertilizer.

photosynthesis: process by which green plants use solar energy to manufacture their food (carbohydrates) from carbon dioxide and water.

polluter pays principle: common-sense idea that the cost of putting right pollution damage should be borne by the person or organization causing that damage, for example in the form of pollution taxes.

polyculture: cultivation of a number of different complementary crops or crop strains together, sometimes in rotation; not as profitable in the short term as monoculture but more sustainable in the long run.

primary forest: forest that has not been commercially logged or otherwise disrupted by large-scale industry.

rainforest: species-rich forest in areas of heavy rainfall.

renewable energy: energy that people can harness and use without depleting natural reserves; for example, hydropower, wind power and solar energy.

Sahel: belt of African countries on the southern edge of the Sahara Desert.

salinization: soil deterioration caused when irrigation water or *groundwater* evaporates and leaves behind a heavy residue of salt.

savanna: open tropical grassland with tall grass and scattered trees and bushes.

scrubbers: flue-gas desulphurization equipment used to curb acidic emissions from coal- and oil-fired power stations.

shifting cultivation: nomadic farming whereby areas of ground are cultivated for one or several seasons and then abandoned, the cultivators moving on to another piece of land; sometimes referred to as *slash and burn*.

slash and burn: see *shifting cultivation*.

solvent: any dissolving liquid.

South: low-income countries of Africa, Asia, the Caribbean, Latin America and the Pacific.

stratosphere: atmospheric layer extending from about 9 kilometres above the Poles and 16 kilometres above the Equator up to about 50 kilometres.

structural adjustments: changes imposed by the International Monetary Fund on the economies of countries it lends money; usually involve market liberalization and reductions in public spending.

subsistence farming: farming for immediate community needs, not for cash.

sustainable: meeting present needs without reducing the ability of future generations to meet their needs.

top-down: widely discredited approach to development and to policy- and decision-making whereby resources are owned or controlled by wealthy and powerful individuals and groups.

transfer pricing: mechanism by which *multinational corporations* arrange prices paid internally between two or more branches to maximize benefits from tax arrangements in different countries.

trickle-down: principle that material wealth generated among rich and powerful groups in a society will gradually seep through to all other groups; see *top-down*.

underground economy: see *informal economy*.

wetlands: bogs, flood plains, mangroves, marshes, river estuaries and swamps.

*wilderness corrido*r: similar to *migration corridor*, intended to allow species greater freedom to range by linking two or more areas of preserved natural habitat.

Notes

1. Food – the Right to Eat

1. Lloyd Timberlake, "The politics of food aid", in Edward Goldsmith and Nicholas Hildyard (eds), *The Earth Report* (London: Mitchell Beazley, 1988), p. 31.
2. Crazy Horse quoted in Dee Brown, *Bury my Heart at Wounded Knee* (London: Picador, 1975), p. 217.
3. John Seymour and Herbert Girardet, *Far from Paradise* (London: BBC Books, 1986), pp. 174-6; Paul Harrison, *The Greening of Africa* (London: Paladin, 1987), pp. 77-8.
4. Seymour and Girardet, op. cit., p. 171.
5. Ted Trainer, *Developed to Death* (London: Green Print, 1989), p. 115.
6. Susan George, *How the Other Half Dies* (London: Pelican, 1986 edn), p. 57.
7. Vandana Shiva, *Staying Alive* (London: Zed, 1988), p. 129
8. *New Internationalist*, no. 194 (April 1989), pp. 16-17; Susan George, *A Fate Worse than Debt* (London: Pelican, 1988), p. 139.
9. Seymour and Girardet, op. cit., p.170; Lloyd Timberlake, *Africa in Crisis* (London: Earthscan, 1988), p. 52.
10. World Commission on Environment and Development, *Our Common Future* (Brundtland Report; Oxford University Press, 1987), p. 120.
11. Gita Sen and Caren Grown, *Development, Crises and Alternative Visions* (London: Earthscan, 1988), p. 52.
12. *New Internationalist*, no. 176 (October 1987), p. 26.
13. Seymour and Girardet, op. cit., p. 179; Goldsmith and Hildyard, op. cit., pp. 157-8
14. Seymour and Girardet, op. cit., p. 180.
15. Frances Moore Lappé and Joseph Collins, *World Hunger: Twelve Myths* (London: Earthscan, 1988), pp. 37-8.
16. Ibid., p. 56.
17. World Bank quoted ibid., p. 43.
18. Senator Humphrey quoted in André Singer, *Battle for the Planet* (London: Pan, 1987), p. 105.
19. Timberlake, "The politics of food aid", op. cit., p. 29.
20. Ben Wisner, *Power and Need in Africa* (London: Earthscan, 1988).

21. *Guardian*, 13.3.90.
22. Lappé and Collins, op. cit., p. 64.
23. *New Internationalist*, no. 206 (April 1990), p. 26.
24. John Medcalf, *Letters from Nicaragua* (London: Catholic Institute for International Relations, 1988), p. 43.
25. Edward Ayensu, "Why can't we feed ourselves?", *The Planet* (companion newspaper to Channel 4 TV series *Battle for the Planet*, 1987), p. 7.

2. Wealth – Greed versus Need

 1. Paul Harrison, *The Third World Tomorrow* (Harmondsworth: Pelican, 1983 edn), p. 304.
 2. Norman Myers (ed.), *The Gaia Atlas of Planet Management* (London: Pan, 1985), pp. 204, 208.
 3. Ted Trainer, *Developed to Death* (London: Green Print, 1989), pp. 9, 14; Worldwatch Institute, *Poverty and the Environment: Reversing the Downward Spiral* (Washington, DC: Worldwatch Institute, 1989), quoted in *Observer*, 19.11.89.
 4. Paul Ekins (ed.), *The Living Economy* (London: Routledge, 1986), p. 18.
 5. Walter Rodney, *How Europe Underdeveloped Africa* (London: Bougle L'Ouverture, 1983), p. 84; Murray Bookchin, *The Modern Crisis* (Philadelphia, Pa: New Society, 1986), pp. 116-17.
 6. Paul Baran quoted in Teresa Hayter, *Exploited Earth* (London: Earthscan, 1989), p. 5.
 7. See Edward Goldsmith and Nicholas Hildyard (eds), *The Earth Report* (London: Mitchell Beazley, 1988), p. 116.
 8. On the early history of Unilever, see Rodney, op. cit., pp. 198-203.
 9. *New Internationalist*, no. 183 (May 1988), p. 22; David Weir, *The Bhopal Syndrome* (London: Earthscan, 1988), p. 130.
10. *New Internationalist*, no. 202 (December 1989), p. 27; Trainer, op. cit., pp. 112-13; Frances Moore Lappé and Joseph Collins *World Hunger: Twelve Myths* (London: Earthscan, 1988), p. 77-8.
11. Goldsmith and Hildyard, op. cit., p. 103.
12. Ibid., p. 127; Richard North, *The Real Cost* (London: Chatto, 1986), p. 130; Lloyd Timberlake, *Africa in Crisis* (London: Earthscan, 1988), p. 68.
13. Timberlake, op. cit., p. 70; North, op. cit., pp. 132-3; *Guardian* 28.9.89.
14. See, for example, Susan George, *A Fate Worse than Debt* (London: Pelican, 1988), pp. 157-61; and *Green Drum*, no. 66 (spring 1989), pp. 14-15.
15. Susan George, *How the Other Half Dies* (Harmondsworth: Pelican, 1986), p. 37.
16. Trainer, op. cit., p. 13; John Seymour and Herbert Girardet, *Far from Paradise* (London: BBC Books, 1986), p. 206. These consumption levels are based on total national resource consumption for all purposes.

17. See World Resources Institute and International Institute for Environment and Development, *World Resources 1988–89* (New York: Basic Books, 1988), table 14.3, pp. 240-1.
18. *New Internationalist*, no. 189 (November 1988), p. 5; J. K. Galbraith quoted in *New Internationalist*, no. 206 (April 1990), p. 21.
19. UNICEF figures quoted in *New Internationalist*, no. 189 (November 1988), p. 9; see also Peter Bunyard and Fern Morgan-Grenville, *The Green Alternative* (London: Methuen, 1987), pp. 246ff.
20. D.L. Budhoo quoted in *New Internationalist*, no. 189 (November 1988), p. 9.
21. See, for example, *South*, July 1989, p. 17.
22. World Bank, *World Development Report 1989* (New York: Oxford University Press, 1989), pp. 204-5.
23. UN Secretary-General Perez de Cuellar quoted in Paul Ekins (ed.), *The Living Economy* (London: Routledge, 1986), p. 17.
24. John Pilger, "Distant voices of dissent", *Guardian*, 12.2.90.
25. See Trainer, op. cit., pp. 48-51.
26. World Bank, op. cit., pp. 200-1.
27. UK Comptroller and Auditor General, *Bilateral Aid to India* (London: HMSO, 1990); for more about the effects of UK and European Community aid, see Teresa Hayter, *Exploited Earth: Britain's Aid and the Environment* (London: Earthscan, 1989).
28. E.F. Schumacher, *Small Is Beautiful* (London: Abacus, 1974), pp. 140, 171.
29. Harrison, op. cit., p. 41; Pat Ellis (ed.), *Women of the Caribbean* (London: Zed, 1986), p. 19.
30. For more on grass-roots organizations in low-income countries, see Alan Durning, "Mobilizing at the grassroots", in Lester Brown *et al.*, *State of the World 1989* (New York: Norton/Worldwatch Institute, 1989), chapter 9.
31. Barber Conable quoted in Lester Brown *et al.*, *State of the World 1988* (New York: Norton/Worldwatch Institute, 1988), p. 21.
32. George McRobie in *New Economics* (New Economics Foundation), no. 6 (summer 1988); Gandhi quoted in Schumacher, op. cit., pp. 27-8; on appropriate development, see, for example, Paul Harrison, *The Greening of Africa* (London: Paladin, 1987); Paul Ekins (ed.), *The Living Economy* (London: Routledge, 1986); and Czech Conroy and Miles Litvinoff (eds), *The Greening of Aid* (London: Earthscan, 1988).
33. Lloyd Timberlake, *Africa in Crisis* (London: Earthscan, 1988), p. 194.
34. Goldsmith and Hildyard, op. cit., p. 220; *Guardian*, 19.12.88.
35. George, *A Fate Worse than Debt*, op. cit., p. 237.
36. Ibid., pp. 242-3.

3. Population and Health

1. André Gorz, *Ecology as Politics* (London: Pluto, 1980), p. 155.
2. *Guardian*, 15.5.90; Paul Harrison, "Every beat of your heart, two

babies are born", *Sunday Correspondent* magazine, 8.4.90; Paul and Anne Ehrlich quoted by Sandy Irvine, letter to *Ecologist*, vol. 20, no. 3 (May/June 1990), p. 119.

3. D. H. Meadows, D. L. Meadows, J. Randers, W. W. Behrens, *The Limits to Growth* (London: Pan, 1972), p. 34.

4. Frances Moore Lappé and Joseph Collins, *World Hunger: Twelve Myths* (London: Earthscan, 1988), p. 25.

5. See Lloyd Timberlake, *Africa in Crisis* (London: Earthscan 1988), pp. 33-4.

6. Paul Harrison, *The Greening of Africa* (London: Paladin, 1987), p. 244.

7. Timberlake, op. cit., p. 36.

8. Norman Myers (ed.), *The Gaia Atlas of Planet Management* (London: Pan, 1985), p. 121; Jorge Hardoy and David Satterthwaite, *Squatter Citizen* (London: Earthscan, 1989), p. 147.

9. *New Internationalist*, no. 179 (January 1988), p. 21.

10. *New Internationalist*, no. 198 (August 1989), p. 18.

11. Myers, op. cit., p. 239.

12. WHO quoted in *Observer*, 8.10.89.

13. *South*, July 1989, p. 61.

14. *Ecologist*, vol. 18, no. 2 (1988), p. 84.

15. Lester Brown *et al.*, *State of the World 1988* (New York: Norton/Worldwatch Institute, 1988), p. 121.

16. *South*, May 1988, p. 73.

17. World Resources Institute and International Institute for Environment and Development (IIED), *World Resources 1988–89* (New York: Basic Books, 1988), p. 30; David Weir, *The Bhopal Syndrome* (London: Earthscan, 1988), p. 143.

18. See Frances and Phil Craig, *Britain's Poisoned Water* (London: Penguin, 1989), pp. 21-9.

19. John Seymour and Herbert Girardet, *Far from Paradise* (London: BBC Books, 1986), p. 151.

20. Brown *et al.*, op cit., p. 7.

21. Estonian Green Party quoted in *Observer*, 17.9.89.

22. See Women's Environmental Network, *The Sanitary Protection Scandal* (London: WEN, 1989); and Edward Goldsmith and Nicholas Hildyard, *The Earth Report* (London: Mitchell Beazley, 1988), p. 134.

23. Lloyd Timberlake, *Only One Earth* (London: BBC Books/Earthscan, 1987), chapter 9.

24. *Earth Matters* (Friends of the Earth), no. 1 (autumn 1988), pp. 2-3.

25. *New Internationalist*, no. 181 (March 1988), p. 26.

26. Rachel Carson, *Silent Spring* (Harmondsworth: Penguin, 1965), chapter 13.

27. See, for example, Dr Rosalie Bertell, *No Immediate Danger: Prognosis for a Radioactive Earth* (London: Women's Press, 1985), pp. 38-44.

28. Dr Edward D. David quoted in E. F. Schumacher, *Small Is Beautiful* (London: Abacus, 1974), p. 15.
29. See Bertell, op. cit., part three; and John May, *The Greenpeace Book of the Nuclear Age* (London: Gollancz, 1989).
30. *Observer*, 21.5.89.
31. Bertell, op. cit., pp. 104-5.
32. Ibid., pp. 70-6; *Greenpeace News*, autumn 1989, p. 10.
33. *New Internationalist*, no. 173 (July 1987), p. 28; Amnesty International, *Report 1989* (London: Amnesty International, 1989), p. 16.
34. *Sunday Correspondent*, 22.4.90.
35. See Anil Agarwal, James Kimondo, Gloria Moreno and Jon Tinker, *Water, Sanitation, Health – for All?* (London and Washington: Earthscan, 1981).
36. Irene Dankelman and Joan Davidson, *Women and Environment in the Third World* (London: Earthscan 1988), p. 35; Myers, op. cit., p. 135; Richard North, *The Real Cost* (London: Chatto, 1986), p. 127; *New Internationalist*, no. 207 (May 1990) pp. 18-19.
37. Agarwal *et al.*, op. cit., pp. 37, 43, 69; Vandana Shiva, *Staying Alive* (London: Zed, 1988), p. 215.
38. See, for example, Myers, op. cit., pp. 194-5; Paul Harrison, *The Third World Tomorrow* (Harmondsworth: Pelican, 1980), pp. 228-30, 368-9.
39. WHO director-general Dr Hiroshi Nakajima quoted in *Observer*, 1.10.89.
40. Carson, op.cit., p. 213.
41. Brown *et al.*, op.cit., p. 122.
42. Ibid., pp. 124-9; World Resources Institute and IIED, op. cit., pp. 30-1.
43. See Richard Body MP in *Green Drum*, no. 61 (winter 1987–8), p. 7.
44. World Commission for Environment and Development, *Our Common Future* (Brundtland Report; Oxford University Press, 1987), pp. 225-6.
45. Ibid.
46. See the Friends of the Earth/*Observer* campaign to clean up hazardous waste sites reported in *Observer* magazine, 4.2.90.
47. Hardoy and Satterthwaite, op. cit., p. 213-14.
48. Brundtland Report, op. cit., p. 216
49. Brandt Commission, *North–South: A Programme for Survival* (London: Pan, 1980), p. 14.
50. *Greenpeace News*, spring 1990, p. 6.
51. Frances and Phil Craig, *Britain's Poisoned Water* (London: Penguin, 1989), p. 118.
52. Goldsmith and Hildyard, op. cit., p. 205.

4. Women – Present Burdens and Future Role

1. Simone de Beauvoir, *The Second Sex* (Harmondsworth: Penguin, 1983), pp. 738, 741.
2. Erich Fromm, *The Anatomy of Human Destructiveness* (Harmonds-

worth: Penguin, 1977), pp. 213-14; de Beauvoir, op. cit., p. 111; Margaret Mead quoted in Joni Seager and Ann Olson, *Women in the World: An International Atlas* (London: Pan, 1986), p. 116.

3. See de Beauvoir, op. cit., pp. 733-4.

4. Seager and Olson, op. cit., map 21, pp. 109, 111; Irene Dankelman and Joan Davidson, *Women and Environment in the Third World* (London: Earthscan, 1988), pp. 15-16; New Internationalist, *Women: A World Report* (London: Methuen, 1985), pp. 22-3; Paul Harrison, *The Greening of Africa* (London: Paladin, 1987), p. 61; Janet Durno and Manabendra Mandal, "Legal rights for poor women", in Richard Holloway (ed.), *Doing Development: Government, NGOs and the Rural Poor in Asia* (London: Earthscan, 1989), p. 57.

5. Durno and Mandal, op. cit., pp. 58, 59, 60.

6. Magida Salman *et al.*, *Women in the Middle East* (London: Zed/Khamsin, 1987), pp. 6, 7, 8.

7. *New Internationalist*, no. 181 (March 1988), p. 8; de Beauvoir, op. cit., pp. 97-113.

8. Dankelman and Davidson, op. cit., p. 69; Paul Harrison, *The Third World Tomorrow* (Harmondsworth: Penguin, 1983), p. 352.

9. *New Internationalist*, no. 181 (March 1988), p. 6, citing Ivan Illich and Anne Oakley.

10. Ibid., pp. 8, 16-17.

11. *Women: A World Report*, op. cit., p. 43; Dankelman and Davidson, op.cit., pp. 71-2.

12. Lester Brown *et al.*, *State of the World 1988* (New York: Norton/Worldwatch Institute, 1988), p. 157.

13. *Women: A World Report*, op. cit., p. 46; Seager and Olson, op. cit., p. 107; Norma Shorey-Bryan, "The making of male–female relationships in the Caribbean", in Pat Ellis (ed.), *Women of the Caribbean* (London: Zed, 1986), p. 71.

14. Robin Morgan (ed.), *Sisterhood is Global* (Harmondsworth: Penguin, 1984), p. 23; Seager and Olson, op. cit., map 31, p. 102; *New Internationalist*, no. 158 (April 1986), p. 17.

15. Seager and Olson, op. cit., p. 103.

16. Dankelman and Davidson, op. cit., p. 9; *Women: A World Report*, op. cit., p. 16.

17. Fromm, op. cit., p. 213.

18. Dankelman and Davidson, op. cit., p. 18; Vandana Shiva, *Staying Alive: Women, Ecology and Development* (London: Zed, 1988), pp. 98, 105.

19. Ester Boserup, *Women's Role in Economic Development* (London: Earthscan, 1989), chapter 1; Shiva, op. cit., pp. 109, 112.

20. Brian Walker quoted in Lloyd Timberlake, *Africa in Crisis* (London: Earthscan, 1988), p. 125; Susan George, *A Fate Worse than Debt* (London: Pelican, 1988), p. 97.

21. See Boserup, op. cit., chapter 3.

22. Dankelman and Davidson, op. cit., p. 14; Shiva, op. cit., chapter 5.
23. *Women, Environment, Development*, seminar report (London: Women's Environmental Network/War on Want, 1989) p. 3.
24. *Women: A World Report*, op. cit., pp. 30, 31.
25. Seager and Olson, op. cit., p. 110.
26. Ibid., map 19; Ivan Reid and Erica Stratta, *Sex Difference in Britain* (Aldershot: Gower, 1989), p. 138.
27. Seager and Olson, p. 109; Gita Sen and Caren Grown, *Development, Crises and Alternative Visions: Third World Women's Perspectives* (London: Earthscan, 1988), p. 75.
28. Morgan, op. cit., p. 17; Latin America and Caribbean Women's Collective, *Slaves of Slaves* (London: Zed, 1980), pp. 181-2.
29. Seager and Olson, op. cit., map 20.
30. Ibid., map 28.
31. Norman Myers (ed.), *The Gaia Atlas of Planet Management* (London: Pan, 1985), p. 187: *Women: A World Report*, op. cit., p. 71.
32. *Women: A World Report*, op. cit., pp. 71-2; Seager and Olson, op. cit., map 22.
33. Anita Desai, "The family – Norway", in *Women: A World Report*, op. cit., p. 108.
34. Seager and Olson, op. cit., p. 112.
35. Ibid., p. 114.
36. Latin American and Caribbean Women's Collective, op. cit., pp. 73, 77, 78.
37. Seager and Olson, op. cit., map 37, p. 119; *New Internationalist*, no. 158 (April 1986), p. 17; *Women: A World Report*, op. cit., p. 65.
38. Buchi Emecheta, "Education – United States", in *Women: A World Report*, op. cit., p. 217.
39. Pat Ellis, "An overview of women in Caribbean society", in Ellis, op. cit., p. 12.
40. Durno and Mandal, op. cit., pp. 60, 61.
41. Paul Ekins, *The Living Economy* (London: Routledge, 1986), pp. 295-303.
42. Paul Ekins, "Growing concern", *Guardian*, 13.1.88.
43. *New Internationalist*, no. 183. (May 1988), pp. 14-15; Lloyd Timberlake, *Only One Earth* (London: BBC Books/Earthscan, 1987), pp. 78 ff.; Susan George, *A Fate Worse than Debt* (London: Pelican, 1988), pp. 223-4.
44. Donald MacKenzie and Judy Wajcman (eds), *The Social Shaping of Technology* (Milton Keynes: Open University Press, 1985); and Margaret Stacey, *The Sociology of Health and Healing* (London: Unwin Hyman, 1988).
45. *Women, Environment, Development*, op. cit., p. 33.
46. Shiva, op. cit., p. 223.
47. *Women, Environment, Development*, op. cit., p. 4.
48. On low-cost appropriate technologies, see George McRobie, *Small*

Is Possible (London: Cape, 1981); and (more recently published) Marilyn Carr (ed.), *The AT Reader* (London: Intermediate Technology Publications, 1985).

5. Human and Civil Rights
1. Julia Häusermann, "Myths and realities", in Peter Davies (ed.), *Human Rights* (London: Routledge, 1988), p. 137.
2. Charles Humana, *World Human Rights Guide* (London: Pan, 1986), p. 1.
3. Murray Bookchin, *The Modern Crisis* (Philadelphia, Pa: New Society Publishers, 1986), p. 161.
4. See Paulo Freire, *Pedagogy of the Oppressed* (Harmondsworth: Penguin, 1972).
5. Figures based on World Bank, *World Development Report 1989* (New York: Oxford University Press, 1989), table 11.
6. See Paul Harrison, *The Third World Tomorrow* (Harmondsworth: Pelican, 1983), p. 257.
7. *South*, December 1987, p. 11; *Green Drum*, no. 67 (summer 1989), p. 17.
8. *South*, December 1987, pp. 9-10.
9. Independent Commission on International Humanitarian Issues, *Indigenous Peoples* (London: Zed, 1987), p. 15.
10. Julian Berger, "Indigenous peoples", in Davies, op. cit., pp. 101-2.
11. *New Internationalist*, no. 184. (June 1988), p. 26; no. 186 (August 1988), p. 5; no. 192 (February 1989), p. 27.
12. *Green Drum*, no. 63 (summer 1988), p. 16; *New Internationalist*, no. 181 (March 1988), p. 27.
13. *New Internationalist*, no. 176 (October 1987), p. 28; *Ethical Consumer*, no. 6 (February/March 1990), p. 25.
14. *Green Drum*, no. 66 (spring 1989), pp. 14-15; for a fuller picture, see George Monbiot, *Poisoned Arrows: An Investigative Journey through Indonesia* (London: Michael Joseph, 1989).
15. World Commission on Environment and Development, *Our Common Future* (Brundtland Report; Oxford University Press, 1987), p. 115.
16. Amnesty International, *Report 1989* (London: Amnesty International, 1989), pp. 13, 108, 114, 122, 125; on Latin American racism see Independent Commission on International Humanitarian issues, op. cit., chapter 2; and Elisabeth Burgos-Debray (ed.), *I, Rigoberta Menchu: An Indian Woman in Guatemala* (London: Verso, 1984).
17. *South*, August 1987, pp. 34-5.
18. *New Internationalist*, no. 189 (November 1988), p. 27.
19. Ricardo Sol Arriaza, "Communication, the church and social conflict in El Salvador", in Elizabeth Fox (ed.), *Media and Politics in Latin America* (London: Sage, 1988), p. 100; see also Robert Armstrong and Janet Shenk, *El Salvador: The Face of Revolution* (London: Pluto, 1982).

20. *South*, July 1989, p. 39; *New Internationalist*, no. 205 (March 1990).
21. Humana, op. cit., p. vii.
22. Amnesty International, op. cit., pp. 31 ff.
23. Noam Chomsky, *Turning the Tide* (London: Pluto, 1986), p. 238.
24. Ted Trainer, *Developed to Death* (London: Green Print, 1989), pp. 144-5.
25. President Bush quoted in Chomsky, op. cit., p. 161.
26. The words of the 1945 United Nations Charter.
27. Michael White, "The secret behind Contragate", *Guardian*, 4.7.87.
28. Trainer, op. cit., p. 167.
29. Barbara Ward, *Progress for a Small Planet* (London: Earthscan, 1988), p. 252.
30. Erich Fromm, *The Anatomy of Human Destructiveness* (Harmondsworth: Penguin, 1977), pp. 575-6.
31. UNICEF, *The State of the World's Children 1990* (Oxford University Press, 1990), p. 7.
32. *New Internationalist*, no. 179 (January 1988), p. 23.
33. Harrison, op. cit., pp. 258-61.
34. UNICEF, op. cit., p. 60.
35. Anthony Swift, "Victims of rescue", *New Internationalist*, no. 194 (April 1989), pp. 13-15.
36. *Earth Matters* (Friends of the Earth), no. 3 (spring 1989), pp. 6-7.
37. *New Internationalist*, no. 203 (January 1990), p. 28.
38. "Colombia – setting a precedent for the world", Gaia Foundation briefing paper, 1989; Peter Bunyard, *The Colombian Amazon: Policies for the Protection of its Indigenous Peoples and their Environment* (Camelford: Ecological Press, 1989).
39. Bookchin, op. cit., pp. 136, 144.
40. Amnesty International, op. cit., p. 15.
41. Sandy Irvine and Alec Ponton, *A Green Manifesto* (London: Macdonald Optima, 1988), p. 86.

6. Working the Land to Death

1. E. F. Schumacher, *Small Is Beautiful* (London: Abacus, 1974), p. 90.
2. Catherine Caufield quoted in Friends of the Earth (FOE) rainforest leaflet; Lloyd Timberlake, *Africa in Crisis* (London: Earthscan, 1988), p. 113.
3. World Resources Institute and International Institute for Environment and Development (IIED), *World Resources 1988–89* (New York: Basic Books, 1988), p. 70.
4. Deforestation statistics used in this chapter are drawn from: Lester Brown *et al.*, *State of the World 1988* (New York: Norton/ Worldwatch Institute, 1988), chapter 5; World Resources Institute and IIED, op. cit., chapter 5 and table 18.1; *New Internationalist*,

no. 184 (June 1988); Earthlife, "Paradise lost", *Observer* special supplement, 1986; Edward Goldsmith and Nicholas Hildyard (eds), *The Earth Report* (London: Mitchell Beazley, 1988); Catherine Caufield, *In the Rainforest* (London: Heinemann, 1985); Patrick Anderson, "The myth of sustainable logging", *Ecologist*, vol. 19, no. 5 (September/October 1989), p. 166; FOE leaflets.

5. FAO reported in *Observer*, 3.6.90; Norman Myers, "Deforestation rates in tropical forests and their climatic implications", FOE paper, 1989.

6. Mrs Thatcher's UN speech quoted in *Guardian*, 9.9.89.

7. Nicholas Hildyard, "Amazonia: the future in the balance" (editorial), *Ecologist*, vol. 19, no. 6 (November/December 1989), p. 208.

8. Tropical Forestry Action Plan quoted in Teresa Hayter, *Exploited Earth* (London: Earthscan, 1989), pp. 46-7.

9. Caufield, op. cit., p. 40.

10. Vandana Shiva, *Staying Alive* (London: Zed, 1988), p. 67.

11. Campaign statement by Forest Peoples' Alliance to President Sarney, 18.1.90; *Green Drum*, no. 62 (spring 1988), p. 14.

12. Caufield, op. cit., pp. 40, 41.

13. Alexander Cockburn and Susanna Hecht, "The jungle and the junta", *Guardian*, 25.11.89; see also the same authors' *The Fate of the Forest: Developers, Destroyers and Defenders of the Amazon* (London: Verso, 1989).

14. Brown *et al.*, op. cit., p. 86.

15. Caufield, op. cit., p. 155; Walter Schwarz, "Smoke signals from the Amazon", *Guardian*, 14.3.89.

16. Brown *et al.*, op. cit., p. 86; "Tropical forests: the facts you should know to save them", ECOROPA information sheet no. 17, 1989.

17. Shiva, op. cit., p. 188; Nicholas Hildyard, "Stop the Nam Choan!", *Ecologist*, vol. 17, no. 6 (November/December 1987), p. 210.

18. *Green Drum*, no. 63 (summer 1988), p. 20; *New Internationalist*, no. 184 (June 1988), pp. 20-1; Walter Schwarz, "Victims of rape in paradise", *Guardian*, 13.3.89.

19. Goldsmith and Hildyard, op. cit., p. 97.

20. Hayter, op. cit., p. 48.

21. Koy Thomson, "Power without the people", *Guardian*, 8.12.89; Caufield, op. cit., p. 41.

22. Anderson, op. cit., p. 167.

23. Earthlife, op. cit., p. 24.

24. Robert Repetto quoted in Anderson, op. cit., p. 166.

25. *New Internationalist*, no. 184 (June 1988), p. 6.

26. Caufield, op. cit., p. 156.

27. Brown *et al.*, op. cit., p. 109.

28. *New Internationalist*, no. 184 (June 1988), p. 20.

29. Lloyd Timberlake, *Only One Earth* (London: BBC Books/Earthscan, 1987). pp. 29-30.

30. Ibid., pp. 39-42.

31. Farmer quoted in Paul Harrison *The Greening of Africa* (London: Paladin, 1987), p. 143; on firewood see Gerald Leach and Robin Mearns, *Beyond the Woodfuel Crisis* (London: Earthscan, 1988).
32. André Singer, *Battle for the Planet* (London: Pan, 1987), p. 25; John Seymour and Herbert Girardet, *Far from Paradise* (London: BBC Books, 1986), pp. 49-62.
33. Soil erosion statistics in this chapter are drawn from: Singer, op. cit., chapter 1; Norman Myers (ed.), *The Gaia Atlas of Planet Management* (London: Pan, 1985), pp. 40-2; Malcolm Smith, "The disappearing planet", *Guardian*, 9.5.85; John Seymour was writing in *Fourth World Review*, no. 38 (1990), p. 8.
34. R. D. Mann, "Time running out: the urgent need for tree planting in Africa", *Ecologist*, vol. 20, no. 2 (March/April 1990), p. 49.
35. Timberlake, *Africa in Crisis*, op. cit., p. 53.
36. Shiva, op. cit., chapter 5.
37. World Resources Institute and IIED, op. cit., p. 225.
38. Goldsmith and Hildyard, op. cit., pp. 209-10.
39. Shiva, op. cit., p. 150.
40. Duncan Poore, *No Timber without Trees* (London: Earthscan, 1989), p. xi.
41. Ibid., p. 196.
42. Anderson, op. cit., p. 167.
43. *WWF News*, April 1990, p. 2.
44. Thomson, op. cit.
45. Anderson, op. cit., p. 166.
46. Jonathan Porritt, "Preserving the treasures of the rainforest" (editorial), *Earth Matters*, no. 7 (spring 1990), p. 1.
47. Timberlake, *Only One Earth*, op. cit., p. 31.
48. Brown *et al.*, op. cit., pp. 175, 176.
49. *Green Drum*, no. 61 (winter 1987–8), p. 16.
50. Brown *et al.*, op. cit., pp. 89-90, 92-3, 100; Timberlake, *Africa in Crisis*, op. cit., pp. 116-17.
51. Harrison, op. cit., pp. 119-20.
52. Brown *et al.*, op. cit., p. 174.
53. Lee Durrell, *State of the Ark* (London: Bodley Head, 1986), p. 92.
54. *Green Drum*, no. 69 (winter 1989–90), p. 24.

7. Water – the Most Precious Resource

1. Rachel Carson, *Silent Spring* (Harmondsworth: Penguin, 1965), p. 50.
2. World Resources Institute and International Institute for Environment and Development (IIED), *World Resources 1988–89* (New York: Basic Books, 1988), pp. 128-9.
3. Armin Maywald, Barbara Zeschmar-Lahl and Uwe Lahl, "Water fit to drink?", in Edward Goldsmith and Nicholas Hildyard, *The Earth Report* (London: Mitchell Beazley, 1988), p. 81; John Seymour and Herbert Girardet, *Blueprint for a Green Planet*

(London: Dorling Kindersley, 1987), p. 26.

4. Barbara Ward, *Progress for a Small Planet* (London: Earthscan, 1988), p. 82.
5. Ibid., p. 83; Jorge Hardoy and David Satterthwaite, *Squatter Citizen* (London: Earthscan, 1989), pp. 193-4.
6. UNICEF, *State of the World's Children* (Oxford University Press, 1990), table 3, pp. 80-1; Anil Agarwal, James Kimondo, Gloria Moreno and Jon Tinker, *Water, Sanitation, Health – for All?* (London and Washington: Earthscan, 1981), p. 144.
7. Hardoy and Satterthwaite, op. cit., pp. 148-50, 164.
8. Judith Vidal-Hall, "Wellsprings of conflict", *South*, May 1989.
9. Anders Wijkman and Lloyd Timberlake, *Natural Disasters* (London and Washington: Earthscan, 1984), p. 7.
10. Ibid., pp. 58-9, 69.
11. Ibid., p. 60.
12. World Resources Institute and IIED, op. cit., p. 132; Irene Dankelman and Joan Davidson, *Women and Environment in the Third World* (London: Earthscan, 1988), p. 31.
13. Vandana Shiva, *Staying Alive* (London: Zed, 1988), p. 197.
14. Lee Durrell, *State of the Ark* (London: Bodley Head, 1986), p. 165; Vidal-Hall, op. cit., p. 23; Shiva, op. cit., p. 151.
15. Shiva, op. cit., pp. 190, 193, 195; much of the following information on dams is drawn from: Richard North, *The Real Cost* (London: Chatto, 1986), pp. 129-34; Lester Brown *et al.*, *State of the World 1988* (New York: Norton/Worldwatch Institute, 1988), pp. 65-6; Goldsmith and Hildyard, op. cit., pp. 103, 126-8; Shiva, op. cit., pp. 184-95.
16. Carson, op. cit., p. 52.
17. Hardoy and Satterthwaite, op. cit., p. 191.
18. Dankelman and Davidson, op. cit., p. 31; Hardoy and Satterthwaite, op. cit., pp. 192-3; Agarwal *et al.*, op. cit., p. 95.
19. *Guardian*, 19.1.90.
20. Maywald, Zeschmar-Lahl and Lahl, op. cit., pp. 81-3.
21. See, for example, Durrell, op. cit., p. 65.
22. Maywald, Zeschmar-Lahl and Lahl, op. cit., pp. 85-6.
23. Friends of the Earth and *Observer*, "Sitting on a pollution time bomb", briefing sheet, 1990.
24. *New Internationalist*, no. 166 (December 1986), p. 28; Goldsmith and Hildyard, op. cit., p. 188.
25. Carson, op. cit., p. 54; Maywald, Zeschmar-Lahl and Lahl, op. cit., p. 85; Frances and Phil Craig, *Britain's Poisoned Water* (London: Penguin, 1989), p. xiii.
26. World Commission on Environment and Development, *Our Common Future* (Brundtland Report; Oxford University Press, 1987), p. 264.
27. Ibid., p. 264; Dr Rosalie Bertell, *No Immediate Danger* (London: Women's Press, 1985), p. 301.
28. Bertell, op. cit., p. 300.

29. World Resources Institute and IIED, op. cit., p. 158.
30. Bertell, op. cit., pp. 302-3; *Greenpeace News*, autumn 1989, p. 12.
31. Goldsmith and Hildyard, op. cit., p. 186.
32. *Observer*, 20.8.89.
33. *Guardian*, 20.8.88, 6.3.90.
34. André Singer, *Battle for the Planet* (London: Pan, 1987), p. 60; Lloyd Timberlake, *Only One Earth* (London: BBC Books/Earthscan, 1987), p. 147; Hardoy and Satterthwaite, op. cit., pp. 192, 210-11.
35. Maywald, Zeschmar-Lahl and Lahl, op. cit., p. 88.
36. Ward, op. cit., pp. 85-6; Seymour and Girardet, op. cit., pp. 24, 27.
37. Seymour and Girardet, op. cit., p. 26.
38. Ibid., p. 30; *Greenpeace News*, February 1988, North Sea pullout.
39. Agarwal *et al.*, op. cit., p. 100.
40. World Resources Institute and IIED, op. cit., p. 132.
41. Ward, op. cit., p. 88.
42. World Resources Institute and IIED, op. cit., pp. 139-40.
43. Friends of the Earth and *Observer*, op. cit.
44. *Green Drum*, no. 69 (winter 1989–90), p. 18.

8. The Atmosphere – the Sky's the Limit

1. Lester Brown *et al.*, *State of the World 1988* (New York: Norton/Worldwatch Institute, 1988), p. 61.
2. Stewart Boyle and John Ardill, *The Greenhouse Effect* (London: New English Library, 1989), pp. 44, 52.
3. Figures on greenhouse gases taken from Stewart Boyle, Linda Taylor and Ian Brown, *Solving the Greenhouse Dilemma*, special report (London: Association for the Conservation of Energy/World Wide Fund for Nature, 1989), p. 5; World Resources Institute and International Institute for Environment and Development (IIED), *World Resources 1988–89* (New York: Basic Books, 1988), pp. 171-2; Boyle and Ardill, op. cit., pp. 10, 11, 52, 60; Brown *et al.*, op. cit., p. 15; Catherine Caufield, *In the Rainforest* (London: Heinemann, 1985) pp. 70-1.
4. John Seymour and Herbert Girardet, *Far from Paradise* (London: BBC Books/Earthscan, 1987) p. 212.
5. IPCC quoted in *Guardian*, 26.5.90; see also World Resources Institute and IIED, op. cit., p. 173.
6. IPCC quoted in *Guardian*, 22.5.90.
7. Boyle and Ardill, op. cit., p. 70; IPCC quoted in *Guardian*, 22.5.90
8. World Resources Institute and IIED, op. cit., p. 159.
9. Brown *et al.*, op. cit., p. 170; Boyle and Ardill, op. cit., pp. 64-5.
10. World Resources Institute and IIED, op. cit., p. 170.
11. Brown *et al.*, op. cit., p. 4; World Resources Institute and IIED, op. cit., p. 178.

12. World Resources Institute and IIED, op. cit., p. 178; *Green Drum*, no. 59 (summer 1987), pp. 22-3.
13. *Earth Matters*, no. 6 (winter 1989–90), p. 5.
14. *Guardian*, 29.2.88.
15. World Resources Institute and IIED, op. cit., p. 175.
16. Boyle *et al.*, op. cit., p. 5; *Earth Matters*, no. 3 (spring 1989), p. 11.
17. John McCormick, *Acid Earth* (London: Earthscan, 1989), pp. 36, 42.
18. Ibid., pp. 14, 15, 16.
19. Don Hinrichsen, "Acid rain and forest decline", in Edward Goldsmith and Nicholas Hildyard, *The Earth Report* (London: Mitchell Beazley, 1988) pp. 76, 78; André Singer, *Battle for the Planet* (London: Pan, 1987), p. 53.
20. Seymour and Girardet, op. cit., p. 147; Norman Myers (ed.), *The Gaia Atlas of Planet Management* (London: Pan, 1985), p. 118; Tom McMillan quoted in Brown *et al.*, op. cit., p. 14.
21. Brown *et al.*, op. cit., p. 15; World Resources Institute and IIED, op. cit., p. 172; Hinrichsen, op. cit., p. 71.
22. McCormick, op. cit., p. 30; Hinrichsen, op. cit., p. 73; Seymour and Girardet, op. cit., p. 153; Environmental Resources Ltd, "Eastern Europe fact file", *Guardian*, 19.1.90.
23. Singer, op. cit., p. 47; Myers, op. cit., p. 118; Seymour and Girardet, op. cit., p. 146.
24. Dr Harold Harvey quoted in McCormick, op. cit., p. 36.
25. World Resources Institute and IIED, op. cit., p. 172.
26. McCormick, op. cit., p. 2; Hinrichsen, op. cit., p. 66; Singer, op. cit., p. 47.
27. McCormick, op. cit., p. 2; Seymour and Girardet, op. cit., p. 150.
28. World Resources Institute and IIED, op. cit., p. 173.
29. Singer, op. cit., pp. 45-6; McCormick, op. cit., pp. 44-6, 47, 48.
30. McCormick, op. cit., p. 65.
31. Brown *et al.*, op. cit., p. 170; World Commission on Environment and Development, *Our Common Future* (Brundtland Report; Oxford University Press, 1987), p. 180.
32. IPCC quoted in *Guardian*, 22.5.90; Dr Mick Kelly quoted in *Guardian*, 1.2.90.
33. Brown *et al.*, op. cit., p. 25.
34. Boyle and Ardill, op. cit., p. 200; *Economist*, 13.5.89, pp. 19-20.
35. *Earth Matters*, no. 5 (autumn 1989), pp. 10-11; Dr Tolba quoted in *Guardian*, 7.11.89; see reports on Bergen (Norway) environment conference, *Guardian*, 15–18.5.90.
36. Boyle and Ardill, op. cit., p. 219; *Economist*, 11.3.89, p. 98; Dr Jeremy Leggett (Greenpeace director of science), "The coals of calamity", *Guardian*, 15.8.89.
37. Brown, *et al.*, op. cit., pp. 43-4, 57.
38. Ibid., p. 41; *Earth Matters*, no. 5 (autumn 1989), p. 11; Boyle

and Ardill, op. cit., pp. 148, 208; McCormick, op. cit., p. 64; Hinrichsen, op. cit., p. 123.
39. Brown, *et al.*, op. cit., pp. 38, 46; Boyle *et al.*, op. cit., pp. 8, 9.
40. *Economist*, 11.3.89, pp. 97-8; *Earth Matters*, no. 3 (spring 1989), pp. 8-9; *New Internationalist*, no. 206 (April 1990), p. 15.
41. Myers, op. cit., p. 136; John Seymour and Herbert Girardet, *Blueprint for a Green Planet* (London: Dorling Kindersley, 1987), p. 91.
42. Brown *et al.*, op. cit., pp. 179-80.
43. Leggett, op. cit.
44. World Commission on Environment and Development, op. cit., p. 201.
45. Ibid., p. 189; *Earth Matters*, no. 1 (autumn 1988) p. 4.
46. Jim Jeffery, "Dirty tricks: how the nuclear lobby sabotaged wave power in Britain", *Ecologist*, vol. 20, no. 3 (May/June 1990), pp. 85-90; "Wave power undercuts nuclear cost", *Guardian*, 1.6.90
47. Myers, op. cit., pp. 128-9.
48. World Commission on Environment and Development, op. cit., p. 198; Brown *et al.*, op. cit., p. 71; Myers, op. cit., p. 128.
49. McCormick, op. cit., p. 65.
50. *Observer*, 3.9.89.
51. *Economist*, 11.3.89, p. 97; *Earth Matters*, no. 6 (winter 1989–90), p. 5.
52. *Observer*, 21.1.90.
53. McCormick, op. cit., p. 69.

9. Habitats and Species – Nature under Siege
1. Norman Myers quoted in Lester Brown *et al.*, *State of the World 1988* (New York: Norton/Worldwatch Institute, 1988), p. 114.
2. James Lovelock, *Gaia: A New Look at Life on Earth* (Oxford University Press, 1979).
3. Lee Durrell, *State of the Ark* (London: Bodley Head, 1986), p. 116.
4. World Resources Institute and International Institute for Environment and Development (IIED), *World Resources 1988–89* (New York: Basic Books, 1988), p. 99; Vandana Shiva, *Staying Alive* (London: Zed, 1988), p. 95.
5. Peter King, *Protect our Planet* (London: Quiller Press/World Wildlife Fund, 1986), p. 35; *Green Drum*, no. 67 (summer 1989), p. 16; Catherine Caufield, *In the Rainforest* (London: Heinemann, 1985), p. 228.
6. Caufield, op. cit., pp. 221, 223; *Observer*, 5.11.89.
7. Caufield, op. cit., pp. 216-17.
8. Victor Scheffer quoted in Norman Myers (ed.), *The Gaia Atlas of Planet Management* (London: Pan, 1985), p. 88.
9. World Resources Institute and IIED, op. cit., pp. 5, 92; André Singer, *Battle for the Planet* (London: Pan, 1987), p. 90; Brown *et al.*, op. cit., p. 106; Caufield, op. cit., p. 244.

10. Caufield, op. cit., p. 61.
11. Brown *et al.*, op. cit., pp. 101, 103.
12. World Resources Institute and IIED, op. cit., p. 94.
13. Ibid., pp. 94-5.
14. *Observer*, 5.11.89.
15. Professor Edward Wilson quoted in Edward Goldsmith and Nicholas Hildyard (eds.), *The Earth Report* (London: Mitchell Beazley, 1988), p. 144.
16. Patrick Anderson, "The myth of sustainable logging", *Ecologist*, vol. 19, no. 5 (September/October 1989), p. 167.
17. Durrell, op. cit., p. 90.
18. Brown *et al.*, op. cit., p. 104.
19. *Green Drum*, no. 67 (summer 1989), p. 16.
20. Durrell, op. cit., p. 104.
21. Ibid., p. 72.
22. *Guardian*, 29.9.89.
23. World Resources Institute and IIED, op. cit., p. 99; *Economist*, 29.4.89, p. 16.
24. Durrell, op. cit., p. 120.
25. King, op. cit., pp. 36-7.
26. Shiva, op. cit., p. 171.
27. John Seymour and Herbert Girardet, *Far from Paradise* (London: BBC Books, 1986), p. 189.
28. *BBC Wildlife*, July 1989, p. 473; Sam Hall, "Whaling: the slaughter continues", *Ecologist*, vol. 18, no. 6 (November/December 1988), p. 207.
29. Professor Cummins quoted in *Guardian*, 31.8.89.
30. Professor Olof Linden quoted in *Guardian*, 20.8.89.
31. King, op. cit., p. 21.
32. World Commission on Environment and Development, *Our Common Future* (Brundtland Report; Oxford University Press, 1989), p. 166.
33. World Resources Institute and IIED, op. cit., p. 103.
34. Brown *et al.*, op. cit., pp. 103, 104.
35. *New Scientist*, 22.10.88, pp. 43-7.
36. *Guardian*, 29.9.89.
37. World Resources Institute and IIED, op. cit., p. 103.
38. Anderson, op. cit., pp. 166-81; World Bank quoted in Brown *et al.*, op. cit., p. 115.
39. Durrell, op. cit., p. 86.
40. Dr John Leger quoted in *Observer*, 8.10.89.
41. World Commission on Environment and Development, op. cit., pp. 162-3.
42. Durrell, op. cit., p. 106; Goldsmith and Hildyard, op. cit., p. 144.
43. *Earth Matters*, no. 6 (winter 1989–90), p. 3.
44. See Professor Tim O'Riorden, "An environmental protection agency for the UK", *Earth Matters*, no. 5 (autumn 1989), p. 5.

10. A World without War?
 1. Archibishop Tutu quoted in Frank Barnaby (ed.), *The Gaia Peace Atlas* (London: Pan, 1988), p. 142.
 2. Ibid., p. 20.
 3. Erich Fromm, *The Anatomy of Human Destructiveness* (Harmondsworth: Penguin, 1977), pp. 155-7, 284.
 4. West German Green MP Petra Kelly in Dr Thomas L. Perry and Dr James G. Foulks (eds), *End the Arms Race: Fund Human Needs* (West Vancouver, BC: Gordon Soules/Seattle: University of Washington Press, 1986), p. 219.
 5. André Singer, *Battle for the Planet* (London: Pan, 1987), p. 129; Perry and Foulks, op. cit., pp. 135, 229.
 6. Helen Collinson, *Death on Delivery* (London: Campaign Against Arms Trade, 1989), p. 82.
 7. Barnaby, op. cit., pp. 46-8, 136.
 8. President Eisenhower quoted in John Cox, *Overkill* (Harmondsworth: Penguin, 1981), p. 152.
 9. *New Internationalist*, no. 190 (December 1988), p. 14.
10. J. K. Galbraith, "The military power: tension as servant; arms control as an illusion", in Perry and Foulks, op. cit., p. 107.
11. US State Department quoted by Bishop Thomas Gumbleton, "The arms race protects the power and wealth of the privileged", in Perry and Foulks, op. cit., pp. 132-3.
12. Dr Rosalie Bertell, *No Immediate Danger* (London: Women's Press, 1985), p. 137.
13. According to the International Institute of Strategic Studies, London.
14. Jonathon Porritt, *Seeing Green* (Oxford: Blackwell, 1984), p. 56.
15. Professor Kosta Tsipis, "Technical and operational considerations of space-based defensive systems", in Perry and Foulks, op. cit., p. 46.
16. Lieut-Gen. Dean Abrahamson quoted in Lester Brown *et al.*, *State of the World 1988* (New York: Norton/Worldwatch Institute, 1988), p. 141.
17. See *New Internationalist*, no. 163 (September 1986), p. 11.
18. Barnaby, op. cit., p. 96.
19. Anthony Sampson, in *Observer*, 14.1.90; Collinson, op. cit., pp. 39, 41.
20. The following figures are taken from: Brown *et al.*, op. cit., p. 148; same authors, *State of the World 1989* (New York: Norton/Worldwatch Institute, 1989), pp. 150-1; Singer, op. cit., p. 125; Barnaby, op. cit., pp. 108, 218; Perry and Foulkes, op. cit., p. 171.
21. *Guardian*, 14.2.90
22. Perry and Foulks, op. cit., p. 97; "The arms trade", Campaign Against Arms Trade leaflet, 1989.
23. Ken Coates, *Think Globally, Act Locally: The United Nations and the Peace Movements* (Nottingham: Spokesman, 1988), p. 122.

24. Michael Albert and David Dellinger (eds.), *Beyond Survival: New Directions for the Disarmament Movement* (Boston, Mass: South End Press, 1983), p. 240.
25. See, for example, Susan George, *A Fate Worse than Debt* (London: Pelican, 1988), pp. 25-7.
26. Brazilian metalworkers quoted in Collinson, op. cit., pp. 106-7.
27. "Above our heads – just!", Campaign for Nuclear Disarmament leaflet.
28. Albert and Dellinger, op. cit., p. 178.
29. E. P. Thompson quoted in *New Internationalist*, no. 163 (September 1986), p. 21
30. Collinson, op. cit., pp. 12, 18.
31. Ibid., p. 91.
32. Brian Urquhart quoted in Barnaby, op. cit., p. 58.
33. Alex Cockburn and James Ridgeway, "An atoll, a submarine and the US economy", in Albert and Dellinger, op. cit., p. 185.
34. Sandy Irvine and Alec Ponton, *A Green Manifesto* (London: Macdonald Optima, 1988), p. 115; Paul Kennedy, *The Rise and Fall of the Great Powers* (London: Unwin Hyman, 1988), p. 510.
35. Admiral (ret.) Eugene Carroll quoted in *Guardian*, 7.6.90.
36. See, for example, Coates, op. cit., chapter 7.
37. Robert McNamara reported in *Observer*, 14.1.90; Pentagon reported in *Guardian*, 14.2.90.
38. Richard Perle quoted in *Guardian*, 30.1.90; International Institute of Strategic Studies reported in *Guardian*, 28.11.89; chair of US House Armed Services Committee quoted in *Guardian*, 24.4.90.
39. *New Internationalist*, no. 202 (December 1989), p. 26.
40. World Commission on Environment and Development, *Our Common Future* (Brundtland Report; Oxford University Press, 1987), p. 303; Palme Commission, *Common Security* (London: Pan, 1982).
41. Campaign Against Arms Trade newsletter, October 1989.
42. Perry and Foulks, op. cit., p. 99.
43. Martyn Halsall, "Peace forces radical change on the armaments industry", *Guardian*, 9.4.90.
44. President Gorbachev quoted in *Guardian*, 28.11.89, emphasis added.
45. Points on the competitive ethos made in the UK Peace Pledge Union's leaflet, "Co-operation".

Recommended Reading

UK magazines and journals

Central America Report (quarterly), 83 Margaret Street, London W1N 7HB.

Ecologist (bi-monthly), 29A High Street, New Malden, Surrey KT3 4BY (subscriptions), and Corner House, Station Road, Sturminster Newton, Dorset DT10 1BB (editorial).

Environment Digest (monthly, with twice-yearly index), Freepost, London SW10 0YY.

Environment Now (monthly), 27 Kensington Court, London W8 5DN.

Ethical Consumer (bi-monthly), 100 Gretney Walk, Moss Side, Manchester M15 5ND.

Everywoman (monthly), 34 Islington Green, London N1 8DU.

The Food Magazine (quarterly), London Food Commission, 88 Old Street, London EC1V 9AR.

Food Matters Worldwide (quarterly), 38–40 Exchange Street, Norwich NR2 1AY.

Fourth World Review (bi-monthly), 24 Abercorn Place, London NW8.

Gaia Magazine (quarterly), 20 High Street, Stroud, Glos. GL5 1AS.

Geographical (monthly), 27 Kensington Court, London W8 5DN.

Green Drum (quarterly), 18 Cofton Lake Road, Birmingham B45 8PL.

Green Line (10 issues a year), 34 Cowley Road, Oxford OX4 1HZ.

Green Teacher (bi-monthly), 22 Heol Pentreheddyn, Machynlleth, Powys, Wales SY20 8DN.

Minority Rights Reports (five issues a year), 29 Craven Street, London WC2N 5NG.

New Consumer (five issues a year), 52 Elswick Road, Newcastle upon Tyne NE4 6JH.

New Internationalist (monthly), 120–126 Lavender Avenue, Mitcham, Surrey CR4 3HP (subscriptions), and 55 Rectory

Road, Oxford OX4 1BW (editorial).

Oxfam News (quarterly), 274 Banbury Road, Oxford OX2 7BR.

Panoscope (bi-monthly), 9 White Lion Street, London N1 9PD.

Peace News (fortnightly), 55 Dawes Street, London SE17 1EL.

Race and Class (quarterly), Institute of Race Relations, 2 Leeke Street, London WC1X 9HS.

Resurgence (bi-monthly), Ford House, Hartland, Bideford, Devon.

Sanity (monthly), 162 Holloway Road, London N7 8DQ.

SCRAM (bi-monthly), 11 Forth Street, Edinburgh EH1 3LE, Scotland.

Spare Rib (monthly), 27 Clerkenwell Close, London EC1R OAT, UK.

Books

Albery, Nicholas, and Yule, Valerie (eds), *Encyclopaedia of Social Inventions* (London: Institute for Social Inventions, 1990).

Amnesty International, *Report* (London: AI, published annually).

Barnaby, Frank (ed.), *The Gaia Peace Atlas* (London: Pan, 1988).

Beauvoir, Simone de, *The Second Sex* (Harmondsworth: Penguin, 1983).

Bertell, Dr Rosalie, *No Immediate Danger: Prognosis for a Radioactive Earth* (London: Women's Press, 1985).

Body, Richard, *Our Food, our Land* (London: Rider, forthcoming).

Bookchin, Murray, *The Modern Crisis* (Philadelphia, Pa: New Society Publishers, 1986).

Boserup, Ester, *Women's Role in Economic Development* (London: Earthscan, 1989).

Boyle, Stewart, and Ardill, John, *The Greenhouse Effect* (London: New English Library, 1988).

Brown, Lester, *et al.*, *State of the World* (New York: Norton/Worldwatch Institute, published annually).

Burgos-Debray, Elizabeth (ed.), *I, Rigoberta Menchu: An Indian Woman in Guatemala* (London: Verso, 1984).

Button, John, *How to Be Green* (London: Century Hutchinson,

Capra, Fritjof, *The Turning Point* (London: Wildwood House, 1982).

Carr, Marilyn, *The AT Reader* (London: Intermediate Technology, 1985).

Catholic Institute for International Relations, *States of Terror: Death Squads or Development?* (London: CIIR, 1989).

Caufield, Catherine, *In the Rainforest* (London: Heinemann, 1985).

Chomsky, Noam, *Turning the Tide* (London: Pluto, 1986).

Coates, Ken, *Think Globally, Act Locally: The United Nations and the Peace Movements* (Nottingham: Spokesman, 1988).

Collinson, Helen, *Death on Delivery: The Impact of the Arms Trade on theThird World* (London: Campaign Against Arms Trade, 1989).

Conroy, Czech, and Litvinoff, Miles, *The Greening of Aid: Sustainable Livelihoods in Practice* (London: Earthscan, 1988).

Cox, John, *Overkill: The Story of Modern Weapons* (Harmondsworth: Pelican, 1981).

Crow, Ben, Bernstein, Henry, Mackintosh, Maureen, and Martin, Charlotte, *The Food Question: Who Gets What and Why* (London: Earthscan, 1990).

Dankelman, Irene, and Davidson, Joan, *Women and Environment in the Third World* (London: Earthscan, 1988).

Durrell, Lee, *State of the Ark* (London: Bodley Head, 1986).

Eavis, Paul, and Clarke, Michael, *Security after the Cold War – Redirecting Global Resources* (Bristol: Safer World Foundation, 1990).

Ehrlich, Paul, and Ehrlich, Anne, *The Population Explosion* (London: Hutchinson, 1990).

Elsworth, Steve, *A Dictionary of the Environment* (London: Paladin, 1990).

Ekins, Paul (ed.), *The Living Economy* (London: Routledge, 1986).

Fight for the Forest: Chico Mendez in his Own Words (London: Latin America Bureau, 1989).

Flood, Mike, *The Potential for Renewable Energy* (Milton Keynes: Open University Alternative Technology Group, 1986).

Freire, Paulo, *Pedagogy of the Oppressed* (Harmondsworth: Penguin, 1972).

Fromm, Erich, *The Anatomy of Human Destructiveness* Harmondsworth: Penguin, 1977).

George, Susan, *A Fate Worse than Debt* (London: Pelican, 1988).

George, Susan, *How the Other Half Dies: The Real Reasons for World Hunger* (London: Pelican, 1986).

Goldsmith, Edward, and Hildyard, Nicholas (eds), *The Earth Report 2* (London: Mitchell Beazley, 1990).

Gradwohl, Judith, and Greenberg, Russell, *Saving the Tropical Rainforests* (London: Earthscan, 1988).

Gupta, Joyeeta, *Toxic Terrorism: Dumping Hazardous Wastes* (London: Earthscan, 1990).

Hardoy, Jorge, and Satterthwaite, David, *Squatter Citizen: Life in the Urban Third World* (London: Earthscan, 1989).

Harrison, Paul, *The Third World Tomorrow* (Harmondsworth: Penguin, 1983).

Harrison, Paul, *The Greening of Africa* (London: Paladin, 1987).

Hayter, Teresa, *Exploited Earth: Britain's Aid and the Environment* (London: Earthscan, 1989).

Hinrichsen, Don, *Our Common Future: A Reader's Guide* (London: Earthscan, 1987).

Humana, Charles, *World Human Rights Guide* (London: Pan, 1987).

Holloway, Richard, *Doing Development: Governments, NGOs and the Rural Poor in Asia* (London: Earthscan, 1989).

Hynes, H. Patricia, *Reconstructing Babylon: Women and Technology* (London: Earthscan, 1990).

Independent Commission on International Humanitarian Issues, *Indigenous Peoples: A Global Quest for Justice* (London: Zed, 1987).

Irvine, Sandy, and Ponton, Alec, *A Green Manifesto* (London: Macdonald Optima, 1988).

Kelly, Petra, *Fighting for Hope* (London: Chatto, 1984).

Kemp, Penny, and Wall, Derek, *A Green Manifesto for the 1990s* (London: Penguin, 1990).

Kidron, Michael, and Segal, Ronald, *The Book of Business, Money and Power* (London: Pan, 1987).

Kidron, Michael, and Segal, Ronald, *The New State of the World Atlas* (London: Pan, 1987).

Kohr, Leopold, *The Breakdown of Nations* (London: Routledge, 1986).

Lappé, Frances Moore, and Collins, Joseph, *World Hunger: Twelve Myths* (London: Earthscan, 1988).

Lappé, Frances Moore, and Schurman, Rachel, *Taking Population Seriously* (London: Earthscan, 1989).

Latin American and Caribbean Women's Collective, *Slaves of Slaves* (London: Zed, 1980).

Lee-Wright, Peter, *Child Slaves* (London: Earthscan, 1990).

Lovelock, James, *Gaia: A New Look at Life on Earth* (Oxford University Press, 1979).

May, John, *The Greenpeace Book of the Nuclear Age* (London: Gollancz, 1989).

McCormick, John, *Acid Earth: The Global Threat of Acid Pollution* (London: Earthscan, 1989).

Medcalf, John, *Letters from Nicaragua* (London: Catholic Institute for International Relations, 1988).

Miles, Rosalind, *The Women's History of the World* (London: Paladin, 1989).

Myers, Norman (ed.), *The Gaia Atlas of Planet Management* (London: Pan, 1985).

New Internationalist, *Women: A World Report* (London: Methuen, 1985).

Patterson, Walter, *The Energy Alternative* (London: Boxtree, 1990).

Pearce, David, Markandya, Anil, and Barbier, Edward, *Blueprint for a Green Economy* (Pearce Report; London: Earthscan, 1989).

Plant, Judith, *Healing the Wounds: The Promise of Ecofeminism* (London: Green Print, 1989).

Porritt, Jonathon, *Where on Earth Are We Going?* (London: BBC Books, 1990).

Rodney, Walter, *How Europe Underdeveloped Africa* (London: Bougle L'Ouverture, 1972).

Roberts, John, *Transport and Society – User-Friendly Cities* (London: Transport and Environment Studies, 1989).

Robertson, James, *Future Wealth: A New Economics for the 21st Century* (London: Cassell, 1990).

Schumacher, E. F., *Small Is Beautiful* (London: Abacus, 1974).

Scott, Gavin, *How to Get Rid of the Bomb* (London: Fontana, 1982).

Seabrook, Jeremy, and Pereira, Winin, *Asking the Earth: Farms, Forestry and Survival in India* (London: Earthscan, 1990).

Seager, Joni, and Olson, Ann, *Women in the World: An International Atlas* (London: Pan, 1986).

Sen, Gita, and Grown, Caren, *Development, Crises and Alternative Visions: Third World Women's Perspectives* (London:

Earthscan, 1988).

Seymour, John, *Complete Book of Self-Sufficiency* (London: Corgi, 1978, reissued 1990).

Seymour, John, and Giradet, Herbert, *Far from Paradise: The Story of Man's Impact on the Environment* (London: BBC Books, 1986).

Seymour, John, and Girardet, Herbert, *Blueprint for a Green Planet* (London: Dorling Kindersley, 1987).

Shiva, Vandana, *Staying Alive: Women, Ecology and Development* (London: Zed 1988).

Shoard, Marion, *This Land Is our Land: The Struggle for Britain's Countryside* (London: Paladin, 1987).

Spretnak, Charlene, and Capra, Fritjof, *Green Politics: The Global Promise* (London: Paladin, 1985).

Timberlake, Lloyd, *Africa in Crisis* (London: Earthscan, 1988).

Timberlake, Lloyd, and Thomas, Laura, *When the Bough Breaks: Our Children, our Environment* (London: Earthscan, 1990).

Toke, Dave, *Green Energy*: *A Non-Nuclear Response to the Greenhouse Effect* (London: Green Print, 1990).

Trainer, Ted, *Developed to Death* (London: Green Print, 1989).

UNICEF, *The State of the World's Children 1990* (Oxford University Press, 1990).

Ward, Barbara, *Progress for a Small Planet* (London: Earthscan, 1988).

Weir, David, *The Bhopal Syndrome* (London: Earthscan, 1988).

Wijkman, Anders, and Timberlake, Lloyd, *Natural Disasters: Acts of God or Acts of Man?* (London and Washington: Earthscan, 1984).

Wilson, Des, *Citizen Action: Taking Action in your Community* (London: Longman, 1986).

World Commission on Environment and Development, *Our Common Future* (Brundtland Report; Oxford University Press, 1987).

Wynne-Tyson, Jon, *Food for a Future* (Wellingborough: Thorsons, 1988).

Index